New Perspectives in
Primary Education

New Perspectives in Primary Education

Meaning and purpose in learning and teaching

Sue Cox

Open University Press

Open University Press
McGraw-Hill Education
McGraw-Hill House
Shoppenhangers Road
Maidenhead
Berkshire
England
SL6 2QL

email: enquiries@openup.co.uk
world wide web: www.openup.co.uk

and Two Penn Plaza, New York, NY 10121-2289, USA

First published 2011

Copyright © Sue Cox 2011

A catalogue record of this book is available from the British Library

ISBN-13: 978-0-33-523573-5 (pb) 978-0-33-523572-8 (hb)
ISBN-10: 0-33-523573-5 (pb) 0-33-523572-7 (hb)
eISBN: 9780335239320

Library of Congress Cataloging-in-Publication Data
CIP data applied for

Typesetting and e-book compilations by
RefineCatch Limited, Bungay, Suffolk
Printed and bound by CPI Group (UK) Ltd, Croydon, CR0 4YY

Fictitious names of companies, products, people, characters and/or data that may be used herein (in case studies or in examples) are not intended to represent any real individual, company, product or event.

The *McGraw-Hill* Companies

Dedicated to the memory of Peter Alan Cox (1955–1969)

Contents

Foreword

It may seem strange to begin a preface to a book on new perspectives in primary education published in 2011 by referring to a government publication dated 1905. That year saw the publication of *Suggestions for the consideration of teachers and others concerned with the work of public elementary schools*. Elementary education was at a hinge in its history. The draconian system of 'Payment by Results' had recently ended and a highly prescriptive national curriculum was being replaced. It became official policy that

> each teacher shall think for himself [*sic*] and work out for himself such methods of teaching as may use his powers to the best advantage and be best suited to the particular needs and conditions of the school. Uniformity in details of practice is not desirable even if it were attainable. But freedom implies a corresponding responsibility in its use.

In the event that elementary school 'spring' did not materialise, except in a very small number of schools. The climate was not right; teacher training was not well developed; research and thinking into elementary education were poor, almost non-existent.

A century on there is a parallel context and a parallel opportunity. The government of the day has promised to develop a far less detailed and prescriptive curriculum; it is reviewing the assessment regime; and it has promised the kind of professional autonomy outlined so eloquently and powerfully in 1905. The opportunity for a primary education 'spring' must be grasped, not lost, this time around.

Hopefully, the climate is ripe for change in a way that it wasn't in 1905. Certainly, teacher education to which Sue Cox and her colleagues have made an important contribution, is well developed and of good quality. Research in primary education, so ably and comprehensively reviewed in this book, is there to be called upon to inform change. Discussion about primary education has never been so well informed.

As Sue Cox stresses, there is a real need for new perspectives on primary education as a whole but crucial to their realisation is a sense of meaning and purpose. Her book provides a framework for thinking about meaning and purpose through a sophisticated exploration of how children learn and how teachers contribute to that learning. She argues that more than ever teachers need to take pedagogical decisions informed by principles and values. She clearly illustrates how participation is key to both children's and teachers' learning and demonstrates from her own research and that of others the benefits of teachers working collaboratively with children in areas such as curriculum and assessment. She does not closely prescribe; she does not dictate; but she does inform and stimulate the kind of responsible and considered thinking necessary for primary teacher professionalism in the early part of the twenty-first century. She provides the kind of thinking that can underlie the idea of professional autonomy over pedagogy so powerfully stated first in 1905 and now so much needed a century on.

Someone invited to write a preface such as this can be expected to say that the book is timely. It is certainly that.

Professor Colin Richards HMI (ret.)

Introduction

Chapter overview

In this introduction I consider how teachers experience change and raise the question of whether they might lead transformation in learning and teaching. I highlight a key distinction between education and schooling and some of the contradictions and constraints that teachers face. In introducing the socio-cultural orientation of this book, the centrality of values in educational practices and issues of rights and power, I aim to open up possible ways of reflecting on and challenging the status quo in practices in English primary schools, which I develop in later chapters. To help the reader get a better sense of the current state of affairs, I explore how primary practices and policy have changed over time.

Change in primary education

For teachers, change, in itself, is not an unusual phenomenon. In fact, it is a central feature of what they do. First and foremost, teachers are involved in the changes that take place in children's lives through learning. Furthermore, they are used to continuously experiencing change in the form of new initiatives in their workplace, often imposed on them by others. A question that is important for this book is whether transformation in primary education can be led by teachers themselves, to realise the kind of changes that they aspire to achieve for children through learning.

There are several ways of looking at this. First, to what extent are teachers actually given the freedom to lead change? This is a political issue and one that is dependent on the point in time in history. Taking the situation at the time of writing, primary schools in England have entered the second decade of the twenty-first century facing turbulent and changing times. The priorities and policies of the Labour government, in power for thirteen years, are being displaced by those of the new Coalition government, elected in 2010. There was an increasing impetus for teacher control under Labour. Many teachers were heartened, for instance, by the prospect of a new National Curriculum, introduced by the so-called 'Rose Review' (DCSF 2009a). In spite of the short-comings of that review (discussed by Alexander 2010), it embraced a very important principle for teachers: that the burden of prescription should be reduced. By tackling the obstacle of too much prescribed content and providing only essential, rather than desirable elements of the curriculum, teachers were to be given full scope 'to shape how it is taught and to supplement it' (DCSF 2009a p. 14). Children and teachers were to be encouraged to 'think creatively "outside subject boxes"' (p. 16). This greater freedom, as it was developing in recent years under the previous government, may in some ways be set to continue. Though it has not been expressed in precisely the same terms, the new government's 2010 White Paper (DfE 2010a) continues to convey a similar message: that teachers are to be released from external control. It outlines a range of steps that will be taken that 'will free schools from externally imposed burdens and give them greater confidence to set their own direction' (p. 24). The White Paper claims that it is the government's ambition 'to reduce unnec-essary prescription, bureaucracy and central control throughout our education system' (p. 37). The government's intentions are, clearly, that teachers will be given increased responsibility for development. There are further questions, of course, about how far teachers will, in reality, be empowered to take the lead and what other limiting factors there might be, as well as wider issues around the ideological differences in motivation and intention of the new govern-ment; but there are indications of further movement towards increased teacher autonomy.

Second, there is the issue of whether teachers are willing to take things forward. There are signs that they appear to be. In anticipation of the new curriculum, some teachers were already enthusiastically exploring alternative ways of looking at their teaching and what goes on in their classrooms. Although they were brought to a full stop in 2010, when the proposals failed to be passed into legislation, arguably, the genie had already been released. I am only speculating here, but there may be new energy amongst teachers to maintain the momentum that was generated for creating their own new visions for the primary classroom.

Third, there are the related questions of what is involved in realising their aspirations for children: what kind of changes should there be and how are they to be made? Are teachers clear about what they hope to achieve for children? How do they view this and how do they see the means of bringing it about? In the chapters that follow, I hope to offer ways of looking at and understanding learning and teaching that will help teachers to address these crucial questions.

Finally, there is the question of whether they have the right to transform education. Teachers are, in our society, democratically accountable to others for whatever they do. Moreover, this does not necessarily mean only other adults. While any transformation in education is pursued ultimately for the good of children, to what extent should teachers also be held directly to account by children themselves?

Placing transformation in education in the context of the wider community, as this final point does, brings me to the way in which the issues will be framed in the discussion in the chapters that follow. All change in education takes place in particular contexts which are social in nature. The underlying premise of this book is that education can be understood in this way – in socio-cultural terms – as social practice. I shall be discussing this further, but, in short, education is shaped and transformed by those who participate in it: by the actions and the ways of talking and thinking of these people in the groups and communities to which they belong – by discourses and cultures. Teachers are, of course, central players, and that is why it makes sense to talk of teachers initiating change, but crucially, so are children.

Schooling and education

While teachers are directly concerned with the transformation of children's lives through learning, they work in the broader social context of the school. I will attempt to clarify, in the chapters that follow, how what teachers do has been shaped by the culture of schooling, which has been characterised by particular ways of acting and thinking. I shall suggest that these may have embodied questionable understandings of how children's learning comes about. They may, also, in some ways, have overlooked children's rights as people and fellow citizens. As I shall discuss, these ways of acting and thinking are quite entrenched in schools. While schools may be in a constant state of flux, this culture and these practices – surprisingly perhaps – have persisted.

To some extent these entrenched practices are a result of the ideological and policy context of schooling within which teachers have been obliged to work, and the power structures that pervade it. As I will argue, this culture of primary schooling in England has been sustained, at least in part, by a performance orientation towards education and a target-driven political agenda (see, for example, Dent and Whitehead 2002; Whitty 2002). Added to this, there has been the overriding expectation, over the past two decades or so, that teachers must comply with policy initiatives (Bottery and Wright 2000; Ball 2004). As a result, the directives from central government and its agencies with which teachers have been continuously assailed during that period have created the ongoing sense of overload and over-prescription across the teaching workforce which the Rose Review acknowledged and the Coalition's White Paper has highlighted. They have undoubtedly limited the opportunities for teachers to exercise their own professional judgement as educators – based on deeper understandings of how children learn, what is important for them to learn and how children themselves are valued. These long-standing practices may, in part, have been sustained by teachers who have not been encouraged to fully enact, acknowledge or articulate what they can offer as educators.

I am intentionally making a distinction here between schooling and education, which is, I shall argue, a significant one. It highlights possible tensions in teachers' lives, between the discourses of their workplace and educational discourses. Many teachers may find that what is expected of them in school does not sit easily with their commitments to deeply held beliefs about education. This would be one reason why they would have welcomed the opportunities provided by a less prescriptive curriculum. However, it is also possible that, by contrast, some teachers no longer experience these sorts of contradiction. It may be, as Andrew Pollard (2001 p. 9) has suggested, that 'hard-edged performance systems and structures' have gradually replaced the educational principles of teachers with a new hegemony – of competitiveness and 'tacit and un-problematised assumptions about how children are deemed to learn'. I shall say more about this later, but the point I want to make here is that if these discourses of the workplace have displaced educational discourses, then principled teacher-led transformation may be impossible to achieve. It is in the spirit of helping to contribute to the renewal of educational discourses and principles amongst teachers that I have written this book.

Socio-cultural perspectives

I set out to discuss key aspects of primary practice in each chapter. My aim is to show that there are discourses other than the hard-edged kind and to explore alternative, socio-cultural ways of looking at primary education – that challenge some of the entrenched thinking and question the values underlying current practices and discourses. These perspectives might provide ways of understanding learning and teaching differently – in terms of participation and collaboration instead of competition, performance and compliance.

As theoretical discourses, these ways of looking at education are not new: as Daniels and his co-authors note, 'it appears as if "we are all socio-cultural theorists now"' (Daniels et al. 2009). For some time, these perspectives have framed the work of educational researchers. Socio-cultural theories of learning are 'assuming an increasingly important position in understanding how children learn' (ibid.). The picture may be rather different, however, from within the primary classroom itself. Some elements of socio-cultural learning theories (as I hope will become clear) are inherent in some of the practices that are becoming more prevalent in classrooms – such as a new emphasis on talk, some aspects of 'assessment for learning' and some of the new directions being taken in early years settings – and may well underlie how some teachers, in the face of the 'new hegemony' continue to think about education. These approaches can be distorted, however, within a target-driven culture in the school context, as I shall show. They can seem at odds with other practices such as national testing and inspection that are currently still imposed on teachers in English primary schools. As for the future, while the current White Paper (DfE 2010a) advocates the removal of targets that are imposed centrally and by local authorities, it continues to emphasise target-setting – albeit by schools themselves. It also proposes that there should be a new minimum 'floor' for all schools to achieve and that formal assessment at Key Stage 2 shall 'promote attainment and progression and ensure schools are properly accountable to pupils, parents and the public for the achievement of every child' (p. 46). Primary schooling, then, remains a world structured by policy makers with a performative agenda that can present challenges to those educationalists and teachers seeking to establish new approaches and to embed new educational principles.

It is more than ten years since Pollard (2001 p. 13), commenting on the development of the socio-cultural perspective and its 'many leads and directions', wrote that 'it will take time for a more integrated set of tenets to become established and presented in forms that are likely to make a direct impact on education policy'. Perhaps during the first decade of this century that aim came closer to being realised. Over a long period of time, researchers such as Wells (for example, Wells 1986; Wells and Chang-Wells 1992; Wells 1999; Wells and Arauz 2006; Wells and Ball 2008; Wells 2009) and Mercer (for example, Mercer 1995; Mercer 2001; Mercer and Littleton 2007; Mercer and Dawes 2008), amongst others, have developed the necessary depth of analysis and synthesis from a socio-cultural point of view to contribute to such a coherent vision, and they continue to do so.

In terms of the impact on policy, some of the officially sanctioned developments during that decade might suggest that the right conditions for achieving more far-reaching changes in the policy agenda were emerging. First, there was an emphasis on responding to and making provision for the needs of all children in the context of concern for child well-being as a whole (*Every Child Matters* DfES 2004), including a focus on the 'voice' of the child. The *Every Child Matters* legislation recognised the need to focus on all children and on the child as a whole person. Second, the publication of an influential report by The National Advisory Committee on Creative and Cultural Education (1999) led to creativity becoming a buzzword in educational circles. There were several moves by central government to allow more flexibility for teachers and to encourage creative teaching. For instance, the Primary National

Strategy (PNS) (DCSF 2003), though somewhat ill-conceived (Alexander 2004; Brehony 2005), was introduced to highlight 'enjoyment' as well as excellence. From the turn of the twenty-first century, then, there was the growing recognition that teachers needed some breathing space, which almost culminated in a new statutory curriculum in 2010. Third, there was affirmation of the importance of Early Years education and how it might influence later stages of schooling through initiatives such as the Sure Start programme, 'Bringing together early education, childcare, health and family support' (DCSF 2009b), and the introduction of a specific phase of education from birth to five called the Early Years Foundation Stage (DCSF 2008).

All these changes suggest that in the first ten years of the century the official agenda became, perhaps, more 'learner focused' than at any time since 1988 when the National Curriculum was introduced through the Education Reform Act. This might have helped to secure a more cohesive integration of policy and educational principle. On the other hand, as I intend to show, the tensions I referred to above were far from resolved, and leave an ongoing sense of uncertainty about the future of Primary Education in England.

Practices and values

Education has become the right of every young person across the world (United Nations Convention on the Rights of the Child 1989). As such it is the concern of virtually every individual and, furthermore, it matters in the societies in which they live. How education is valued is an open question, given that the different interests in education and the different beliefs and values that individuals and groups come to hold are generated in social contexts, or in what Lave and Wenger (1991) and Wenger (1998) have called 'communities of practice'.

It is, perhaps, useful at this early point to clarify this notion of a community of practice as it underpins much of the discussion that follows in subsequent chapters. As Lave and Wenger explain, in the context of 'activity theory', which informs their analysis, it does not necessarily imply a fixed, clearly identifiable or located group who are 'co-present' (in each other's presence). As they make clear: 'It does imply participation in an activity system about which participants share understandings concerning what they are doing and what that means in their lives and for their communities' (Lave and Wenger 1991 p. 98).

The term 'community' is 'a slippery one . . .' (Wells 2004 p.71). As Wells goes on to explain:

> However, in the context of activity theory it has a very specific meaning. It refers to those who, as members of the same activity system, are motivated by the same 'object' (Leont'ev, 1981) and who,

although through different actions, contribute to the achievement of that object.

Although this may sound rather abstract, the discussion in the chapters that follow will draw on this theoretical point of view and will develop aspects of it. Suffice to say here that while in educational contexts these may be communities at the localised level – of, say, the institution of the school, and the local community – or academic or researcher communities, or those at the more centralised level such as national government or national interest groups, they are groups that have an interest and involvement in specific educational practices or goals or are concerned with specific activities that are part of learning and teaching.

The centrality of the values base of education should be clear. It is an important idea that will underlie the discussion from the socio-cultural perspective. As practices – as 'activity systems' – learning and teaching involve agency on the part of the participants. Any action requires a decision at some level on what to do: on whether to take one course of action or another. These are not autonomous decisions in any absolute sense, but are shaped by the community of practice in which they are made and embody its values. Assuming that education is seen as a 'good', then it would make sense that any individual's actions would be predicated on judgements about what is 'right', or what is most 'important' within the community of practice. Given that values are developed collectively across groups and communities where individuals have overlapping understandings and purposes, this does not imply that learners and teachers are constantly and consciously weighing up their decisions about what to do every minute of the day. In order to act at all on any shared endeavour, even, say, at the level of holding a conversation, there are shared, tacit assumptions about how to proceed. But, it does imply that there are grounds for actions that may also be more consciously worked out (Peters 1958).

If a teacher holds themselves responsible for their actions and gives the actions specific direction, then conscious engagement with the values that underpin them becomes more important. This goes back to the possibilities for teachers to lead educational transformation. The Coalition government ministers may emphasise that teachers are to take responsibility for leading their own and others' development by sharing effective practice, but 'effective' is a values-based word. In accounting for their actions and, furthermore, in developing their vision for children's learning, a teacher needs to have an understanding of what they are doing, of why they are doing it and its implications: their justification will be expressed in terms of values of one kind or another. Awareness of inherent values potentially enables a teacher to take a course of action that will realise particular aims. In other words, a *reflective* teacher would consciously engage with the values base of what they do. This opens the way for ensuring that they are engaging in educative practice, rather than merely schooling.

Rights and power

I have already indicated that there are issues of relative power and that this gives rise to tensions. Differences in power within and between different communities add complexity to how values are generated and held, and how they are played out in practice. Teachers' actions and values may be facilitated or constrained by the degree to which they do, or do not, hold power. To pick up on the distinction between education and schooling, decisions for action that teachers make, informed by their values as educators, may not always be achievable, even within the world of the classroom where teachers ostensibly make many of the decisions. Their priorities might be at odds with what is valued within the school. To take a straightforward example, in a teacher's judgement it may be important for their Year 6 class to have the opportunity to paint and draw, but this may conflict with the school's need to focus on revision in literacy and numeracy to gain high levels in the SATs (Standard Assessment Tests) in literacy and numeracy. If schools are to be given increased powers under new legislation, this kind of institutional control over teachers may actually increase: despite the avowed intentions to reduce external control, there will be the pressures of reaching the minimum floor of perform-ance, for instance.

These matters of rights and power are central and complex. As I've already indicated, from the point of view of teachers, the pace of change and the need to process the volume of information that accompanies any recommenda-tions and policies may have prevented them from considering alternative perspectives. When the requirements are heavy, and are imposed on them, unreflective compliance to the external agenda can seem the only option. Perhaps a starting point is the assumption that, even where they do not hold power, teachers would rather be reflective professionals, conscious of the values inherent in their day-to-day actions, than unreflective operatives in a wider system. This does demand that they ask penetrating questions about what those values are. To the extent that they do hold power – whatever that is to be in the future – it is imperative to address the central questions concerning the direction in which they should take their practice: what are their aims and principles to be?

There is every reason, in these uncertain times, for teachers to seize the initiative, as educators, to be willing and equipped to generate changes within their pedagogical practices that are educationally principled. Their rights to do so will always be contestable. However, where their rights are constrained in the interests of those who do not necessarily prioritise children or children's *education* then, arguably, those constraints should be challenged.

Where primary teachers are and how they got here: the child-centred era

It is useful to explore some of the background to where primary teachers find themselves at the present time, so that new practices can be seen in the context of those of an earlier era and the shifts in thinking and policy from which they have emerged. This historical perspective is important if we accept the premise that education is a social practice, shaped by both history and culture.

Some teachers, whose experience stretches back into the 1970s and 80s, may feel they have recently been witnessing something of a pendulum swing. Others, who have more recently joined the profession, may see current developments as radical new ideas. Neither of these positions is in itself adequate for the challenges of the present. If nothing else, learning from what has gone before, rather than simply re-adopting past practices or starting as if from scratch, may help to avoid some of the pitfalls that were encountered in earlier decades.

Since there has been a renewed focus on 'creative teaching' and on more learner-focused approaches, an appropriate starting point is to consider the powerful influence of the Plowden Report on primary teaching (CACE 1967). In the late 1960s the 'Plowden era' brought in a period of apparently child-centred – or progressive – approaches to learning and teaching that continued to influence forms of 'good practice' into the 1970s and beyond. They may still resonate clearly with older teachers facing the current changes. Insofar as they were based in theory, these followed a Piagetian understanding of children's development (which I shall discuss further in Chapter 1), but Plowden made little use of any empirical research. Rather, the report was a set of recommendations, based on values that placed the child at 'the heart of the educational process' (ibid. p. 9). Their coherence depended on a long history, bound up with changing conceptualisations of childhood over the centuries that had found expression in their original form in the works of philosophers such as Rousseau (1762) and educators such as Froebel and Montessori. In terms of educational policy recommendations, also, these were not new ideas. The same sort of values had informed the Hadow Report of 1931 (Board of Education 1931). But in the 1960s, which was a period of re-appraisal of old values and practices following the post-war era – rejection of some and revitalisation of others – as well as a time of increasing affluence, these were perceived as major shifts in thinking. A more liberated approach to life provided a context in which Plowden values could flourish. The practices that emerged in the classroom during the period following the publication of the Plowden Report seemed to hold the potential to foster freedom, equality of opportunity, autonomy and creativity: the curriculum integrated traditional subject areas and was built around children's needs and interests and teaching was envisaged as a free-flowing response to individual children. Learning was organised around the principle of 'the integrated day' (where there was no fixed timetable of lessons subject by subject, but a programme that flowed across the whole day and the whole curriculum). Teaching was characterised as facilitation of processes such as learning through play, learning by discovery, and growth. New state school buildings were designed on 'open plan' lines, with interconnecting areas rather than closed, single classrooms. The state school system itself was challenged, by thinkers such as Illich (1971) Reimer (1971) and Postman and Weingarter (1969) who inspired 'de-schoolers' and 'free-schoolers'. They were following in the footsteps of progressive educators such as A. S. Neill (1962) who believed the formal school system to be, by its very nature, restrictive of children's freedom to learn and had set up the independent free school Summerhill. (Such schools were not funded by the state, unlike the free schools being set up under the present Coalition government.) Inspired by these radical educationalists, other independent free schools began to appear – though some were short lived – organised around children's choices and preferences, giving precedence to children's rights.

Competing conceptions of education

Around the same time, the London School of philosophers of education was articulating a liberal-humanist conception of education to provide an ethical and analytical framework for practice. They developed a specific conception of aims for education (Peters 1966; 1973). This was not necessarily at odds with the democratic values that broadly underpinned the Plowden approach: Peters' *Ethics and Education* (1966) – prescribed reading in the early 1970s for most teachers in training – was firmly grounded in a democratic framework of values. Considered in the light of Peters' arguments, however, 'Plowden' thinking and methods clearly displayed some theoretical inadequacies and conceptual confusions. Dearden's writings on the philosophy of primary education (1967; 1968; 1976) and Peters' (1969) *Perspectives on Plowden* similarly exposed inconsistencies and flaws.

One of the claims of the London philosophers was that what children learned could not be decided by children themselves – not on the grounds that this was inadvisable, but that it was conceptually incoherent. Dearden (1968), for instance, was pointing out that children's education could not be equated with a biological process of growth and that 'need' is an evaluative term: the direction of children's intellectual 'growth' and the identification of their needs is dependent on human values and is not a matter of human nature.

This was a challenge to those who believed that the teacher's role is to respond to needs, as if these were 'given'. Furthermore, Hirst (1973) argued that what children 'needed' to learn could be established on epistemological grounds – on the basis of the nature of knowledge itself. I shall return to this in Chapter 7, but, in brief, Hirst was claiming that a worthwhile curriculum must be construed in terms of human rationality – and the different disciplines of thought on which this is based. Criticism of the Plowden method of 'learning by discovery' followed from this, on the grounds that it was illogical to assume that the human disciplines of thought and enquiry and the knowledge they generated could somehow be discovered from interacting with the material environment rather than with other reasoning human beings (Dearden 1967).

At the time that these philosophers of education were developing their ideas, another contrasting school of thought was emerging. Social scientists also began to raise questions for educationalists. Their new 'sociology of knowledge' recognised knowledge as a social construction (see for example, Berger and Luckman 1966; Young 1971). For them, knowledge was constructed and re-constructed by those generating and using it, in different historical and cultural contexts. From this point of view it would similarly not make sense to assume that, in the classroom, knowledge could be 'discovered' by children through their first-hand experience of the world alone, without engaging with other people. (I shall discuss this further in Chapter 1 and later chapters.) But as far as the nature of knowledge was concerned, their position ran counter to that of the philosophers. From the social scientists' perspective, it was not plausible to construe particular disciplines of thought as universally worthwhile and valid – for all time and for all peoples – as the analytical philosophers were attempting to do. Rather, knowledge – what it was, what was valued and what counted as knowledge – was forever in a state of flux.

These theoretical accounts are significant, as they provided a different way of interpreting what children should be learning in schools. Whereas the philosophers were arguing that the Plowden focus on children's 'needs and interests' was logically incoherent, and that knowledge and the curriculum can be rationally defined, the sociologists were suggesting a more open-ended account of how curriculum decisions are made, grounding them in social practices and power relations. What constituted a curriculum was more about who held the power to decide than it was about the nature of knowledge itself. Whose agenda was to be promoted was not to be settled by providing analysis of the concepts of education. From the social scientists' perspective, the philosophers' accounts were seen as stipulated ideas rather than essential truths, in reality shaped by specific social, political, historical and cultural conditions. From this perspective, if the Plowden model was seen to be deficient, this would be more a question of cultural conceptions and priorities – of dominant practices and discourses, of ideology and power – rather than philosophical necessity.

Primary education in practice – the 1970s and 1980s

Plowden ideas began to be challenged in practice and progressivism began to give way in the late 1970s. The so-called Great Debate about education initiated in 1976 by Jim Callaghan, who was prime minister at the time, reflected the political and public perception that the primary education sector was not delivering and that there was a need for clearer aims and objectives. There was a sense that the system was in a state of collapse, triggered by events in one particular school (William Tyndale) where a seemingly extreme version of child-centred methods had led to a public enquiry (Auld 1976). The view that children should be the arbiters of their learning was called into question. Accountability for the use of public funds demanded something different from, or more than, was apparently being achieved in the child-centred classroom. There were, at that time, no standardised measures by which this could be judged.

In some schools and classrooms, aspects of the ethos and tenets of primary practice that emanated from the child-centred movement persisted into the late 1980s. Indeed, they may have endured into the 1990s. Some teachers, particularly those who had been young and idealistic in the early 1970s continued to hold on to child-centred notions of good practice in principle, if not always in practice. Their ideas about teaching were influenced by the Plowden legacy and its concerns with social justice. They were motivated by beliefs about the rights of the child, perceptions of the oppression of schooling and visions of radical approaches to education. Such teachers continued to value the child's 'ownership' of their learning, the integrated curriculum and the integrated day, and individualised and group-based activities. The classroom environment was deemed to be a key feature of children's self-directed learning – providing resources for learning that prioritised first-hand experience. Ideally, it was rich in artefacts – books and displays. While the 'basics' of Maths and English – or 'language' – may still have been given a distinctive focus, much of the curriculum was organised around themes or topics and teachers would produce plans in the form of 'spider diagrams' or 'topic webs' that linked activities in different curriculum areas to a central idea. These may have been supplemented by records of the activities and of children's learning. It was significant that some head-teachers placed more emphasis on records than plans, at this time, in the belief that the learning often occurred in response to spontaneously arising events or interests. Specific, almost symbolic, features of 'good' classroom practice became widespread: the handcrafted books containing children's work, made by the children, with sewn pages and covers. These, and the carefully double or triple-mounted work, and rich and carefully constructed classroom display, came to signify a kind of orthodoxy of child centred-ness. However, as I shall discuss more fully in later chapters, it is questionable

– even where these practices did occur – how far they embodied new forms of pedagogy, rather than simply changes in the way classrooms and learning were organised.

The post-1988 era

It was the Education Reform Act of 1988 that, perhaps more decisively than anything else, marked the end of an era that many teachers who lived through it might look back on with nostalgia or disbelief. Their feelings may, in part be due to a sense of the loss of their autonomy and control, which they valued very highly. In many respects, teachers – and children – had much more say in what went on in their classrooms before 1988 than they have ever had since. It was through the 1988 Act that control was centralised under national government and later, in 1990, that Local Management of Schools devolved the control of school spending to head teachers and governors, removing control from Local Education Authorities. Prior to that, local authorities were able to respond to local needs in diverse ways and a number of local education authorities were a leading influence on good practice, such as the West Riding of Yorkshire, Leicestershire and the Inner London Education Authority. Ideas were also generated and disseminated through the Schools Council, and there was a network of Teachers' Centres, often dynamic and influential places where teachers shared ideas and found resources and where professional development could be pursued on a localised level through courses and activities. Prescriptions for practice from beyond the classroom were tentative. In short, developments were less 'top down': they were not coordinated nationally and initiatives were not imposed on schools by central government as they have been since 1988.

It would be wrong to assume, however, that the 1970s and 1980s were some kind of golden age. In any case, it transpired that the Plowden vision was not, in actuality, widely realised, and the child-centred revolution was seen by some (Richards 1999, for example) as more of a myth than reality. Richards, writing in 1979, suggested that The Primary Survey (DES 1978) was largely responsible for de-bunking the Plowden myth. It revealed that

> 'the primary school revolution' has not been tried and found wanting but never been tried at all except in a small number of schools; most primary school teachers have not responded in the 'open', flexible, imaginative way curriculum developers assumed they would . . . The current curriculum is revealed as scarcely more than a revamped elementary school curriculum with the same major utilitarian emphasis.
>
> (Richards 1999 p. 28)

Similarly, large-scale research in classrooms began to show what was actually going on. Maurice Galton and his colleagues discovered mismatches between rhetoric and practice through their ORACLE research project (Galton et al. 1980). The research led by Peter Mortimore revealed some superficial, routinised practices (Mortimore et al. 1988). There were clearly varying degrees of commitment to child-centred principles. In some schools the pre-established practices of a more rigid timetable and a more teacher-directed approach may have persisted and in others the principles may have been distorted in practice by practical difficulty, with 'individualised' teaching resulting in unchallenging worksheets or working through textbooks, and queues of children waiting for attention. 'Topics' could become loose collections of conceptually unrelated activities with little depth or purpose. Some good practice was undoubtedly going on, that could have been well justified in terms of democratic values and coherent principles for learning and teaching, but this was by no means universal. The sense that the whole system needed reform took hold, based to some extent on the evidence of research as well as on the emerging view that too much teacher autonomy could undermine children's entitlement to good educational provision.

The call for more control of the curriculum that resulted from the Great Debate was framed initially by left-wing principles of ensuring that every child had an equal and consistent entitlement to high-quality education, but it was taken up with a different purpose by Thatcher's Conservative government in 1979. The move towards a centrally determined national curriculum gathered pace during the eighties, when Thatcherism was at its height. A state-controlled curriculum may seem inconsistent with conservative policy, usually in favour of de-centralising power – but it was pursued within a neo-liberal agenda. While government maintained a focus on the perceived need to 'raise standards', its underlying motives for controlling the curriculum were to create a market (Lawton 1994). I shall discuss this further in Chapter 2, but in short, more standardisation meant that schools could be compared against each other. Standard assessments across all schools would quantify outcomes from the same curriculum content, providing a measure of the relative success of schools across the country. Along with a policy that allowed parents to choose their preferred school (open enrolment), a standardised National Curriculum would create competition and compel schools to strive to be better.

The National Curriculum

These policies became law through the 1988 Act and the process of developing and introducing a National Curriculum began. Teachers today are utterly familiar with the concept of a statutory curriculum, but, at that time, this was breaking completely new ground. Working parties were set up for each subject area and included experts in each field. The discussions and public consultations were extensive – indeed, it might be regarded as remarkably so, in comparison with today. The process, however, was not without controversy. For example, the selection of members of working parties sometimes clearly reflected a particular political bias, such as the appointment to the English working party of Brian Cox, who had been an author of the so-called Black Papers (for example, Cox and Dyson 1969) which were highly critical of progressive education. (It is interesting to note that this particular appointment in the end backfired as Cox radically changed his views during the National Curriculum consultation process!)

The subject-centred approach, in which programmes of study were designed for all phases – primary through to secondary – in discrete areas, was a new departure for primary schools. It meant that subjects were seen in isolation from each other, which was a quite different approach from the cross-curricular way in which the primary curriculum had been conceived post-Plowden. Room for manoeuvre was very limited: the legal proviso that the National Curriculum was not intended to represent *all* that would be taught in schools (the 'whole' curriculum covered more) may well have seemed irrelevant to those trying to fit the National Curriculum into the available hours. As each working party sought to ensure that its own subject area was properly represented, the lack of a holistic overview meant that the curriculum that was introduced into schools was inevitably going to be very full, and probably fragmented, from the start.

What was achieved, at this stage, was a thorough overhaul of what was considered to be the valuable knowledge, understanding, skills and processes of each subject area. In this, the working parties were informed by those who were well versed in their subjects. It might seem that this was a time of filling out what Hirst had earlier outlined as the necessary components of the curriculum and a clarification of the nature of the disciplines. In fact, however, the structure of the curriculum was not given any epistemological justification. Deciding on the structure of the new curriculum seemed to have been regarded as unproblematic and was, as many commentators have noted (e.g. Ball 1994), ultimately a reflection of the traditional curriculum of the 1904 Education Act (albeit with a few additions, such as technology).

Assessment, accountability and control

While the National Curriculum provided the standard content, a Task Group on Assessment and Testing, chaired by Paul Black, set out to devise methods of assessment that could capture the wide-ranging knowledge, understanding and skills that were specified in the curriculum. It may surprise some readers that each of the ten curriculum areas had its own ring binder of requirements and guidance. As well as numerous 'Attainment Targets' in all subjects (now considerably reduced in number), there were hundreds of 'Statements of Attainment', against which primary teachers were expected to assess children's learning. The assessment process devised by Black's working party was based on complex forms of standard assessment designed to preserve the established principles of good primary practice (as they were then perceived) in a new context of standardisation, accountability, targets and measurement. At first, it required extensive teacher assessment, which was to be carried out through 'tasks' rather than pencil and paper tests. (At this point the 'T' in SATs stood for 'tasks' instead of 'tests'.) These entailed an individualised approach that would thoroughly assess each child's thinking, using teacher observation of activities. For instance, the Science assessment in Year 2 entailed teachers observing, assessing and recording the learning of each child undertaking a floating and sinking investigation. The first round of KS1 (Key Stage One) SATs, however, inevitably showed that this was an unrealistic goal and 'tasks' were soon replaced with externally devised 'tests'. In any case, such detailed assessment of individuals' learning was not essential to the purposes of assessment under the new market model, which was primarily to provide comparative data across schools (see Chapter 2). Once testing was established, league tables followed – initially created by the media – to rank schools according to their performance.

Along with the new arrangements for curriculum and assessment came Ofsted inspections. Again, inspection was symptomatic of much tighter control over schools and teachers and was important to the creation of the education market: it would ensure that parents had the necessary information to choose their child's school in the new era of 'open enrolment'.

There remained one important element that was not subject to legislation – and that was the *way* in which the curriculum was taught. This stayed under the control of teachers and schools. As there was no legal requirement to teach in a particular way, in the wake of the introduction of a crowded curriculum some primary teachers continued to teach through 'topics'. The conventional structure of the National Curriculum, however, carried implicit messages about the value of much older, traditional ways of teaching the curriculum. It soon became a policy focus to establish a subject-centred approach to teaching with a traditional subject-based timetable that reflected Conservative preferences. In 1992 the government commissioned an enquiry into the primary curriculum, led by Alexander, Rose and Woodhead (who became known, ironically, as the 'three wise men') and the subsequent report (1992) was used by the then Secretary of State for Education, Kenneth Clarke, to promote subject-based approaches to teaching. The effect was that primary schools increasingly organised their day around a subject-centred timetable rather than teaching through topic.

While it was beyond the remit of government to prescribe how the curriculum should be organised and taught, messages were effectively disseminated through Ofsted's judgements of good practice. Indeed, over time, Ofsted has been an efficient means of ensuring that schools and teachers comply with government recommendations. In fact, a culture of compliance (Gleeson and Husbands 2001) became well established during the 1990s, so that when the Literacy and Numeracy Strategies were introduced (DfEE 1998; 1999b) teachers took them on board, even though they were not legally obliged to do so. The Strategies prescribed in minute detail how teachers should plan, organise and teach literacy and numeracy 'hours' and provided strict guidelines as to not only how a lesson should be structured in three, timed parts but also what exactly should be going on. The burden was on schools to show that they could raise children's performance by other means, and in the face of Ofsted inspectors it was a brave school that took that risk.

Calls to slim down the overloaded curriculum began soon after its inception and quite quickly led to the Dearing review (Dearing 1993). As a consequence, a new version of the National Curriculum was introduced in 1995 with a promise of no further interventions for five years. In 1997, however, when the New Labour government came into power, education was destined for further overhaul. The Prime Minister, Tony Blair, made this clear with his famous mantra 'Education; education; education'. The promise of a period of calm was broken when the new focus on the basics was identified as the key to raising achievement and the Literacy and Numeracy strategies were brought on stream. The National Curriculum was cut back again for 2000 (DfEE 1999a), giving teachers more discretion over coverage to make space for the Strategies but, close on the heels of the new version of the National Curriculum of 2000, came the schemes of work devised by the QCA (Qualifications and Curriculum Authority). Again, these were very detailed templates for lessons in the different curriculum areas. Even though they were non-statutory, the climate of compliance led many schools to adopt these exemplars as their curriculum plan.

I shall return to this more recent history in later chapters, but for the purposes of this introduction, it is enough to note that by the twenty-first century, the prescribed and performance-driven approach signalled values that were very different from those of the child-centred era. The expectation that teachers would conform and comply and achieve the required outcomes was now firmly embedded. There was a clear sense that end results – extrinsic ends, such as 'level 4' SATs scores and a high-ranked position for the school in the league tables – were taking precedence over other values in education.

Concluding reflections

This brief, historical overview sets the scene for appraising future developments in learning and teaching in the primary phase. It should help to show how current practice and thinking and possibilities for the future have been shaped and how teachers can learn from the past.

There are indications that new practices have been emerging in primary schools. More 'creative' approaches, however, need to be theoretically coherent, and the underpinning values need to be clearly articulated if the pitfalls and the fate of the 'progressive' education of the past are to be avoided. The same must apply to the greater diversity of practices envisaged by the current government if they really are to bring worthwhile changes.

It will become clear, however, in the chapters that follow, how the testing regime and the pervasive target-orientated policies and their underlying values continue to obstruct the transformation of primary education. In a culture that has been shaped by the 'performance' agenda, the dominant teaching and learning practices are in conflict with the more flexible approaches that have begun to develop and might yet be realised. I shall explore and challenge these instrumental practices and consider the alternatives in the chapters that follow.

An underlying position of this book will be that education is best served by investigating and working with educational principles and values rather than by responding to imposed expectations of compliance and performance. In the book as whole, I shall discuss, from socio-cultural perspectives, the ways in which children's transformation through learning comes about and how teachers can support it. I argue for an approach to the transformation of schools that is grounded in the idea that principled action provides the way forward for primary *education* and, in order to develop that, the discussion will be approached with a critical focus on the current context of the school and its discourses of *schooling*. Underlying the discussion is the notion that good practice is constructed in educational contexts – it is work in progress rather than a prescription to apply pre-defined templates. Professional knowledge and understanding is a matter of enquiring, reasoning and reflecting and is not a result of knee-jerk responses, 'copying and pasting' or ticking boxes. Above all, it is assumed that change must meet the overriding challenge to ensure that the time children spend in their primary school makes a positive difference to their learning and lives.

Issues for teachers

- What are your visions for primary education?
- How do people in your professional community and your workplace context talk about their practice?
- How do you see your rights as a teacher and the rights of the children you teach?
- How do you see 'performance' practices and discourses impacting on what you do?
- What do you make, at this point, of the distinction between schooling and education?
- How do you see practices and values being shaped in school? In the local community? By central government?
- How do you see recent developments in practices and policies in schools?
- Reflecting on your values and principles as a teacher, to what extent are they consistent with your practices?
- How do you think your practices and values and the way you understand learning and teaching are influenced by those practices and ideas of the past that are discussed in this Introduction?

1 Children as thinking learners

Chapter overview

In this chapter, I look at how theories of learning have changed over time. As well as showing the inadequacy of the models of teaching that are derived from behaviourism and its underlying conceptions of children, my aim is to explore alternative accounts and their implications. I look at contrasting ideas, where children are seen as active in their own learning, and compare the constructivism of Piaget with the social constructivism of Vygotsky and Bruner. This brings into focus the issue of language and how children make meaning in the social and cultural contexts which are shaped by language users. I discuss how Lave and Wenger (1991) have developed these ideas to show how learning is situated in social practices. This introduces the possibility that being a teacher is more a matter of being a fellow participant in the 'socially situated activities' that constitute learning than of 'acting upon' children to bring learning about. These ideas will be developed further in later chapters.

Looking at learning

In the Introduction, I explained some of the background to the current situation in English Primary Schools, where teachers are under pressure to deliver results. The difficulty with this emphasis on outcomes and performance is that it inevitably affects the way teachers teach. Put bluntly, in the context of the drive to 'raise standards', the purpose of the work teachers do in the classroom can sometimes simply be the improvement of children's responses to a test paper. It can seem that as long as their pupils are able to come up with the right answers to the questions asked, the teacher's job is done. In Chapter 2, I shall say more about instrumental values in schools and classrooms to see how what teachers do, or feel compelled to do, is shaped by this dominant culture in schools. In this chapter, I look at how children learn, in order to show how teachers' practice is framed by theories and values. How children's learning is understood and how children are valued have implications for how teachers might change their practice and ultimately challenge and change the existing culture of learning and teaching in schools.

Dickens fictitious character, Gradgrind, in *Hard Times* (Dickens 1969, first published 1854) is often used as an illustration of a teacher working in a school system dominated by performance. Gradgrind, under the watchful eyes of the government inspector, ridicules one of his pupils, Sissy Jupe, for being unable to give the formal definition of a horse. He turns to another child, Bitzer, who can recite it perfectly:

> Quadruped. Graminivorous. Forty teeth, namely twenty-four grinders, four eye teeth, and twelve incisive. Sheds coat in the spring; in marshy countries sheds hoofs too. Hoofs hard, but requiring to be shod with iron. Age known by marks in mouth.
>
> (p. 50)

Bitzer's response is what Gradgrind was looking for: he can regurgitate what he has learned off by heart. But Sissy cannot. Dickens implies, however, that despite disappointing Gradgrind, Sissy does know all about horses – because she has grown up with them. Her father, Sissy says, 'belongs to the horse riding' – or, as Gradgrind describes him, he is a veterinary surgeon, a farrier and a horse breaker. The story implicitly raises the question: what is understood by learning? Is it simply 'changed behaviour' – a case of the learner being able to do something they couldn't do before? Bitzer would meet this criterion. His response shows that he can do what the teacher has asked him to do – give a definition of a horse. He has, apparently, acquired a certain ability or skill. He may not, however, have any *understanding* of what he reels off to Gradgrind and the inspector. There is nothing in his performance that categorically and unambiguously indicates that he knows what is meant by 'graminivorous' or 'grinders' – terms which he confidently includes in his definition. Sissy, on the other hand, being familiar with horses and having a very clear idea of 'a horse', may not know that a horse is graminivorous, but she would know what it eats as this is part of her everyday experience. Sissy would understand what 'horse' means in a way that Bitzer may not.

Dickens' satire works because the reader will assume that Sissy has learned all about horses from her informal experience. But how did Sissy learn? On one level, this can seem an unnecessary question. She simply lives around the animals. The question repays analysis, however, as how it is answered carries with it implications for teachers' practice. There is more to the process than merely absorbing or 'abstracting' ideas from experience of the material world – as if concepts already exist, in some way, in the physical environment itself; as if they are already 'givens'. On this view, the idea, or concept, of 'horse' and, in contrast, the concept of 'sheep', for example, and the dividing lines between them, are simply present in the world: Sissy would see a horse in the real world and would simply extract the idea of what it is, acquiring a mental category to which the term 'horse' can be applied, along with all the other ideas she holds about horses. The assumption here is that the development of her thinking – her learning – would be an individual, private matter. This does not provide a very adequate explanation, however. How does she know to which mental category the term applies?

An alternative explanation, that concepts are acquired through others pointing out that this is a 'horse' and that is a 'sheep' (ostensive definition) also falls apart: how is she to identify which specific aspect of her perceptual experience is being referred to as horse, as distinct from, say, its colour 'brown', or some other feature of it? Again, this account seems to call for a pre-existing mental category, to which the label of horse can be applied, in which case, it takes us back to the question of how that is acquired.

Behaviourist learning theory

Gradgrind, in his role as a teacher in a particular sort of school system, was not interested in the way that Sissy had come to know the characteristics of a horse from her everyday activities and without his specific instruction. For Gradgrind, the children are merely 'pitchers' that he must fill with facts. He is not concerned with what is going on in the children's lives or in their heads – only with making sure that they can recall what he has taught them. His is the sort of mode of instruction that, according to Vygotsky, cannot lead to the development of concepts but, rather, 'substitutes the learning of dead and empty verbal schemes for the mastery of living knowledge' (Vygotsky 1987 cited in Daniels 2007). His efforts to elicit particular behavioural responses from his pupils reflect the kind of 'learning theory' that was developed some time ago by behaviourist psychologists such as Skinner (1938). There is insufficient space here to explore their ideas in depth – but put simply, for these theorists, learning rests on the idea that a stimulus causes a response. Bringing about learning requires some external means of 'acting upon' the learner – providing the conditions that would produce the desired response and reinforcing that response through reward and punishment.

Children as active in their own learning

An alternative view of learning rests on a different set of ideas which challenged behaviourist accounts. Rather than seeing learning in causal terms – and the learner as being 'acted upon' – children themselves are understood to be active in their own learning. They come into the world with a propensity for finding out how it works and for making sense of it. They already have the neurological means and the mental facility to make this possible: to be able to categorise what they experience – to recognise similarities and differences. This gives them the capacity to form concepts, which are the mental constructs through which they bring order into their experience.

One way of looking at the process of learning, then, is as the active construction by the learner of a mental model. It was Piaget who developed the idea of the child as active in the process of learning in this way. This was a major contribution to theories of learning. From a Piagetian perspective, the child's development occurs through physically interacting with the environment and the problems it presents: thought was internalised *action*. On this account, the child's knowledge and understanding are built through schemes of activity that the child develops through exploration and practical problem solving. Existing activity schemes enable the child to 'assimilate' a new experience and to 'accommodate' it. In other words, as a learner encounters a new experience they incorporate it into their existing activity schemes. When they meet new experiences and ideas that they cannot easily accommodate to their existing schemes, they re-model the schemes so the new experience can be incorporated. In this way the activity schemes that the child develops are constructed by the child, using what they already 'know' to make sense of the new. This constructive process takes place as the child acts in and on the world around them.

Wood (1998 p. 53) provides a useful illustration of the process which I shall quote at length to help explain it:

> Objects become 'known' and 'recognised' in terms of the actions that serve to *assimilate* them to the fulfilment of intentions. So, for example, a bottle may be known and perceived in terms of activities like grasping, bringing it to the mouth, sucking and swallowing. To the extent that any new 'container' can be assimilated successfully to these schemes in order to fulfil the desire to drink, then it too will be 'known' in terms of 'bottle-related' actions . . . in Piagetian terms, every act of assimilation involves an element of *accommodation*. Piaget uses the term to refer to the changes, often minor ones that have to be made to pre-existing schemes of activity in order to make possible the assimilation of a new experience. Imagine, for example, the infant

trying, for the first time, to pick up and drink from a full, pint-sized container. She tries to assimilate this new object to her existing schemes of grasping and drinking but finds that the new object *resists* her efforts and begins to tilt and spill . . . The child cries out or in some way requests assistance. Her father helps her to lift the container until it is in a position that enables her to fulfil her intention to drink (to assimilate the object). She has now *accommodated* her activities to this new experience. The realm of objects that can be assimilated to the activity of drinking is now split into those that can be assimilated by the original schemes of grasping and drinking, and those that require other means (e.g. a call for help) to enable assimilation.

Wood suggests that she may discriminate between these two classes by size at this stage, although this experience provides the foundations for the concept of weight. When new experiences cannot readily be assimilated this leads to mental 'disequilibrium', 'cognitive conflict' or 'cognitive dissonance'. The structure of the child's thinking 'adapts' to create a new state of equilibrium – new mental schemes are developed and this is how learning proceeds. Through his observations, Piaget concluded that children pass through a series of *stages* in their development, moving from the 'sensori-motor' (where they begin to link their physical activity with their senses) to a stage where they are 'opera-tional' and can act on the world. At first the child learns through operations that are 'concrete' – or practical – but as the child matures they are able to think in the abstract, or through 'formal operations', through their internalised activity schemes. This maturational approach meant that, for Piaget, child development resembled a biological process. As such, these stages of development were common to all children – regardless of their social and cultural experience.

I have over-simplified complex ideas that could only be fully appreciated through a study of Piaget's work, but my summary should provide enough of an explanation to show that the way in which learning is understood has implications for what teachers do. Piagetian ideas were clearly influential in the era of child-centred teaching at the time of Plowden that I discussed in the Introduction: they provide a theoretical explanation for the practice of giving children space and time to explore an environment that has been enriched with sensory and practical experience. To foster children's development there would need to be provision of materials and resources for children to manipu-late in order to find out how the world works and to develop the requisite concepts to help them understand it. The idea of 'stages of development' following a pre-determined path of progression gave rise to the idea of 'readiness'. For example, for a Piagetian teacher in the Plowden era, there was little point in expecting a child to engage with logical thought or abstract ideas before they were ready.

The importance of play in this process of development is clear – to learn, children need to be able to interact with and act upon the world. Play offers opportunities for trying things out. It provides the context and the vehicle through which those activities that may have serious purpose or consequences in the 'real world' can be tried out experimentally by children. Learning occurs 'heuristically' or by discovery. For a Piagetian, this 'hands-on' approach to learning is crucial, both at the early sensori-motor stage and later at the 'concrete operational stage'. The teacher, in this context, would have an important role in facilitating learning, making rich and stimulating provision with plenty of opportunities for practical problem-solving, but could otherwise stand back. They would need to make sure that experiences they provided took account of children's readiness to learn – in other words, that they were appropriate to the child's level of development – and they would ensure children could work at their own pace, without undue intervention or instruction.

Social theories of learning

The context for learning, however, is a social one. Learning does not take place in isolation. Children watch and hear what others do and say. As I've already pointed out above, however, learning from experience is not just a matter of absorbing concepts from the environment. The philosopher Wittgenstein (1953) helped to provide a way of avoiding these conundrums around learning, which had occupied philosophers for years. He argued that how people think – the way they classify and conceptualise the world – is integrally related to how people use their language: 'The meaning of a word is its use in the language' (p. 20). Sissy would have come to know what a horse is in the company of her father. Being around horses would have meant that he would have been talking about them and Sissy would have learned to talk about them too. As Hamlyn argued, in his analysis of how understanding comes about:

> It is not just that [the child] comes to see similarities and differences (although he [sic] no doubt does just this), but that some of these are given importance by the roles which they play in relationships with others, particularly of course his mother or whoever it is that is responsible for the child's nurture in a given culture.
>
> (1978 p. 102)

The language or languages used by a social group help to shape the way that the group conceptualises their experience of the world; the way the world is ordered and classified is shaped by the way a group uses a particular language – or, by how that group participates in what Wittgenstein referred to as a particular 'language game'. People's conceptions, and their perceptions too, on this view, are shaped according to how the language is used in situations where the 'rules' for its use are shared within a 'form of life'. So, from this perspective, the idea that concepts can somehow be absorbed by an individual from their environment in isolation from others – which, as I suggested above, does not seem to make sense – is superseded by the idea that concepts are generated through using the language with other people. Learning a language is not a matter of clothing pre-existing concepts with words – privately and independently of others, as the 'abstraction' idea would suggest. Wittgenstein showed that the idea of 'private languages' is a contradiction in terms. The ways in which an individual classifies and categorises the world are themselves shaped by the way others give meaning to their experience through language.

From this point of view the social context of learning is a community of language users. When Sissy talks of horse-breaking, she understands this activity in terms of the language of horse breakers. She is using language appropriately in the context, although others not familiar with the practice may not fully understand the way she is using 'breaking'. Similarly, when a child learns, for instance, to say 'get down' when she climbs off a chair, she understands her actions in terms of the language used by those around her. Piaget was by no means unaware of the significance of language. But, for Piaget, it is active inter-action with the environment that structures the child's thinking, rather than language – in a sense, the activity schemes are established independently of language and are unaffected by it. As Wood explains, for Piaget, the child's use of language is determined by the way the child's thinking has been structured through activity. As Bruner (1986 p.144) puts it: 'For Piaget, language *reflects* thought and does not determine it in any sense. That the internal logic of thought is expressed in language has no effect on the logic itself.' The ways the child can use language are therefore limited by the stage of development they have reached as a result of their physical interaction with their environment.

Wittgenstein's philosophical account, then, brings the social context and language into sharper focus in accounts of learning. In terms of psychological theory, Vygotsky, similarly, has been very influential, giving a different emphasis to the role of language from Piaget. Vygotsky's ideas began to have more of an impact in the educational field in the 1980s (although he worked and wrote in the 1930s) and have become increasingly significant since. Bruner, too, understood learning as a social process. For Bruner, culture and the social aspect of life are quite clearly the means through which individuals make meaning (Bruner 1986, 1996). From Vygotsky's and Bruner's 'socio-cultural' perspective, the Piagetian model appears to have serious shortcomings. The world a child encounters cannot be seen as a place of neutral objects with which the child interacts and which present problems to be tackled. Instead it is seen as having already been interpreted and given meaning by others. Indeed, it is difficult to discuss the nature of a neutral world, as any discourse is already interpreting it and giving it significance in particular ways. The world, as it is experienced, then, is an interpreted world, made meaningful by those who live in it. As Bruner argued:

> Most of our encounters with the world are not. . . . direct encounters. Even our direct experiences, so called, are assigned for interpretation to ideas about cause and consequence, and the world that emerges for us is a conceptual world. When we are puzzled about what we encounter, we renegotiate its meaning in a manner that is concordant with what those around us believe.
>
> (1986 p.122)

It is through the categories, classifications and forms of representation that are languages, that children construct meaning. The world, with its material arte-facts and its social practices, including language, constitute the resources – or the tools (Vygotsky 1978) – for learning. It is through interaction with those who make, and make use of, those resources that the child learns. From this perspective, when a child is puzzled by the container she cannot lift, she builds a new concept of containers that are too big, in a context where others are already making those distinctions in their use of language. As Wittgenstein's work showed, children's learning is shaped within a community of language users, who already use language in ways they have learned.

Both Piaget and Vygotsky, then, shared an understanding, as develop-mental psychologists, of the centrality of the child's activity in the process of learning, but Vygotsky saw the role of language differently. Whereas Piaget presented a constructivist account of learning, Vygotsky provided a social constructivist view. What is distinctive about Vygotsky's ideas is that language is, in itself, one of the activities that helps to construct thought; a tool through which thinking – the higher intellectual processes such as planning, evaluating and reasoning – comes about (Wood 1998). As Wood (p. 31) explains:

> Note that these processes are *culturally* formed in social interaction. Looked at in this way, language does not simply *reflect* or represent concepts already formed on a non-verbal level. Rather, it structures and directs the processes of thinking and concept formation themselves.

Vygotsky's analysis, then, resonates with that of Wittgenstein. It is not a case of labelling pre-existing concepts with language – thought is, rather, *constituted* by language. As Bruner (1986) points out, Vygotsky recognised the potential of language for shaping the culture as well as for transmitting it – he highlighted its generative role: 'Piaget's [view] expresses his faith in the inherent logic of thought and subordinates language to it. Vygotsky's gives language both a cultural past and a generative present' (Bruner 1986 p. 145).

It is all language users, including children, who contribute to shaping the culture in this way.

While he acknowledged the significance of Piaget's work, ('. . . Piaget's accomplishments were gigantic' [Bruner 1986 p. 147]), Bruner himself explored the possible limitations of Piaget's view that the development of thought has an 'internal logic' that is not determined in any sense by language. Bruner was certainly building on the work of Piaget, but was also inspired by Vygotsky's work, which he saw as a 'provocation to find a way of understanding man as a product of culture as well as a product of nature' (Bruner 1986 p. 78). In the preface (p. X) to his later book he wrote:

> you cannot understand mental activity unless you take into account the cultural setting and its resources, the very things that give mind its shape and scope. Learning, remembering, talking, imagining: all of them are made possible by participating in a culture.
>
> (Bruner 1996)

Like Vygotsky, he saw that communication and language were pivotal in the formation of thought. From this perspective, he emphasised the central role of other people in a child's learning:

> I have come increasingly to recognise that most learning in most settings is a communal activity, a sharing of the culture. It is not just that the child must make knowledge his [sic] own, but that he must make it his own in a community of those who share his sense of belonging to a culture.
>
> (Bruner 1986 p. 127)

He shares Vygotsky's view that language embodies cultural history, and that it is also more than 'being simply a vehicle for the transmission of cultural history'. (Bruner 1986 p. 143). Language users, within a culture, actively construct the categories, classifications and forms of representation that are the languages and discourses that constitute that culture.

Learning as 'situated'

Lave and Wenger (1991) were also influential in taking social theories of learning further. Significantly, these theorists showed how social situations are necessary to explaining learning itself. They developed the idea that learning is integral to social and cultural contexts. In taking this approach they were challenging the conventional view of learning – including that of Piaget – that it is primarily a cognitive process whereby the individual internalises knowledge. For Lave and Wenger, the cognitive accounts presume a dichotomy between inside and outside. Their argument is difficult to convey in a few words, but they suggest that on the cognitive accounts, the emphasis is on the changes within the individual. Though learning 'takes place' *in* a social context, on those accounts, this context is not part of the explanation of learning itself. From Lave's and Wenger's point of view, the cognitive accounts would beg the question: what *is* this learning process that occurs in a social situation and involves other people? How can it be described or explained? For them, a social theory of learning relates to cognition in social situations in a different way. As they explain it:

> learning is not merely situated in practice – as if it were some independently re-ifiable process that just happened to be located somewhere; learning is an integral part of the generative social practice in the lived-in world.
>
> (p. 35)

In other words: 'learning is an aspect of all activity' (p. 38). On their argument, because learning cannot be understood in any other way than in terms of social situations, it can only be understood in terms of their particularities. It challenges the very idea of generalisation. In other words, the social context provides the explanation of the process of learning not only in a general sense: a social theory of learning, they suggest, situates cognition in *specific* social practices in particular times, places and cultures – or, to use their terminology, in 'communities of practice' (see Introduction). In short, and at risk of misrepresenting the subtlety of their argument, it is not a matter of 'learning' occurring through participation *in* 'social practices'; rather, learning *is* participation in social practices. As Sfard (2009 p. 47)) puts it, this is 'learning-as-participation'. It is not a matter of learning *by* doing; learning and doing are indivisible. It is by participating in the activities of the communities to which the child belongs that they actively and literally make sense of their experience and transform their worlds. I hope, in the following chapters, to illustrate these ideas and to clarify them further.

Social theories of learning – implications for child development

Once it is acknowledged, then, that learning is located in social and cultural contexts, there is a shift from the Piagetian view of the child as a 'lone scientist' to that of a socially situated learner, which means that the construction of thought becomes a shared venture. The worlds that the child interacts with are more than tangible, physical environments: they are conceptualised worlds. This also means that the idea that the growing child passes naturally through the 'developmental stages' that Piaget identified – and that this is a process common to all children – becomes less convincing. The socially situated view of learning unsettles the assumptions about paths of development that follow a seemingly biologically determined course. Development is shaped by the specific activities of the particular social groups within a culture that include the child, so it is in no way fixed or universal. To summarise, the child gives order and sense to their experience – they construct their worlds – in the company of others and in the context of the patterns of meaning making that have been established in the social and cultural groups to which they belong.

The socio-cultural accounts, then, call into question those approaches to teaching (which were advocated during the Plowden era) that focus on the facilitation of a child's interaction with their material environment so they can progress through predictable stages of development. As I noted in the Introduction, at the time when ideas about 'learning from experience' and 'learning by discovery' were being widely disseminated in schools, philosophers such as Dearden (1967) and Peters (1969) were already warning of the possible conceptual confusions that I've mentioned above. From a psychological perspective, researchers were showing that when the experiments and observations that Piaget carried out were conducted rather differently, then different results were achieved. Margaret Donaldson, for instance, showed that if the experimental tasks were contextualised differently – if they were set up so that the child participants could make more sense of them – the children could act in ways that did not conform to Piaget's predictions (Donaldson 1978). When children were better able to interpret the task or the language that was used during the experiment, they could exceed what might be expected of them according to Piaget's theories. It seemed that the social experience of the child and the social and linguistic context of the task made all the difference to what the child could do. What seemed like a failure to reason was instead a failure to understand the task. Again, learning was shown to be not so much dependent on the child's stage of development but on the specific characteristics of the context.

Researchers, then, were showing that there are cultural assumptions built into accounts of development. The ways in which children learn, and what they learn, are neither universal nor static. These challenges to Piaget's thinking now permeate educational research. John Matthews, for instance, has exposed the assumptions that are embedded in the way Piaget charted the development of children's visual representation. Piaget saw its natural course leading towards the unquestioned end point of visually realistic representation, but, as Matthews (1999) pointed out, visual realism is a cultural convention. As a way of representing the world through drawing, painting and sculpture, it is not an immutable end point of human maturation, but is culturally and historically defined.

Changing views of learning and children: implications for teaching

As I shall go on to explore further in later chapters, socio-cultural views of learning lead to approaches to teaching that are very different from Gradgrind's methods, or even, possibly, from those of some primary school teachers today who follow those traditions (those who are concerned only that children should produce the right responses in a SATs test, for instance). These newer approaches require the teacher to engage with the child as a thinker – with the child's mind.

It is worth pausing here, as this suggestion in itself, might seem a questionable or even unintelligible idea to some. Another person's mind is, after all, inaccessible to others. Maybe, in the end, the behaviourist's approach makes more sense. In reality, the argument would go, it is only behaviour that can be accessed so perhaps teachers can do no more than to try to change behaviours. This argument points the way to the sort of scientific mind-set that behaviourists adopted. Experiments would determine which conditions (of stimuli and reinforcement) would produce the intended behavioural results, potentially giving scientific predictability to teaching and learning. Behaviourists, then, would be concerned with what children 'do', but – and this is significant – only in the limited sense of manifest behaviours. They would focus on the skills that children acquire and demonstrate as these are readily observable, unlike children's understanding. This model of learning and teaching perhaps remains attractive to those who want to set targets and improve outcomes, as I shall discuss more fully in Chapter 2. It can appear to offer objectivity, because it focuses on what can be observed. It promises predictable outcomes and measurable results – the focus on changed behaviour entails a straightforward comparison of what the child can do now with what they could do before – all 'objectively' observable. All these features add up to a simple, 'mastery' based, linear, input-outcome view of teaching and learning that seems achievable in the practical classroom situation.

When it is acknowledged, however, that teachers are ultimately concerned with children's minds, and the development of understanding, things are more complicated. There are obvious pitfalls in exclusively focusing on behaviours as the equivalents of thought. Behaviour is, clearly, very ambiguously related to mental life (Dearden 1976). It was evident in the example from Dickens that Gradgrind cannot be sure whether Bitzer understands what he was saying, or whether he is only reciting 'by heart'. Similarly, does the fact that a child can skilfully call out the words from a page equate to them understanding what they read? When a child sits still facing the teacher does it necessarily mean they are making sense of what they hear? This means too, that how behaviours themselves are identified is far from objective. Is the child reading? Are they listening? What behaviours imply, then, and even what they are, is all open to interpretation. As socio-cultural accounts make clear, inferences are always grounded in cultural assumptions – in these last examples, in assumptions about what is understood as 'reading' and 'listening'.

For teachers, the idea of pre-specifying behavioural outcomes may seem straightforward but, as should now be clearer, it is actually highly problematic. As Dearden argues, it 'may be feasible enough for isolated physical or practical skills, such as doing a handstand or planing some wood. It will still have some feasibility if what we want is simply verbal responses to questions that we put. But the further we move from such relatively unambiguous bits of behaviour, the more impractical and unreliable this hard-headed search for certainty will become' (p. 23). I shall come back to these issues in Chapter 2.

Returning to the idea that children are active in their own learning, from this perspective what children 'do' acquires a much broader significance. As the discussion in this chapter suggests, the activity of teaching entails finding ways of engaging with children as motivated people with intentions and feelings, who are actively developing their ideas. This also potentially accords them much more respect than when the teacher concerns themselves only with their behavioural responses. Given that Bruner holds the view that learning is embedded in and contributes to the making of culture, it is perhaps not surprising that he saw earlier theories and pedagogy, such as behaviourism, as products of the culture and related them to the views of childhood prevailing at that time. He pointed out that earlier characterisations of the child all implied that the young were somehow deficient:

> The pedagogy that resulted was some view of teaching as surgery, suppression, replacement, deficit filling, or some mix of them all. When 'learning theory' emerged in this century, there was added to the list a further 'method', reinforcement: reward and punishment could become the levers of a new technology for accomplishing these ends.
>
> (Bruner 1986 p.124)

By pre-supposing that children are deficient, teaching methods that are based on a behaviourist theory of learning carry with them particular ways of valuing children. The teacher holds the power in determining the direction of the learning and in controlling the processes that will bring it about. The child is not valued as a self-determining agent in their learning: they are an object in the educational process rather than a subject. In short, such methods have implications for the way children are seen as *persons*.

Dickens' fictional character of Gradgrind reflected some of the social practices of the time – cultural norms and values that carried similar assumptions about his charges. He was duty bound to satisfy the educational inspectors through the children's performance. Dickens presents a caricature, but clearly Gradgrind had little interest in Sissy Jupe as a person, who was living in a world that held meaning and value for her – he declared that he was not the least interested in her father's occupation. Her lived experience, her interests, knowledge and understanding were of no consequence. From the socio-cultural perspective, it becomes clear how, in the case of Sissy Jupe, her knowledge of horses was not so much simply a result of her experiences of those animals in her home environment, but her membership of a family who worked with horses. If only Gradgrind had understood the significance of that to her learning, he would have realised how much she knew. But this was not his concern.

Bruner draws attention to the way the kind of cultural norms that Gradgrind's practice represents have survived over time. Writing in 1986, he contrasted his own vision of education with

> traditions of pedagogy that derive from another time, another inter-pretation of culture, another conception of authority – one that looked at the process of education as a *transmission* of knowledge and values, *by* those who knew more *to* those who knew less and knew it less expertly.
>
> (Bruner 1986 p. 123)

I shall go on to discuss more fully in Chapter 2 and beyond, how the culture of schooling in the twenty-first century has continued to sustain such practices – typified in the past by the instilling of information and the modelling of a narrow range of skills. Teachers today will still recognise what Bruner is describing here. Primary school practices continue to place excessive emphasis on transmission (Alexander 2010) and teachers are still pre-occupied with outcomes. Furthermore, a school and classroom culture of transmission creates a situation where respect for children as people is compromised, setting up the possible tensions between teachers' values and practices (to which I referred in the Introduction). By contrast, in emphasising that children learn as active meaning makers, in social contexts, the social constructivist view of learning calls for a responsive approach to children, rather than a didactic one.

When learning is theorised within a socio-cultural framework, it becomes clear how children's learning might be limited by outdated transmission modes of teaching. From this perspective, the cultural norms and values of the school are highly significant. As I have said, from the point of view of Lave and Wenger (1991), the patterns of meaning making that have been established in the social and cultural groups to which children belong – the 'communities of practice' in which they are active participants – *constitute* the children's learning. This includes the practices in the school contexts in which children live out a considerable part of their lives. From this point of view, learning is understood not just in terms of the process of the individual constructing their knowledge, and how they are supported in doing this – for instance by their teachers' pedagogical actions – but in terms of the features of the social practices in which learners are participating. In contrast to more conventional views, this focuses attention on 'the structure of social practice rather than privileging the structure of pedagogy' (p. 113). In other words, schools and classrooms must be seen in the round as the source of the learning that is going on, rather than looking in isolation at what children and teachers are doing. From this perspective, it is crucial for teachers to gain insight into the culture of the school and classroom. They need to be clear about the contexts in which they and the children are going about their daily lives – the nature of school and classroom practices and values in all their aspects – if change is to be achieved.

Concluding reflections

Children's learning can be seen from different perspectives: the way it has been described and explained over time has changed. Piaget's constructivist way of explaining learning displaced behaviourist accounts, and in turn has given way to social-constructivism. The socio-cultural challenges to the way learning is construed have significant implications for approaches to teaching. From this different perspective, how the child's thinking develops depends on the social and cultural practices, the ways of talking and thinking of the social and cultural groups in which the child lives and learns; it is the shared practices of meaning making that account for children's learning. The social and cultural practices of the communities of which the child is a member, and in which the child participates, include those of the school and classroom. These situations are worlds where meanings are shifting, changing, forming, re-forming within the communities that construct and use them: languages and discourses are constructed in multifarious ways.

If both the development of the child and the content of their learning are products of the activities of social groups to which they belong, of their culture and history, then teachers do not stand outside children's learning and influence it through their chosen pedagogical actions. They are an integral part of the situation. Whatever they do is integral to children's learning. Given that others' ways of acting, talking and thinking – their practices or discourses – provide the means that children use to give meaning to their experiences and to construct their ideas about the world, the way that other people act and interact with the child will make all the difference to the child's meaning making. I shall discuss these ideas further – and what they might mean for learning and teaching in the primary school – in the chapters that follow. If some of the practices of primary schooling seem reminiscent of aspects of the culture of a different age, what are the implications for children and what are the alternatives?

Issues for teachers

- Arguably, whatever you do in your classroom embodies theoretical assumptions of one kind or another. Reflecting on your own practice, what theories of learning might be implicit in your own actions as a teacher?
- Having read this chapter, what are your initial thoughts about how you might change what you and the children do in your classroom to take account of any changes in how you understand children's learning?
- How would you describe the culture of your classroom from the point of view of the different participants?

2 Means and ends for learners and teachers

Chapter overview

In Chapter 1, I explored theories of learning where children are seen as active meaning makers in social contexts. I drew attention to what this theoretical framework means for children's learning, for ways of valuing children and also for teaching, contrasting it with other theoretical approaches. I suggested that some of the current teaching practices in schools may be reminiscent of those of earlier times which invoke behaviourist learning theory. In this and the next chapter, I explore some of the emerging ideas further. In this chapter, I focus mainly on the political and ideological contexts in which the existing dominant – or 'currently privileged' (Burke and Hermerschmidt 2005) – practices have taken hold and explore how these practices manifest themselves in those contexts. Discussion of these wider contexts inevitably throws up the question: what is school meant to be for? I discuss how the 'market based' ideology, that currently frames educational practice, sidelines this critical question altogether. This does not help those concerned with children's education to make decisions about what to do. I hope to show that, in looking more closely at their practice from the alternative perspectives I am presenting, teachers might see possibilities for different decisions for action that reflect different values. I develop this discussion further in Chapter 3 to begin to show how teachers might re-form their practice.

A market-driven system

I have been referring to the pressure on teachers to produce results and suggested that this emphasis on outcomes and performance can have particular consequences for the way teachers teach. It sets up a tension with alternative ways of understanding how children learn and it embodies assumptions about children that can be disrespectful of their agency and their rights as thinking people. When we see children from the alternative perspectives, as active meaning makers and as participants in social practices, this raises questions for teachers around what they do and how they value children. But educational policy has continued to push teachers in the other direction. In this chapter, I want to explore further how schools have sustained practices that seem to be out of touch with newer ways of thinking about learning and with ways of valuing children that are now enshrined as rights of the child (United Nations Convention on the Rights of the Child 1989).

There is, perhaps, a tendency on the part of policy makers to assume that their particular way of thinking about education is self-evident and universal. The discussion so far has already begun to suggest, however, that what is apparently 'given' or neutral can, instead, be seen as grounded in particular discourses. From this perspective, current policy and practices are seen as framed within specific ideologies. Arguably, it is the dominant ideological context of the open market and the culture of performativity (Elliott 2001; Ball 2001; Whitty 2002) that has given rise to difficulties and contradictions in primary education.

At the heart of the market-based system is the familiar dynamic of supply and demand: the product that is being offered to the consumer must meet what the consumer demands. On the demand side, there must be opportunities for choice: the consumer will select from what is offered on the basis of its quality in relation to their needs. In the marketplace this requires measures of quality – indicators by which schools can be compared and 'successful' schools identified by the consumer. A competitive ethos is generated by public demand for the best schools and, in order to survive, the less successful schools must do better. In the eyes of the policy makers, the need to maintain a share of the market drives all schools to continue to raise their standards: as the weaker schools catch up, the stronger ones must strive to stay ahead.

The measures of comparison that are currently used in England are the outputs in terms of SATs results (which are used to create 'league tables' of schools) and the results of Ofsted inspections. It follows that the system obliges all schools to ensure that they measure up in terms of these indicators: schools will inevitably focus attention on their performance in these areas to maintain their place in the market. In the performative culture in which schools operate, according to Elliott (2001) these auditing systems are required to make performance 'transparent to the public's gaze'. They 'aspire to provide perfect information about the workings of the organisation' and assume 'fixed and immutable standards against which to judge performance' (p. 194). Quality is measured in terms of cost-effectiveness. As Elliott explains it: 'The organisation's over-riding goal is to optimise performance by maximising outputs (benefits) and minimising inputs (costs) and thereby provide "value-for-money". Lyotard calls this the "principle of performativity"' (p. 193).

In the education system as they currently experience it, teachers are driven, then, by the national policy agenda, to maximise and objectively measure outcomes. As a consequence, it is not surprising that the outcomes-orientated model of teaching and learning, to which I referred in the Introduction and Chapter 1, persists and that the values associated with it continue to dominate.

Although there has been a plethora of initiatives to improve practice, these have all been within this countervailing performative system of inspection, testing and league tables which are seen as major factors working against developments (Webb and Vulliamy 2006; Wyse and Torrance 2009). There is considerable public disquiet around testing and commentators routinely make the case that initiatives for developing the curriculum are stifled by the current regime, particularly the SATs at Key Stage 2 (Reay and Wiliam 1999; Hall et al. 2004). A recent government review of testing, carried out under the Labour Government, resulted in the Education Secretary at the time, Ed Balls, accepting the recommendations that SATs in English and Maths should be retained in the short term, while Science tests would be scrapped. In the longer term the advice was that the remaining SATs should be replaced with teacher assessment. At the time of writing, the Coalition government was undertaking a review of Key Stage 2 Testing and Accountability under Lord Bew (DfE 2010b). This is probably not before time. Teachers' opposition to the SATs regime has been continuously growing – reportedly to the way the test results are used by government rather than to their use for assessment of learning (Shepherd and Williams 2010) and in 2010 the unions voted for a boycott with an estimated 7000 of England's 17,000 primaries taking part. Feelings were already running high in condemnation of the continuation of the external testing regime at the National Association of Headteachers conference in 2009 (Brookes 2009) and the teacher unions have sustained their campaign, now exerting pressure on the new Coalition government to change the situation. The general secretary of teaching union the NUT, Christine Blower, has taken the stance that the SATs regime is a breach of children's human rights (Marley 2010). Comments in the media are frequent. Tanya Byron (2009) in the *Guardian*, for instance, expressed a common concern, that children are 'blocked by an education system that narrows the definition of achievement because it is built around targets and testing and staffed by creatively compromised and disempowered teachers'.

The purposes of testing and the nature of the tests

If all that matters is success in a test, clearly much depends on the way that the test is constructed and the criteria that are used in assessing success. It might be assumed that in the context of market forces, the test would reflect what the consumer wants from education or schooling as they conceive these things. The criteria of measurement used, if they are to act as the indicators of the quality of the product they are getting, would be responsive, one might imagine, to the parent's need to know how well their child is doing and how well a school is helping them to improve. However, when the system is set up to focus exclusively on outcomes the issue of *what might be meant* by 'doing well' is not necessarily raised. In the market context, the primary function of the performance indicators is, after all, simply to provide clear measures of comparison of output. Where the quality of the product stands or falls only by the measured outcomes, theoretically there is no obligation to question what is tested and how it is tested. In other words, test items and procedures need not reflect any particular educational principles or strategies. A test in a particular subject, for example, need not be informed by a valid theory of learning.

As I mentioned in the introduction, however, when the education system was opened to market forces by Margaret Thatcher's conservative government, it was recognised that some standardisation of the product was required if comparative measures were to be applied across the whole system. There was also concern to introduce some structure into what children should be learning. As I also mentioned, the child-centred movement faltered on the perception that children might not be learning anything worthwhile or useful, that the curriculum was too loosely based on children's 'needs' and 'interests' and that a prescribed curriculum was needed. There was a body of political opinion that could not entertain the idea of child-centredness to any degree. The perception was that giving direction to what children should be learning would keep teachers in line, particularly those who had adopted a laissez-faire or anything-goes approach.

The Conservative government, then, introduced the National Curriculum to serve several purposes. It enabled central government to set up systems of accountability, creating a common product so that the effectiveness of delivery could be measured and compared across schools thereby providing a way of bringing teachers under central government control. In addition, it established the body of knowledge and skills that children would learn. Along with the introduction of open enrolment (that allowed parents to choose their children's school) and the introduction of local management of schools, the state-controlled, centralised curriculum helped to create the education market.

In this respect, this is not a 'free' market system as such. (It is a 'very strange one' (Ball 1994).) In a system driven by the ideology of the free market, the product – education or schooling – is shaped by the vagaries of that market. In theory, an open market with an exclusive focus on the consumers' demands would require schools to provide whatever their clients desired. In contrast, a prescribed curriculum imposes certain limits. It means that the tests, that are the measure of quality, must take account of the nature of that curriculum. To this extent the tests are governed by a specific, statutorily defined account of subject knowledge. The status and veracity of this account, however, is a matter for debate.

In the reality of the performative climate, too, the extent to which the tests actually reflect the complexities of the knowledge, skills and processes of a subject, even as represented in the National Curriculum, is questionable. But the need for this can be overridden by the accountability agenda. Research carried out by Daugherty et al. (2008 p. 251) revealed 'just how influential the political imperatives for system-level accountability can be'. Where the emphasis is on comparing performance across the system as a whole, the validity of the test in relation to the subject matter is not the issue. It is

> more a question of how valid the test is as a source of data on system performance. Predictably, perhaps, this affects how teachers and students regard both the teaching that leads to the test, and the test itself, with pedagogy geared increasingly towards enhancing pupil performance.
>
> (p. 251)

Importantly, in the context of a market-based ideology, a prescribed curriculum does not, then, guarantee that the product-led measures of performance take account of how children learn. More specifically, it does not – and, I suggest, cannot – do justice to the view of children's learning as active meaning making. Where education and schooling remain subject to market forces with the quality of the product offered measured by outcomes, the processes of learning are significant only inasmuch as they are instrumental in achieving those ends. As a consequence, much about the child's learning may go unrecognised and much classroom activity may rest on unexamined assumptions about learning.

An objectives-driven approach to teaching

As I have pointed out, the system does not provide for any checks on how children experience school and the curriculum; their activities are inevitably influenced by the market-led ethos. It is the school's and the teachers' job to simply deliver the prescribed programme and outcomes. The very word 'delivery', now so common in educational discourse, in itself suggests a pre-packaged product that simply has to be passed on to the learner. To reiterate, as a national programme, the 'effectiveness' of the delivery could be measured through performance and compared across schools. Given this context, it is hardly surprising that an instrumental model of planning for teaching, driven by 'learning objectives', became established in the primary classroom. In the context of statutory 'programmes of study' which lay down what children should learn, this may, indeed, appear to make incontrovertible sense. It may be as well to explore this idea, and how teaching to objectives became established, before offering a critique.

The objectives-driven model of planning (see also Chapter 7 and 8) rests on the assumption that the intended learning outcomes determine what will happen in any teaching episode. Lesson activities are designed with the specific intention of achieving the prescribed objectives. This provides a quite straightforward model of teaching and learning where the end point – the target or the objective – is pre-determined and teaching is focused on achieving that in the most effective or efficient way. As well as identifying the intended outcome of a lesson, the objectives are the starting point from which the process and content of the lesson follow and the success of the teaching methods adopted can be judged on the basis of their effectiveness in bringing about the intended learning. Metaphorically, it is a form of planning that can be represented by a straight line. As I noted in the introduction, the early incarnations of the National Curriculum programmes of study were laid out in great detail, providing an extensive framework for determining objectives and the content of lessons. In addition, there were the 'Attainment Targets' along with numerous 'Statements of Attainment' against which learning was to be assessed. It is worth pointing out that these were distinct from the 'programmes of study': they were always intended to be a tool for assessment, not a planning template to determine the content of lessons. They readily lent themselves, however, to being super-imposed as 'outcomes' at the planning stage.

As the curriculum became less detailed during the 1990s, there was perhaps more scope for schools and teachers to determine the learning objectives for themselves, although, by the turn of the present century, the literacy and numeracy strategies introduced further layers of prescription. Whether it was through the programmes of study, the attainment targets, the detailed content and objectives of the Literacy and Numeracy Strategies or the QCA schemes of work, objectives-driven planning became the dominant practice. As well as preserving the attractive simplicity of the linear model it also suited the wider institutional and educational culture which required that targets be reached at certain times in a child's educational career. It promised progression and efficiency.

The approach has clearly been encouraged by Ofsted through the criteria used in classroom observations. It seems remarkable that such inspection criteria have, apparently by stealth, overridden the statutory guarantee (enshrined in the 1988 Education Act) that teaching methods cannot be prescribed, but – as if this were the only method available – it is now the norm for the teacher to set lesson objectives and to plan their teaching around them.

This, then, is the pedagogical practice at the everyday classroom level that has come about as a result of the prioritisation of outcomes. It echoes the 'behavioural objectives' movement that originated in the USA in the 1950s (Tyler 1949; Bloom 1956) in response to behaviourist learning theory. In this earlier era, the view that learning was a matter of changed behavioural responses meant that educational success would be defined as the acquisition of behaviours or skills. It held the prospect of a technology of teaching that could be scientifically refined (see also Chapter 1). As learning outcomes would be identified through specific forms of behaviour, the programme of teaching and learning would be based on an ordered, pre-specified sequence of these 'behavioural objectives'. The scientifically motivated quest to ensure that objectives were always expressed in terms of clear, observable behaviours demanded finer and finer distinctions to be made between responses, fragmenting the programme of teaching and learning even further, and possibly trivialising the outcomes.

It is interesting that in the UK, this kind of model of learning and teaching took some time to take hold, though interest had begun to grow in the 1960s. As Blenkin and Kelly noted (1981), the School Council developed projects such as Science 5–13 and introduced the concept to practising teachers – albeit, tentatively – through its publication *With Objectives in Mind* (Schools Council 1972). Even in the 1970s and 80s, when there was some disquiet around the content of the curriculum there was, nevertheless, strong opposition to the objectives-driven model. Alternative approaches which focused on planning around educational processes rather than products or outcomes (Stenhouse 1975; Eisner 1969, 1985) were more consistent with the progressive educational ethos at the time. Eventually, however, with the development of the new, post-1988 framework of values and practices that I have been describing, an objectives-led orthodoxy emerged and then became entrenched, even if it did not conform strictly to the edict that objectives must be expressed in purely behavioural terms.

Objections to objectives

Social-contructivist learning theory that, by contrast, does justice to the child as an active meaning maker sits uncomfortably within a market-led, target-driven system, but at the same time provides an alternative perspective from which it can be challenged. From this alternative point of view, the discrete items of learning that characterise the linear approach can appear de-contextualised. Outcomes-driven teaching seems to render the content potentially meaningless to the child and the process hit-and-miss, as both what is taught and how it is taught may not be appropriate to an individual child's developing conceptions. Furthermore, the child's control of their learning is eclipsed as there is no recognition of the child's active and constructive role in meaning making. (I shall come back to this in later chapters.)

A fundamental problem with the objectives-driven approach is that it is not possible to make accurate predictions of educational outcomes. An immediate objection is that it does not readily accommodate the imaginative or creative aspects of learning, where outcomes are, by their nature, unpredictable. Obvious areas that might come to mind are those associated with the arts. An alternative position, however, and one from which critics such as Eisner and Stenhouse argue, is that this applies to all areas of knowledge – that all knowledge is a tool for creativity:

> Education enhances the freedom of man [sic] by inducting him into the knowledge of his culture as a thinking system. The most important characteristic of the knowledge mode is that one can think with it. This is in the nature of knowledge – as distinct from information – that it is a structure to sustain creative thought and provide frameworks for judgement.
>
> (Stenhouse 1975 p. 82)

The objections, then, rest more on the way in which learning and knowledge are understood than on the simply practical difficulties of predicting outcomes. Stenhouse makes the inherently open-ended character of education itself explicit in his next statement:

> Education as induction into knowledge is successful to the extent that it makes the behavioural outcomes of the students unpredictable.
>
> (p. 82)

The objectives-driven approach may suit the performative agenda of measurement and control, because it can appear to provide clear indicators of learning, and, also therefore, the effectiveness of teaching. If the primary purpose is for the child to gain specific 'learning outcomes', then the measure of the *teacher's* success is the child's positive result: the teacher is effective as long as the target is reached by the child. The cycle of accountability is complete. But, following Stenhouse's arguments, in reality this is a chimera. As I suggested in Chapter 1, it is seemingly impossible to 'observe' a child's understanding with any certainty; relating evidence definitively to learning outcomes is problematic. Furthermore, outcomes depend on time and context (see for example, Elliott

2001 and Drummond 2003). As Elliott points out, assessments that focus on clarity

> conceal the complexities of the teaching–learning process and in doing so fail to yield evidence about the real impact of teaching over time. At any point in time evidence of impact will inevitably be partial and provisional.
>
> (Elliott 2001 p. 197)

To illustrate some of these limitations of an outcomes-driven approach and the difficulties of assessing or measuring the achievement of the intended learning in a concrete way (see also Chapter 1), take a hypothetical example where the objective is for the child to understand the life cycle of a frog. The child is given the task of representing the life cycle through a drawing, to provide observable evidence of their achievement of the objective. Say the child has been able to produce a drawing that shows several frogs at different stages of development that matches, reasonably well, what the teacher is expecting to see. In this case, on the evidence of the child's performance, the teacher may assume that the child has achieved the intended scientific understanding – the objective has been successfully met and the teaching has therefore been effective. It remains an open question, however, whether the child has represented the same creature in various stages of metamorphosis or whether they think they have represented several discrete creatures, each with its own distinctive form. It is impossible to discriminate between these different conceptions on the evidence of the drawing itself. Furthermore, while the child *may* be demonstrating scientific understanding of the phenomenon of the life cycle, they could simply have memorised the drawing and reproduced it. The point I am making is that, if the focus is on the end result as the indicator of learning and, in this case, the child's performance fulfils the criterion of reproducing the diagram, no further questions need be asked about the child's learning. The learning that has gone on may in fact amount to learning how to reproduce a diagram rather than understanding the development of a frog, but this goes unacknowledged. What has been missed by focusing on the outcome is any attempt to establish the way the child has understood the biological process.

This example highlights the difficulty posed by an exclusive focus on the achievement of an objective, a difficulty that is illuminated by Stenhouse's comment on the nature of understanding: it 'cannot be achieved. It can always be deepened' (Stenhouse 1975 p. 94). This point was reflected by a group of student teachers I once worked with, in the very early stages of their four-year initial teacher education course, who felt intuitively, and very strongly, that teachers could not assess what children had learned – only what they were learning.

Teaching to the test

The belief that it is possible to provide clear indicators of success in learning and teaching in the form of measurable, evidence-based outcomes leaves the way open for the teacher to employ whatever methods best realise the desired product. An efficient means, for example, may be for the teacher to encourage the child, in the case described above, to memorise the diagram by having them copy it over and over, offering suitable reinforcement to encourage the desired response. In this example, from the teacher's point of view, the need for the child to produce the correct response to the test may override the need to find out about the child's understanding of the science. Similarly, for a Maths SAT, the teacher *may* use drill or rote learning of algorithms, so the child can produce an accurate answer to a sum. If a teacher uses this approach exclusively, however, they will have no insight into the child's conception of the mathematical operation.

Where value is placed on the 'end' of passing the test, there is clearly pressure on teachers to teach in what appears to be the most efficient way (Elliott 2001; Wyse and Torrance 2009). Again, the accountability agenda can take over. In discussing evidence both from the UK and the USA of the rises in test scores that can be achieved simply from implementing test-based accountability systems, Torrance (2002) questions the validity and meaning of those rises. He says:

> What is most likely to have led to increases in scores, is practising for the tests. All international research evidence, gathered over many years, not to mention personal experience and common sense, suggests that this is what happens when 'high stakes' tests are encountered in educational systems; i.e. when teachers and students are faced with tests which carry significant consequences for student life chances and teacher accountability, very significant time and energy will be devoted to test preparation.
>
> (p. 10)

This is identified as a persisting problem by many commentators. Mary Bousted, general secretary of the Association of Teachers and Lecturers, at the time of writing, was quoted as saying that 'any method of assessment which is used to judge teachers, schools and pupils like this will have the same outcome – children being taught to the test' (*The Independent* 3.08.10).

To return to the point I made earlier in this chapter, we can see how the performative culture has created a system of schooling that can undermine, rather than enhance children's education. It is an enduring problem. In his critique of the objectives approach back in the 1970s Stenhouse was making it clear that the imperative of accountability and control was embedded in a political discourse, rather than an educational one:

The demand for objectives is a demand for justification rather than simply description of ends. As such it is part of a political dialogue rather than an educational one. It is not about curriculum design, but rather an expression of irritation in the face of the problem of accountability in education. I believe that politicians will have to face the fact that there is no easy road to accountability via objectives.

(Stenhouse 1975 p. 77)

Values and ends

When learning is valued and conceived in terms of its outcomes, there is nothing *inconsistent* in finding the most efficient ways of realising those ends. We often hear, when politicians discuss education, that teachers should be guided by 'what works'. This begs a crucial question, however: 'works with respect to what?' As I have implied, this may seem unproblematic from an outcomes-driven perspective. What works from this point of view is simply whatever brings about the desired end result. The reply to the question is likely to be 'with respect to the pre-specified outcomes'. While the plea to focus on what works can appear to be un-contentious, it is, at the very least, unhelpful. There are broader critical questions: 'what are we trying to achieve?' 'To what further ends do these pre-specified outcomes relate?' 'How can we say what has worked unless we have first of all clarified what it is we are aiming for?' Furthermore, the discussion of the examples above suggests that these outcomes can conceal assumptions about learning and teaching: as I have implied, outcomes-driven practices tend to reflect a view of learning derived from the kind of behaviourist psychological theories that I discussed and critiqued in the previous chapter.

To summarise, in the context of this broader question, the market model imposes a particular vision of what goes on in schools. Since the market-led and target-driven discourse and practices of teaching prioritise outcomes, pre-determined by the prescribed curriculum, the activities of teaching and learning are merely the technical means of achieving those ends. These means are *valued* only in terms of how effectively or efficiently they achieve particular ends: in other words, they are valued instrumentally. The ends themselves are valued as commodities. Value is not placed on 'becoming educated' – engaging in the practices that make a difference to how a person thinks and who they are. Instead, education is valued as some 'thing' to be acquired (having an education). As such, in the marketplace, its worth is dependent on its exchange value. The example of a child's performance in a SAT will again provide a useful illustration. A Year 6 child learns how to perform in the test; their performance merits a level 4; as a 'level 4' the child acquires a certain status that may later be converted to further rewards, such as a place in 'top sets' in secondary school; this confers certain advantages in achieving GCSE (General Certificate in

Secondary Education) and then A level success, which ultimately earns them a place at university, and so on. Similarly, the child's achievements bring advantages to the school. The level 4, collectively with others, leads to a good place in the league tables for the school, which results in popularity with parents, a sustained intake of pupils and secure (and less stressful) jobs for the teachers. At each stage, what is achieved has value in relation to what it can be traded for. This chain of exchange, of using one 'product' to acquire another, means that the value of education and whatever learning is going on is always seen in terms of some other 'good'. It is valued for what else it may procure; for ends that are extrinsic to learning itself. This acquisition of goods in pursuit of further goals can lead to a situation of 'infinite regress' where at no stage are any of the 'goods' valued in themselves, for reasons that are intrinsic to them.

Furthermore, this means that within the market-driven system, any demand for justification of those ends is wholly contingent on the conditions of the market. This tends to rule out any disinterested consideration of the ethical implications of both the ends to be achieved and the means employed – the unacceptable pressure that the testing regime imposes on children, for instance. It could well encourage teachers to use strategies which, while maximising efficiency and getting the results, are morally inappropriate, such as manipulative strategies that are akin to bribery, where children are given material rewards for achieving the desired outcomes. The focus on the end result seems to devalue children themselves: the children become the means for producing the desired output, and their well-being can, in effect, be marginalised as the school pursues its goal of success and survival in the market place. If this situation is indefensible, then questions need to be asked from this ethical perspective. What are the 'goods' that are being pursued and what are the ethical implications of the means that are used to achieve them?

The overriding question that was discussed in Chapter 1, in relation to the way that children's learning is theorised, arises again in relation to this discussion of the prevailing values of the market: how should we value children? Are they merely objects in a performative system rather than subjects in an educational one? Is it acceptable that, as people, their identities are appropriated by what might amount – from a cynical viewpoint – to a system constructed to secure electoral votes as a public response to education's contribution to a commodity-based economy? Are they valued only as the producers and consumers within the competitive global culture of economic growth? In short, is it right that educational aims are left to be determined in the marketplace, where market values are assigned to the 'goods'?

The need for a moral dimension in educational thinking has been an enduring issue for philosophers of education. For both John Dewey (1916) and Paulo Freire (1972), for example, education was linked to democratic values. In England, Richard Peters (1966) located educational values in a democratic framework of equality, freedom and respect for persons. Similarly,

John White (1982; 1990; 2007) and Patricia White (1996) have consistently argued for the need to address the ethical base of education and have kept educational values and aims in sight over many years. In the last years of the labour government there were, at least, signs that thinking about broader educational values and aims had begun to shape educational policy. The 2000 version of the National Curriculum introduced a clear statement of aims (although White 2005 notes the mismatch between the aims and the regulations around the subjects). The QCA Futures project invited debate around questions about aims and values, asking, for example, how school subjects contribute to wider aims and values and how the curriculum might better equip pupils for the roles and responsibilities of global citizenship. The previous government's Rose Review (DCSF 2009a) – as well as the Cambridge Review of Primary Education (Alexander 2010[1]) saw the identification of aims – the question of what education is for – as central. At the time of writing it remains to be seen how this sort of thinking will be taken up by the Coalition government.

Means are not value neutral: means as ends

The alternative framework of theory and values I am proposing gives a different emphasis to the 'means' of teaching. When theorised from the outcomes-driven, performative perspective, means are construed narrowly in technical, functional terms. On the other hand, when they are theorised from a socio-cultural perspective as practices, there are other possibilities, too. What teachers do, from this perspective, need no longer be determined by extrinsic ends. Rather than being seen as value-neutral instruments for bringing about further desired learning outcomes, the means can be valued as ends in themselves. Teaching strategies can be construed in terms of 'principles of procedure' rather than technique or method (Peters 1973; Stenhouse 1975; Blenkin and Kelly 1981). Peters, for instance, argued many years ago that the means by which people have become educated do in fact contribute to the content of their education: the way that teachers work with children (treating them with respect for instance) can constitute what children learn. Children will also learn – in the context of the ways in which knowledge itself is developed as well as how it is taught – the principles of procedure that are pre-supposed in activities such as science and history, for example.

[1] The *Cambridge Primary Review* was a comprehensive enquiry and review of evidence led by Robin Alexander and a team of academics, researchers and teachers, launched in 2006. Its findings were published in 31 interim reports and the final report *Children, their World, their Education* (Alexander 2010). Arguably, the Labour Government's own Independent Review (the Rose Review) was triggered by Alexander's review and was used to sideline the latter's recommendations.

There must be respect for evidence and a ban on 'cooking' or distorting it; there must be a willingness to admit one is mistaken; there must be non-interference with people who wish to put forward objections; there must be a respect for people as a source of argument and an absence of personal invective and contempt for what they say because of who they are. To learn science is not just to learn facts and to understand theories; it is to learn to participate in a public form of life governed by such principles of procedure. In so far, therefore, as a person is educated scientifically, he [sic] will have to absorb these principles of procedure by means of which the content of scientific thought has been accumulated and is criticised and developed. He must take this sort of social situation into his own mind. Indeed, the mind of the individual is largely structured by the principles of procedure of such public situations in which he participates.

(Peters 1973 p. 25)

I shall say more about this in later chapters. Peters was a rationalist; he was not arguing from a socio-cultural perspective. Nevertheless, in common with socio-cultural theorists, he recognised the centrality of 'social forms of life' – of 'social practices' (although he doesn't refer to them this way) in learning and education. His argument, that the means or processes of education – or the practices – are inextricably linked with *what* children learn, to this extent chimes with the socio-cultural view. According to Peters, it is this that 'makes any attempt to conceive it [education] as taking means to an end, or as developing a product by means of processes, quite inappropriate' (Peters 1973 p. 25).

In later chapters, I shall explore further, from the socio-cultural perspective, this indivisibility of means and ends – of what teachers do and the values their actions embody, on the one hand and what children learn, on the other. Peters was making the point that the means of education can legitimately be seen as aims: since the processes of teaching and learning are imbued with values and principles, they can be understood in terms of what educators might intentionally be trying to achieve for children's learning. I should point out, however, that drawing attention to means as aims – emphasising procedural knowledge or 'learning how' – does not rule out consideration of other content or aims. Learning of this kind must always take place in particular contexts. Procedural knowledge does not develop in a vacuum. For instance, learning how to carry out fair tests in Science, say, must be contextualised by testing something in particular – so there is always the question of what meanings and knowledge children are constructing besides the procedural. There are further decisions to be made about these other sorts of aim.

In the discussion in subsequent chapters, I shall show how, from a socio-cultural perspective, decision making about what children should learn, and why, would itself be located in specific cultural contexts and communities of practice, and I will question whether decisions should rest only with the adult participants. Following up the point I raised in the Introduction I shall note, however, that to adopt this socio-cultural perspective is to take a very different line on how those decisions are made compared to that of rationalist philosophers such as Hirst and Peters (see Chapter 7).

Focusing on meaning making

A shift from the behaviourist interpretation of learning and from performative, instrumental values, then, can have significant implications for how teachers teach and how they understand their teaching. Mary Jane Drummond (2003) provides a vivid and illuminating example of what happens when the emphasis moves from the child's performance, to their actions and thinking. This is an appropriate example to use here, as this different way of seeing what is going on is applied to a situation where the outcomes are meant to be the focus: seven-year-old Jason is undertaking a fairly traditional sort of maths test. It serves to make the point, as Drummond intends, that what a child is achieving can be judged very differently when the focus is on the child's meaning making rather than on how he is measuring up to the desired outcomes. Looking at his test performance in terms of his answers to the questions, they would be judged to be incorrect and Jason's performance would be rated as a failure. What Drummond shows, however, through careful analysis of how Jason might have interpreted the test items, is that he has made good sense of the questions in terms of his existing knowledge and conceptions and has demonstrated intelligent use of appropriate strategies. Her analysis shows what he *has* successfully learned. For instance:

> He has learned to listen and follow instructions carefully, as closely as he can, though his short-term memory does sometimes let him down. In question 1, for example, he was asked to write in numerals the number two hundred and fifty-two . . . he has almost done so, writing two, a hundred, and forty-two. He has learned to stay with a task and complete it.
>
> (p. 2)

This quotation gives a flavour of Jason's responses and Drummond's interpretations of them. He has shown some, though limited, mathematical knowledge and understanding of mathematics, but he has also shown persistence in the face of challenges, application in solving problems and has found ways of making some sense of the unfamiliar:

... I believe there is substantial evidence that, against what must be, for him, inconceivable odds, Jason is struggling to make sense of the test, and what his head-teacher is asking him to do. His mathematical understanding is still too scanty to be of much use to him, but he uses all the other clues he can get. This is, I think, a remarkable achievement, and a tribute to Jason's persistence, to his longing for meaning.

(p. 8)

To consider Drummond's example from the perspective of the social constructivist view of learning that I discussed in Chapter 1, it is clear that Jason is showing his strengths as a learner. A teacher who is looking for accurate outcomes would be disappointed: he has been unable to meet the criteria of the test. For such a teacher, he would not be demonstrating that he can 'do' the sums accurately. I use the word 'do', here, only in the limited sense of his performance or behaviour, which does not match what is required: he has not mastered the necessary changes in behaviour in response to the sums that would, on a broadly behaviourist view, indicate that learning had taken place. Things look rather different, on the other hand, to Drummond and to the kind of teacher who sees Jason as an active meaning maker. They know that Jason is attempting to do what mathematicians do and is trying very hard to make sense of that. Although it is clear that he does not have the requisite kind of mathematical understanding to be able to solve the problems, Drummond has shown that he has been successful in actively constructing meaning as best he can. He is drawing on his existing ways of understanding both mathematics and test taking that he has previously learned as a participant in those activities. He is using them in ways that he deems to be appropriate in the present context of taking the maths test. The teacher who is aware that learning is situated in specific social practices will see, then, that a child like Jason is not only doing their best to make sense of the content of the test, but is learning what is entailed in doing a test.

As well as focusing on the child's thinking, the teacher who looks at children's learning in this way is also looking differently at the child as a person. She is not seeing them as deficient in their ability because they cannot pass a test or meet the learning objectives. The focus is not on what the child cannot do, but on what they can do – and 'do' in the much broader sense of using the conceptual tools and resources available to them to solve the problems as they perceive them. I would go further and suggest that even here the words 'can do' are not quite appropriate. They remain framed in a particular paradigm of assessment that suggests there are pre-determined abilities, some of which have been 'acquired' – and, even if only by implication – some which have not. It is still a measurement of sorts, against criteria that are held by others. To shift even more decisively to a focus on the child's meaning making, it is better to refer to what the child *is doing*. This keeps the focus neutral and descriptive rather than judgemental. It allows for a clear focus, from teachers, on interpretation, unclouded by appraisal, and for response that is not directed by pre-determined expectations.

Correspondingly, this approach implies a way of valuing the child as an equal – as a fellow human being who has strategies for learning and, as with all of us, whose learning is founded on their existing experience and understanding. So, when the teacher sees the child's actions as the observable evidence of their strategies for making sense of the unfamiliar in terms of what they already know, and sees what they do as an opportunity to investigate the child's thinking, rather than to make judgements about it, the result can be a shift in the balance of power between child and teacher. The teacher is no longer the authority who holds all the answers, but the enquirer who must find out – in this case of a child taking a maths test for instance – how the child is dealing with what they encounter as they participate both in mathematics and in test taking.

I am not suggesting, here, that there is no value in the child coming to understand how others make sense of the world, and to see their own abilities, understandings and knowledge in relation to those of others who already know how to use systems of thought and enquiry such as mathematics, as in the above example. As I have already said, learning to use them is part of what educators aim to do. I shall go on to say more, later, about these systems as cultural tools and resources that have already been, and continue to be, socially, culturally and historically developed, and how they provide the means for children to construct new knowledge and to enrich their understanding.

I am suggesting, however, that the value that is placed on these tools or resources or systems of thought is not the 'be-all and end-all'. Rather than making judgements only as to how a child measures up, in what they can do, to the standards implicit in those subjects, teachers might consider, instead, how their own actions measure up in responsively supporting the child's learning. This offers a different orientation to teaching and different sorts of aim. Rather than simply, by hook or by crook, aiming to get the children through their SATs tests, to raise the league table profile of the school or attempt to achieve all the prescribed learning objectives, teachers would have a more divergent approach to what they were doing. They would aim to engage with children as people and individuals, adopting more open, investigative and receptive attitudes to what children are doing and learning. Introducing children to valued means and practices – the tools and resources of the culture – would become an integral part of their activities as teachers. I shall say more about these ideas in the remaining chapters.

A way forward for teachers?

The instrumental, technical relationship between means and ends has led to a particular conceptualisation of teachers' roles – that it is not their concern to make the judgements about what the ends should be, or indeed about pedagogical strategies. When their focus is merely to apply whatever techniques 'work' in achieving the prescribed goals, they are acting as technicians rather than professionals (Schon 1983). Professionalism, on the other hand, implies judgement, but successive national initiatives have increasingly removed from teachers the opportunities to make professional decisions. As Ball has argued: 'There is the possibility that commitment, judgement and authenticity within practice are sacrificed for impression and performance' (Ball 2001 p. 214). As government policy has increasingly limited the influence that teachers might have on what they teach and how they teach it – as they have become ever more micro-managed – the scope to make sensitive and receptive interpretations of, and responses to, children's actions has been further eroded. Such initiatives as the Literacy and Numeracy Strategies, for instance, might appear to have been driven as much by the policy makers' desire to make the curriculum 'teacher-proof' as they were to ensure that the 'right' material was taught and the decreed objectives were achieved.

As a consequence – and here I am fleshing out what I mentioned in the Introduction – teachers may find their practice conflicts with their own sense of the rights of others in a democratic society, with their respect for children as fellow citizens and with their desire for social justice and more equal relations between themselves and the children. On these grounds alone, teachers might question and reject teaching to the test and the objectives model of teaching. They may feel their professional judgement and moral principles are compromised. There is plenty of evidence in teachers' blogs to suggest that their feelings run deep: 'There are other alternatives [to SATs] that are viable and do not stress and pressurise our abused and channelled children' (Onthespot 2010).

Many readers may recognise these reactions. From personal experience, I know many reflective teachers who discuss them on university masters-level courses, or in conversation with student teachers in their classrooms. Only recently a student teacher explained why she was feeling unhappy: 'I feel as though I cannot be the kind of teacher I want to be.' Teachers have experienced the contradictions between the need to comply and conform and to produce results in a target-driven system, on the one hand, and the need to be true to the way they value children on the other. This is when 'teaching to the test' is not so much a sign of teachers' commitment to hard-edged approaches (Pollard 2001 – see Introduction) as a way round the demands imposed on them. As Elliott has argued, one response to the pressures of 'performance auditing' in the performative culture has been resistance through playing games with performance indicators, or 'creative compliance' (Elliott 2001).

Such games involve the cynical production of auditable performances, such as when teachers 'teach to the tests' in the full knowledge that the outcomes of good teaching are rarely made visible by test results.

(p. 202)

Teachers may intuitively know what 'good teaching' is, but the existing culture of schools and schooling may be preventing it from flourishing.

Seen from the socio-cultural perspective, however, teachers' decisions about their actions, whatever they may be, are grounded in the practices and values of the communities to which they subscribe or belong. They might recognise, therefore, the possibility of acting in other ways, identifying with different communities of practice, with different values. The practices of the wider community at the present time may be characterised by performative methods and values. To the extent that teachers are part of that community they may feel obliged to follow such practices. There are, undoubtedly, issues of power around the regulatory hold that such communities have on teachers. However, the fact that teachers can participate in communities that prioritise *educational* practice and can relate with groups of like-minded educators is not to be overlooked. Furthermore, they do retain a good deal of control over many of their minute-by-minute pedagogical decisions for action within their classroom communities. As I noted in the Introduction, the signs are that there may be increased opportunities to exercise this kind of local control – this does appear to be a key feature of the present government's agenda. Given that children are also members of the classroom community, and given the profound implications of classroom practices and teachers actions for children's learning, arguably teachers need to be particularly mindful of what goes on within them, and, as I have been suggesting, should therefore ensure that changes are educationally principled. I shall be discussing all this further.

Concluding reflections

The outcomes-driven approach, it seems, leaves a lot to be desired, both in terms of the market ideology that sustains it and the learning theory it endorses. It does not demand of teachers or, indeed, facilitate either engagement with the child's thinking or with the child as a person, or ethical appraisal of what teachers do – even though they may be professionally inclined to prioritise these approaches to their work.

When teachers are driven by targets, and they feel their practice is geared towards achieving the given results, they can feel under pressure to tick the box and move on, regardless of the child's meaning making. They are required only to bring about changes to what a child can do and, insofar as the primary school agenda remains dominated by SATs, perhaps only in the minimal sense of those changes that are required by particular test items. Such modification of behaviour may be deemed sufficient from the behaviourist perspective. By contrast, where understanding of learning is informed by socio-cultural theory, it is appropriate that teachers would aim to give close attention to the child's activities as a maker of meaning and to their participation in cultural practices. Where teachers build communities where there is a sense of the rights of the child and children are valued as persons and citizens, there is the possibility for more democratic educational strategies.

Teachers may have been compelled to comply with the centralised agenda in a performative culture, and to refine and hone their methods to deliver the given ends, giving them little encouragement and opportunity to develop alternative communities of practice and to reflect on key questions about learning, action and values. There have been signs, however, that the practical debate about aims and values has re-emerged in the twenty-first century. It is to be hoped that, within current and future educational reforms, this will continue and space might be made for teachers to be able to create those new communities of practice and, with a different understanding of how means and ends are interconnected, to collaboratively re-shape their teaching in less instrumental ways.

Issues for teachers

- Reflecting on your own practice as a teacher, to what extent do you think your decisions about what to do are governed by the need to ensure that children are successful in tests and/or that they meet externally imposed criteria and targets? How do you feel about this?
- To what extent is your teaching driven by objectives? What do you think about this?
- How do you see the difference between education as a commodity to be acquired, or as an entitlement to learn?
- In reflecting on your values and aims, to what extent do you place value on children's learning itself? To what extent, by contrast, do you place value on the extrinsic rewards that their success might bring – either for the children or for yourselves or the school?
- How do you value children? How do you think your response to this question relates to your responses to the previous questions?

3 Means for making meaning – children taking part; their worlds taking shape

Chapter overview

In this chapter I develop further the discussion of how children's learning can be understood, firmly grounding it in children's participation and meaning making. As I noted in the Introduction, my position is that this different kind of understanding of what children do can provide a new framework for teachers' decisions for action that divorces decision making from prescription and can encourage a break with the habits of compliance. This framework prioritises, instead, pedagogical judgements and teaching that is grounded in principled action. I look at how children, in the context of their activities, purposefully and actively construct meaning through representational practices of all kinds. I consider the idea that people's worlds are jointly created and what might be meant by this. I discuss the implications of this for what teachers do and look critically at interpretations of working in the 'zone of proximal development' (Vygotsky 1978). The discussion in this chapter again highlights the implications for the traditional balance of power in suggesting a shift for the teacher, from being in authority to being responsive and collaborative.

More about learning: means and ends from the learners' point of view

As I have tried to show, the values and theories that are embedded in the prevailing practices in the wider educational community – which are currently endorsed through the testing regime and its market-based ideological context – shape school and classroom practices. Although the standards agenda is still paramount (DfE 2010a), grass-roots opposition has been threatening the survival of the testing regime and has gathered momentum. Key Stage 2 SATs, at age eleven, were, at the time of writing, under review. Furthermore, the effects of the global economic recession may yet destabilise commitment to the values of the marketplace, so it is possible that teachers' desire for change will be part of wider cultural shifts. In the discussion so far, I have attempted to expose the inadequacies of target-driven agenda both in terms of children's learning and how teachers think of children. The perspectives I have been exploring offer opportunities for conceptualising learning and teaching, and establishing the directions it might take, that are different from those presented by the linear model where pre-specified objectives are set by the curriculum and the teacher. These alternative, socio-cultural ways of theorising learning lead teachers to give attention to children's active engagement in meaning making in social contexts and to fully engage with children in order to support their developing thinking: to be 'contingently responsive' (Wells and Chang-Wells 1992 p. 60; Gallimore and Tharp 1990; Bruner 1996).

In the preceding chapters, I argued against a functional relationship between means and ends in education. This was with regard to the way in which the process of learning was configured in relation to the extrinsic goal or objective. This is not to say, however, that there is no functionality intrinsic to the activities of learning themselves. On the contrary, the perspective on children's learning that I am advocating takes seriously the *child's* intentions and purposes – the child's own goals and how they actively pursue them. Again, this was highlighted by Bruner, whose work (building on that of Piaget) developed a focus on 'the role of function' (Bruner 1977 p. xiii) in learning. Bruner was, in fact, critical of Piaget for moving away from the 'functional concern' that initially informed his work. He questioned his neglect of 'the adaptive "reasons" that impel or motivate the intellectual activity' of the child. For Bruner, it was a specific shortcoming of Piaget's ideas that '[t]here was no place for use and intention, only for an analysis of the products of mind taken in the abstract.' (Bruner 1986 p. 147). In other words, Bruner was criticising Piaget for over-emphasising the *structure* of children's mental development. Bruner, by contrast, was concerned to ground learning in use and intention, which is also to acknowledge that it occurs in specific contexts: that it is shaped by what children intentionally *do* in the particular situations in which they find themselves. These contexts are shaped by patterns of activity and the social and linguistic practices of the social groups and communities in which children are growing up. (See also Chapter 1.)

To develop the ideas that I introduced in Chapter 1 about the role of language, it is important to point out that 'linguistic practices' can be considered in the broadest possible terms. It is perhaps most useful to think of *representational* practices children engage with, which include verbal language but are not restricted to that. The forms of representation that children use for their meaning making are many and varied. Current thinking and research acknowledges this and shows how children use all the resources available to them – not just the verbal – to intentionally bring order and meaning to their experiences. It shows how children use the materials in their environment, manipulating them to create signs through which they both represent and construct meaning.

John Matthews' investigations and ideas (1999; 2003), for instance, focused on the way in which visual mark making, of various kinds, is used by the child to represent meaning. He argued that the first marks made, with a finger on a steamy window, or with a crayon on paper, for example, are far from meaningless scribbles: from the first realisation that marks have the potential to carry meaning – from the first gestural marks the child produces, such as those made by smearing spilt food, for instance – the child goes on to use mark making as a way of encoding their understandings of the world as they experience it in specific contexts. Matthews' discussion of the drawing activity of three-year-old Ben provides an example:

> In a series of drawings at 3 years and 3 months, the zig-zag is an important element, and Ben plays with the variations in denotational meaning which occur due to changes in context. For example, he uses it to represent a tail of a dog or a fox or, with slight variations, to represent a stairway.
>
> (1999 p. 101)

As I mentioned in Chapter 1, Matthews challenged the Piagetian view that children were moving through predictable developmental stages in learning how to draw; in particular, he rejected the idea that they were following a predetermined path towards the endpoint of 'visual realism' – of being able to produce an accurate rendition of the object being drawn. As he goes on to say, in relation to Ben's drawings:

> In these drawings the link with entities in the external world is only provisional; a useful pivot around which many plays and interplays on structure and meaning, text and context can be formed.
>
> (Matthews ibid.)

Children's early drawing might seem deficient in terms of its visual verisimilitude – in other words, it may not 'look like' any object in the world – but this is a normative criterion. The point is that 'visual realism' is not a universal and neutral, or 'culture free' end point, but is a cultural construct.

As Bruner pointed out, to say 'that a theory of development is "culture free" is to make not a wrong claim but an absurd one' (1986 p. 135).

Matthews argued, then, that the significance of drawing can be construed differently in terms other than visual realism: it can be seen as the process of using means of representation – in this case, mark making – through which children are actively making meaning and developing their own thinking. Children are not so much learning how to make a conventional, accurate drawing – in the way that many people might understand 'learning how to draw'. Rather, their participation in drawing activity is a *means* of learning; it is one way – amongst a very broad range of ways – of representing and constructing their conceptualisations. From this perspective, the place of drawing in children's learning is seen not so much in terms of *producing* 'a drawing' – creating an end product or a new object – but as 'engaging in drawing' as activity. It is clear, from observing children when they are drawing, that this is, indeed, their focus. A drawing will go through many transformations as a young child plays with mark and meaning, as Ben's drawing activity showed. The child's engagement with and exploration of the process of encoding and decoding was also evident in my own observations and analysis of children's drawing activity. For example:

> During the course of drawing activity the marks made were often interpreted many times by the children. Sometimes a child might encode an idea through a mark which they then decoded in a different way. (This was evident in the verbal commentary of the children as they drew.) The stimulus could be something extraneous to the drawing itself. For instance, Jake drew several arcs above each other and identified his drawing as a rainbow. At that moment someone near to him sneezed and he decided that the drawing now represented a sneeze. On other occasions the drawing itself could suggest a new idea, prompting additional mark making or a modification of the original marks. Rory's drawing illustrated this point. He was playing with, and closely observing, a model zebra. Rather than observing the object from a fixed viewpoint (a culturally specific way of looking that he has yet to learn about), he inspected it from all angles, turning it around in his hands. As he drew he stated that he needed black and white. Having drawn some vertical black lines, he then declared: 'It's raining – it's all rain coming down.' He then added further short vertical lines over the paper in response to this idea.
>
> (Cox 2005 p. 119)

Clearly, in this example, the children's intentions can be interpreted not so much in terms of the completion of the drawing as an objective representation of an idea or an observation, but in terms of *using* visual representation to construct meaning as they act in and on the world. To use Vygotsky's terminology (1978), children's activity is *mediated* by drawing.

> When a child is including, or excluding, features of the world in a drawing and when they are encoding and decoding intentions in their drawings in a playful and on-going way, they are experimenting with the language of materials and marks and building concepts at the same time. From this perspective, drawing is a form of language (see Goodman 1976), which carries meanings in ways which are semiotically specific to it.
>
> (Cox 2005 p.193)

As the child discovers the possibilities and power of this representational practice, they use it intentionally and purposefully in specific situations in the social, interactive world in which they live. As I emphasised in Chapter 1, the child's environment is a social and cultural one, as well as physical. In other words it is already laden with meaning. The active interplay that can be observed, as the child continues to transform their drawings, is that between the child's own sign-making and its context – between the child's representational activities and the social and cultural environment. It is the evidence of children's minds at work – of their learning-in-action.

The same goes for spoken language. As Barnes (1976 p. 28) suggests 'communication is not the only function of language'. He refers to one child's utterances full of hesitations and changes of direction, which, he explains, as communication may leave 'something to be desired'. He says:

> The hesitations and changes of direction have a different function: we usually call it 'thinking aloud'. Talking her way into a problem is enabling this girl to monitor her own thought, and re-shape it. Talk is here a means for controlling thinking.

Children, then, engage with the activities of drawing and spoken language and their meanings within the specific social and cultural contexts in which they are living their lives (Stetsenko 1995). In participating in the activity of drawing, they construct their own representations and develop their thinking, making use of their own existing conceptual resources and the resources of the culture as they experience it. These resources, or tools, are not only the physical 'stuff' – the artefacts and materials – but the range of sign-making systems that can be used to represent and conceptualise their worlds. These are the 'mediational means' (Wertsch 1991) that have been socially and historically constructed (Vygotsky 1978).

To reiterate, this is sign making in all its forms, including the verbal. Kress (1997) is one researcher who draws attention to the multiplicity of ways in which children construct meaning using both physical and cultural tools. He explores the 'multi-modal' and multi-media nature of the mediational means that children use. They use whatever is to hand, both materially and conceptually, transforming what is around them for their own purposes. When, for example, children use pillows, blankets, chairs and dolls (p. 19) in their play they are giving these objects complex meanings; they are using them to represent and communicate in the context of their activities. For Kress, 'pillows and blankets are in this respect as important as coloured pencils and paper: the former encourage a disposition towards taking everything as being potentially meaningful . . .' (p. 98).

All this is in contrast to the accounts of earlier researchers. For instance, some researchers of children's drawing (e.g. Kellogg 1969) intentionally isolated drawing from the children's oral commentary and the social interactions that accompanied drawing activity. These researchers' exclusive focus on the drawings themselves misses the significance of drawing as one representational practice amongst the many that children use to make sense of their experiences. Their view indicates a very different understanding of children's development, focused as it is on the characteristics of the drawings, and an adult's conventional interpretation of these, rather than on the child's interpretive activities.

Some philosophical issues

Once development is seen instead in terms of socially situated and motivated activity, which takes many forms, the significance of close observation of children's meaning making in all its variety and in its particular contexts becomes clear. Whether these observations are carried out by researchers – or by teachers – they provide the evidence of how children interact with the world around them: how they bring to bear what they know and understand on the new or unfamiliar; how they actively invent ways of representing it; how they actively engage with and interpret the representational and communicative practices of the social group and actively use its mediational resources both to realise and to shape their own purposes.

In so doing, their active construction of meanings also creates new possibilities for interpreting the world within the communities to which they belong and in this way, as participants in those communities, children themselves contribute to the shaping of the culture and its practices. As Wertsch claims (1991 p. 8): 'When action is given analytic priority, human beings are viewed as coming into contact with, and creating, their surroundings as well as themselves through the actions in which they engage.'

While the kind of ideas generated by the research of people like Matthews and Kress, to which I have referred above, have a long history, they do seem grounded in *new* perspectives on children's learning, if only in that they are at odds with some of the practices that have commonly prevailed in some classrooms. As I have already suggested in earlier chapters, the present approach encourages teachers to focus primarily on their own actions as teachers – on teaching that produces particular outcomes from their pupils. It is a directive approach. As Bruner (1996 p. 56) put it: 'It is blankly one-way: teaching is not a mutual dialogue, but a telling by one to the other.' By contrast, these alternative perspectives on children's learning suggest that teachers should tune in to children's meaning making; they must see what goes on in the classroom as more of a collaborative venture where the children are initiators as well as the teachers, where children engage with what the culture provides and where, in turn, they contribute to the shaping of that culture.

From this alternative point of view, meanings are constructed jointly, through interaction between individuals and their worlds; through dialogue between children and other people in the social situations in which they live. It is this that that allows for the realisation of what Bruner talks about as 'possible worlds' (Bruner 1986). His is a bold claim; he envisages a new breed of developmental theory:

> it's central technical concern will be how to create in the young an appreciation of the fact that many worlds are possible, that meaning and reality are created and not discovered, that negotiation is the art of constructing new meanings by which individuals can regulate their relations with each other . . . The power to recreate reality, to reinvent culture, we will come to recognize, is where a theory of development must begin its discussion of mind.
>
> (p. 149)

This vision is a radical one. It raises philosophical issues that have been at the core of debates about knowledge – particularly in recent decades, in the era of 'postmodernism'. Bruner's words invite educators to question further the relationship between children's meaning making and the world they live in. What is that world? His theme of the collaborative creation and recreation of reality suggests that his constructivist theories of mind and learning embrace wider theories – of 'philosophical constructivism'. To get a sense of what might be meant by this, it can be contrasted with the idea of 'philosophical realism' which relates to the common-sense perception that 'reality' exists independently of human beings' representations of it. Philosophical constructivism calls into question this apparently self-evident idea. For the philosophical constructivist, the real world can only be construed in terms of the different ways in which it is described, using the different systems of description or representation that have been invented. In this respect, Bruner's ideas reflect those of Nelson Goodman (1978) – that reality is made rather than found. This might seem a rather extreme view and Bruner pointed out that it is difficult to accept the epistemological questions Goodman's ideas raise. Bruner's thinking was, nevertheless, clearly influenced by his Harvard colleague. He wrote: 'whatever the limitations of Goodman's proposals, he has made clearer a concept of mind to be specified not in terms of properties, but rather as an instrument for producing worlds' (Bruner 1986 p. 104).

Such broad philosophical debates can seem remote from the world of the classroom and some teachers might protest that their work is very firmly grounded in a real world. First, they might argue that they work in the real world of a legally and institutionally regulated environment, where they are required to teach the National Curriculum, 'delivering' prescribed content and achieving particular outcomes. Second, flights into philosophical constructivism may seem to undermine the very bedrock of their work: that there is a real world and that it is their role to help children to gain access to it. As I've already suggested, the existing culture of schooling is centred on practices where there are those who teach and those who are taught. Bruner's vision – and the philosophical questions it raises – challenge what might be the underlying tenet of teaching for many teachers: that there are certain things that children need to know and understand, that these are, moreover, simply 'givens' and that the teacher's job is to ensure that children acquire that knowledge and understanding.

But, to take this a step further, it has to be remembered that these apparently common sense ideas, which have been such a powerful influence on teachers' everyday actions, can themselves be located within a philosophical frame – the sort of philosophical realism that asserts the incontrovertible existence of a real world, unproblematically accessed by systems of representation and knowledge. From the point of view of realism, very broadly speaking, the development of knowledge depends on applying these systems to discover more about that pre-existing reality. What is found out corresponds with what there is 'out there' to know. The pedagogy that derives from this approach assumes this transparent relationship between what these systems reveal about the real world and that real world itself: the descriptions directly reflect the reality they describe. Educating children is then seen as the teacher-driven enterprise of providing them with this knowledge – teaching them about what is already known about the real world and how to find out more about it. This common-sense framework, however, may well seem more comfortable and acceptable than the alternative point of view, which suggests that the world is constantly under construction and re-construction. It may seem extreme to dispense with the idea of a real world altogether which, carried to its logical conclusion, seems to invalidate the very idea of education, at least as it is traditionally understood.

The issues here are complex, as Bruner shows, and the common-sense, realist perceptions are clearly open to challenge. But there are those who argue that it is not necessary to adopt 'philosophical constructivism' as the only alternative to philosophical realism. Holma (2009) has shown that Scheffler, for example, does not subscribe to the certainty of knowledge from the realist perspective, but, nevertheless, does not abandon the possibility of a real world. According to Holma, Scheffler accepts that there are different worlds – plural realities – in the sense that there are multiple systems for *describing* reality. He rejects, however, the view that there is no real world that exists apart from the constructions of human minds and communities. Scheffler's sticking point, as Holma points out, is that

> . . . he cannot accept the idea that 'we create or shape the things to which our words refer' (Scheffler, 1997 p. 196). In Scheffler's view: 'In making the true statement that there were stars before men, we do not also make the stars that were there then' (ibid.).
>
> (Holma 2009 p.333)

In other words, there are those who argue for pluralist versions of reality but who also hold that knowledge and learning are not completely relativistic; whose arguments do not presuppose that it is wholly a matter of the real world being 'made up' by human beings and their systems of knowing and understanding.

Socio-cultural theories – implications for teachers as mediators

Where do the research into children's learning and the related philosophical debates lead teachers regarding approaches to their teaching? At this point I shall try to clarify further what it means for teachers to adopt a responsive, collaborative approach to children and the reasons why this is an appropriate pedagogical stance. I have hopefully, begun to show how, from the socio-cultural perspective, human beings, through their relationships with one another, in communities of meaning makers, create ways of making sense of their experience of a real world. People make the real world accessible and communicable to each other through their representations and descriptions of it. They learn through engaging in these practices of representing and describing – of knowing – the world, with other people. In other words, learners use the socio-cultural resources that they encounter in the communities to which they belong and the communities' activities in which they participate. (I shall say more about these practices later.)

From this perspective, the possibilities for the creation of meanings – the construction of new conceptions and knowledge – are in the hands of both learners and teachers. (This need not, however – as I've noted above – imply that the worlds of meaning they jointly create have no grounding at all in a real world beyond those constructions or inventions.) Children's meaning making, then, takes place in specific, social contexts and is in part shaped by the practices, tools and languages of the communities to which the child belongs. It must also be borne in mind that, on this analysis, the teacher is bringing their own interpretations to children's actions. The teacher's own constructs shape their responses to the child's meaning making in those contexts. To the extent, however, that the child and teacher are members of the same communities of practice there are possibilities for shared and negotiated meanings. As Barnes (1976 p22) has put it: 'Classroom learning can best be seen as an interaction between the teacher's meanings, and those of his [sic] pupils, so that what they take away is partly shared and partly unique to each of them.'

On this kind of account, knowledge is not a product in the commodity sense (see Chapter 2), owned by the already initiated, to be acquired by the learner. It is a product in the sense of being made or created by the members of the social group, including the young, who actively take part in making a culture's meanings and constructing knowledge. Knowledge is not pre-determined and cultures are shaped between community members. Those who participate in activities (the 'community of practice') construct and re-construct their worlds. For Lave and Wenger (1991 p. 33), 'agent, activity and the world mutually constitute each other'.

This view directly challenges the assumed authority and power of the instructor, suggesting instead a more equal relationship between learner and teacher. It implies a classroom as a learning community: it calls for a more democratic space, where children's active engagement is prioritised and where teachers actively help children determine the direction of their own activities. I shall say more about this later, but already it is clear that a case can be built for teachers to reconfigure their responsibilities, stepping away from their authoritative role, to participate in children's meaningful activities; to engage with them as thinking people with their own intentions and to be responsive to children's possibly idiosyncratic learning pathways.

As I shall discuss more fully later, children come to school as learners with their own purposes, who have already been participants in other, everyday social contexts. They do not come to school 'uneducated', only 'unschooled'. Their everyday concerns are often playful: their activities do not necessarily conform to adult practices or adult expectations, but are exploratory and, by their nature, unpredictable.

From the socio-cultural perspective, then, the one-way transmission mode of teaching clearly comes under strain. The objectives-driven, linear model does not readily accommodate divergence from the pre-ordained agenda. The teacher, in maintaining the focus on the achievement of the objective must ensure that activities stay on track. Children may struggle to make sense of the prescribed activities, as was illustrated by Drummond's example of Jason (see Chapter 2). In these situations, the onus is on the child to make connections with their existing conceptions and knowledge; the child is in the position of having to interpret the demands of the task and the intentions of the teacher. From the alternative, socio-cultural point of view, this expectation clearly becomes less tenable.

Interpreting Vygotsky's 'zone of proximal development'

It would not be fair to presume, however, that a teacher working within the existing culture of objectives-driven teaching necessarily and always adopts a one-way transmission mode of teaching and makes no effort to provide contexts for activities that help children to interpret new ideas in terms of the familiar. On the one hand, it is common practice for adults who interact with children to make these connections. On the other hand, many teachers may have learned from Vygotsky's theories that they can take the child's learning beyond what they can already do unaided, into the 'zone of proximal development' (ZPD). The ZPD marks out what children can achieve with the support of others:

> It is the distance between the actual developmental level as deter-
> mined by independent problem solving and the level of potential
> development as determined through problem solving under adult
> guidance or in collaboration with more capable peers.
>
> (Vygotsky 1978 p. 86)

Wood, Bruner and Ross (1976) introduced the term 'scaffolding' to refer to the way the teacher, or any more experienced other person, might support the child's learning in the ZPD so they can accomplish tasks they would not have been able to learn how to do alone. They showed that with such support, chil-dren can achieve more than would be predicted by Piaget's developmental theory. Scaffolding entailed the tutor using a variety of tactics that would 'keep the child involved in task activity long enough for them to figure out how to do it for themselves' (Wood 1998 p. 99). The researchers identified two key features of such support: offering immediate help when the child struggled and reducing it when the child was succeeding so as not to hold the child back (p. 100).

Wood himself notes the limitations of this approach, particularly because it focuses on learning in adult–child tutoring situations which have different characteristics from naturalistic interactions, where, by contrast 'it is usually the child, rather than the adult, who initiates interactions and sets the shared agenda' (p.100). He turns to Rogoff's more inclusive concept of 'guided partici-pation': 'In guided participation, children are involved with multiple compan-ions and caregivers in organised, flexible webs of relationships that focus on shared cultural activities . . . [which] provides children with opportunities to participate in diverse roles' (Rogoff 1990 pp. 97–8, cited in Wood 1998 p. 101).

Moll (1990) also takes a critical stance towards the way in which Vygotsky's ZPD may be interpreted. He describes (p. 7) how the ZPD is usually characterised as:

1   Establishing a level of difficulty. This level, assumed to be the proximal level, must be a bit challenging for the student but not too difficult.
2   Providing assisted performance. The adult provides guided practice to the child with a clear sense of the goal or outcome of the child's performance.
3   Evaluating independent performance. The most logical outcome of a zone of proximal development is the child performing independently.

He warns against making the assumption that classroom activities represent ZPDs just because they have the three characteristics identified above. Indeed, this would mean that instructional practices such as rote drill-and-practice could be held up as examples. Moll argues that this was not what Vygotsky had in mind. This use of the ZPD results, he suggests, from conceptualising it as 'the teaching or assessment of discrete, separable, skills and sub-skills' (p.7).
    As he explains:

> a problem in applying the concept of the zone to the analysis of classroom instruction is that a definition of the zone emphasising the transfer of knowledge, and especially of skills, by those knowing more to those knowing less, may characterise virtually any instructional practice.
>
> (p.7)

He uses the skills-based approach to the teaching of reading to make his point. He contrasts this method, where reading skills are atomised and taught discretely, with a very different way of teaching reading that had emerged at the time he was writing: the 'whole language' approach. The thinking – which was much more in tune with Vygotsky's ideas – was that reading should be contextualised, so that it was taught through authentic, meaningful, functional uses of language. To make his case, Moll cites Cole and Griffin (1983):

> 'Skills are always part of activities and settings, but they only take on meaning in terms of how they are organized. So, instead of basic skills, a socio-historical approach talks about *basic activities* . . .'
>
> (Moll 1990 p.8)

It is the emphasis on creating meaning, rather than on the teaching of specific skills that is the key to the ZPD for Moll. The emphasis is not on 'independent

performance after guided practice . . . but the ability of the children to participate in qualitatively new collaborative activities' (p.13). This is why in some
classrooms children are learning to use reading and writing through making
lists to go shopping or reading recipes to bake cakes with their teacher or to
engage in the activity of sharing and enjoying stories with adults.

Moll's suggestion that it is easy to miss the point of the ZPD, because of
the pervasiveness of the skills perspective, remains as relevant today as it was
when he was writing. In the current mandatory approach to teaching phonics
(synthetic phonics), for instance (DCSF 2007a), it is assumed that reading can
be reduced to a set of skills, that these should be taught discretely and that this
is the best means for teaching literacy. Phonics programmes may well be built
around progression, ensuring that each step is at an appropriate level of difficulty for the child, but, following Moll, this would be an example of a different
kind of instructional practice than Vygotsky's theories suggest. Moll argues,
instead, for environments in which 'different types of "literacies" can be developed and learned.' (Moll 1990 p.8). This is an approach that is very much a part
of critical discussion of the teaching of literacy today (the 'new literacy'
approach). It entails 'the creation of social contexts in which children actively
learn to use, try, and manipulate language in the service of making sense or
creating meaning'. Moll suggests, in a similar way to Rogoff, that the zone
should be thought of in terms of

> the child engaged in collaborative activity within specific social envi-
> ronments. The focus is on the *social system* within which we hope
> children learn, with the understanding that this social system is
> mutually and actively created by teacher and students. This
> interdependence of adult and child is central to a Vygotskyan analysis
> of instruction.
>
> (Moll 1990 p. 11)

This is very different from the linear model of instruction where someone
other than the learner attempts to *direct* the learning – controlling the learner's
activities through setting objectives. Instead of employing the one-way
teaching methods of the linear model, the teacher working with a socio-
cultural understanding of the ZPD would think in terms of the child's activities and the way those are contextualised. They would see learning in terms of
the child's participation in what is going on around them (see Chapter 1).

It is important to raise this, as many teachers will have heard of
Vygotsky's zone of proximal development and may have transposed
the idea into their teaching. It is clear from Moll's analysis that it is
inappropriate to bolt on the concept of the ZPD to existing skills-based,
performance-led practice. In a context of linear, objectives-driven teaching
where knowledge and skills are often de-contextualised, it is most likely

that it will be misinterpreted in the ways Moll describes and used as a justification for 'top-down' instruction.

Alternative frameworks for teaching

Moll's analysis of Vygotsky's ideas is significant and I shall return to it later. It helps to show that the kind of teaching that will take learning forward entails the diagnostic appreciation of the child's meaning making in context, through close observation and engagement. It focuses teachers' attention on children's actions, on the representational strategies that the children use in specific situations and on those situations themselves. Instead of seeing the child from the outside, the teacher tries to enter the child's thoughts (Bruner 1996 p. 56). This calls for the teacher to be immersed in the situations and contexts in which the child is actively making meanings. It has to be remembered that these may be the imaginative constructions of the child (take for example, a role-play scenario created by the child), and so demand a further layer of interpretation. It is the teacher's responsibility to seek in-depth insight into the child's activities, their purposes and intentions.

The teacher's role, then, is not just a passive one of providing for self-chosen activity in a 'stimulating environment' and then standing back – as the Plowden or Piagetian teacher might have thought – with the expectation that the child, as a 'lone scientist', will make their own 'discoveries'. For all the reasons I have discussed, that is no longer an adequate account of learning or teaching; nor is the view that teaching is the single-minded pursuit – even with the provision of structured support – of given objectives. Rather, the teacher's role is to collaboratively support the child's engagement with the resources of the culture. The teacher is already immersed in the discourses that the child enters and knows how to make practical use of the tools available within the culture: they are familiar with its ways of sense making and thinking; its modes of enquiry through which its plural representations of reality and fields of knowledge are constructed; the processes of investigation and creation and the skills that are employed within these practices. As Bruner (1996 p. 20) argued:

> Reality construction is the product of meaning making shaped by traditions and by a culture's toolkit of ways of thought. In this sense, education must be conceived as aiding young humans in learning to use the tools of meaning making and reality construction, to better adapt to the world in which they find themselves and to help in the process of changing it as required.

The teacher can act as a guide for children. To adopt a metaphor, the teacher enters into the child's own learning journey as a partner, a respectful companion of the child, and supportive in helping them to build their own pathways through the terrain. To reiterate, this is very different from an outdated behaviourist model of teaching, of training the child, for instance, to achieve a certain level of skilled performance. Vygotsky suggests that this latter sort of process does not develop what he defines as intelligence – the ability to solve problems independently. It disregards the crucial factor that 'human learning presupposes a specific social nature and a process by which children grow into the intellectual life of those around them' (Vygotsky 1978 p. 88). As Vygotsky argues, by working with others, in the ZPD, children can go beyond their independent capabilities: 'children are capable of doing much more in collective activity or under the guidance of adults'.

In summary and to sustain the metaphor, children do not merely get taken on the journey. Learning, as I have presented it, is grounded in activity. It is a matter of the child both physically and mentally taking part in the activities going on in the situations in which they find themselves. This is not just the kind of activity that teachers might come up with to occupy children or keep them entertained, but the meaningful activities that are part of life within a culture. The children's journey is a shared venture: their teacher is a fellow participant in it.

As I have suggested in both the previous chapter and in this one, from this socio-cultural, participative perspective, the classroom becomes a place that affords the possibility of more democratic relationships between teacher and children: a place where activities, and thus the direction of the learning pathways, are negotiated between them, in partnership.

Concluding reflections

If learning is grounded in what children actively encounter in social situations and in their intentional, motivated action, this suggests a shift away from current, dominant pedagogical approaches. It does not only entail a very different level of engagement with the child – as a person and a thinker – from that of the prevailing methods. It also demands that children's intentions and motivations are taken seriously as they participate in activities. It should be clear that when learning is understood in terms of what children do, it is contextualised within the actualities of children's lives and the decisions for action that they themselves make. It is about what they learn to do in specific contexts; of them as an individual exploring and challenging the possibilities of their social as well as their physical environment, in all their particularities and complexities.

Children are predisposed to learn and their learning both results from their own intentional activity and feeds into it. This implies a pedagogical approach based on learning as 'doing', not interpreted in the narrow behav-ioural, or acquisition-of-isolated-skills sense, nor in the laissez-faire, being busy sense, but in the constructive sense of providing 'activity for learning'. The child engages in purposeful activities, interacting with those around them. The teacher neither 'acts upon' the child, nor takes a non-interventionist approach. Rather, as a fellow participant, they support the child in identifying their own purposes, and help them to make use of the cultural practices or tools to achieve them. Teachers have a role in modelling those practices and in helping children to navigate those social and cultural resources in their meaning making, respecting children's motivations and intentions.

From this perspective it is the obligation of the teacher, as educator, to ensure that their actions are responsive to the child's own actions and purposes. From this point of view the more simplistic view of teaching as a one-way process of transmission and elicited performance is replaced by appreciation, on the part of the teacher, of the complexities of the social and collaborative activities that human beings engage in; of how children are purposefully participating in them and of the nature of children's own purposes. The teacher's active role is to share in those activities so that they can both under-stand the child's intentions and can help the child realise them, using the cultural resources which the teacher knows how to use. I shall say more about all this and how it might be achieved, in the context of the classroom culture, in the following chapters.

Issues for teachers

- To what extent are you aware of children's own intentions and purposes in their activities?
- When you closely observe children in action, in what representa-tional practices do they engage? How are they using these multi-modal means to mediate their activities?
- How would you describe the ways in which you support children's learning?
- How have you thought of and applied Vygotsky's idea of the zone of proximal development in your teaching? Looking critically at how it can be interpreted, how might you see it differently?
- How do you create contexts for collaborative activity in your own classroom?

4 Interacting and communicating to learn

Chapter overview

In this chapter, I look more closely at the relationships between children and teachers, paying particular attention to the patterns of interaction between them and also exploring communicative practices in classrooms (particularly talk), to consider these in relation to the culture of learning and teaching within the primary school and beyond it. I shall try to bring into sharper focus the implications of school activities for children's learning from the point of view of this participatory account of learning. I shall review the evidence to show that there are particularly resilient patterns of interaction that perpetuate the existing, performative culture of 'school' and contribute to the conflict of values and practices that some teachers experience. I shall explore the community of practice of English primary schools from the point of view of classroom communicative practices, which tend to be of a kind – as I shall show – that can inhibit children's propensity to participate and collaborate in self-directed meaning-making activities and, furthermore, in the activities of the wider culture that the school ostensibly offers.

Learning as participation

I have already tried to show that children can be seen as thinking people engaged in intentional activity to make meaning, and the teacher, as Bruner puts it 'is concerned with understanding what the child thinks and how she arrives at what she believes' (Bruner 1996 p. 56). I have tried to make it clear that when this 'first person perspective' (ibid.) is analysed in socio-cultural terms, how and what the child comes to think and know is not a result of 'one-sided' (Rogoff 1994) activity on the part of the teacher. Rather it is dependent on children's participation in activities within specific social and cultural situations and the communities of practice (see Introduction) to which they belong. In this chapter, I say more about this, so that patterns of communication in school might be understood in a way that is different from how they are often seen, which might open up new ways for teachers to interact with children.

As I have argued, from this different perspective, learning is 'an integral and inseparable aspect of social practice' (Lave and Wenger 1991 p. 31). Participation and collaboration are central to learning. Learning in this sense cannot be a choice between 'learning through doing' and learning through some other means. Learning *is* doing and children learn *in* doing (ibid.). It is implicit in this view that learners engage interactively as participants in particular practices. These practices are social in nature: they embody particular social relationships, values, meanings and purposes.

When Lave and Wenger explain learning as participation, they do so in terms of 'legitimate, peripheral participation'. People learn in the process of engaging with activities along with other members of the community of practice, whatever the nature of that community and its practices. According to Lave and Wenger, their participation is 'peripheral' in the sense that they are newcomers. They engage with full participants, who already have shared understandings of the activities; who shape them and are shaped by them. From this analytical perspective, as Lave and Wenger have made clear, it is participation in collaborative activity that constitutes learning. For Lave and Wenger, there is no activity that is not situated (p. 33); 'peripheral' does not imply a periphery and a centre (p. 36) and no participation is illegitimate. The three elements of legitimate, peripheral and participation are not to be considered in isolation from each other; each defines the other and in combination they create community membership (p. 35). Legitimacy is important in that it highlights the complex social relationships within and between communities in terms of power. Furthermore, these relations become part of the learning: 'The form that the legitimacy of participation takes is a defining characteristic of ways of belonging and is therefore not only a crucial condition for learning, but a constitutive element of its content' (p. 35).

The meaning and force of these ideas in relation to children's learning will become more apparent in this chapter.

As I have already suggested, in relation to teaching, to take this point of view is to locate the individual in the context of the activities, beliefs and values, forms of discourse, and patterns of interaction of the wider group. It is to see thinking in the same way as Vygotsky did, as Moll – referring to the work of Minick – succinctly puts it: 'as a characteristic not of the child only but of the child-in-social-activities with others (Minick 1985)' (Moll 1990 p.12).

Understanding the learning that is going on would rest on understanding how children participate in the activities of a 'community of practice', such as the school (Lave and Wenger 1991). Moreover, as I have highlighted in earlier chapters, this socio-cultural analytical perspective places the school in relation to the wider world.

In being social, practices are always inter-subjective, communicative and dialogic. (See Street 1993, for example, cited in Barton and Hamilton 1998.) The child actively uses verbal language to help them make sense within the social contexts in which they are participating (see Chapter 1). Crucially, if teachers accept Lave and Wenger's analysis, then talk or dialogue takes on a different significance from the common-sense conception that they are *vehicles* for learning – instead, as social practices, they *are* learning. As Lave and Wenger (1991 p. 109) explain it: 'For newcomers, then, the purpose is not to learn *from* talk as a substitute for legitimate peripheral participation; it is to learn *to* talk as a key to legitimate peripheral participation.'

Learning and schools

From the socio-cultural perspective, then, schools and classrooms are particular communities of practice, amongst others in the wider world. On this view, there are no grounds for prioritising schools, over other social contexts, as the specific sites where learning takes place. All social contexts – or communities of practice – afford opportunities for participation in their respective activities and, therefore, for learning. It is true that schools exist as communities specifically set up with pedagogic purposes, which might explain why, from a traditional perspective 'learning' is understood as what goes on in the school setting or some similar institutional context. As Lave and Wenger (1991 p. 54) note, 'the activity of children learning is often presented as located in instructional environments and as occurring in the context of pedagogical intentions'. A key distinction (and one which will become clearer in Chapter 7) that is central to Vygotsky's thinking is that the discourse in school

> represents a qualitatively different form of communication because words act not only as means of communication, as they would in everyday discourse, but as objects of study. In classroom interaction, the teacher directs the children's attention to word meanings and definitions and the systematic relationships among them that constitute an organized system of knowledge.
>
> (Moll 1990 p. 10)

This marks out the difference between 'everyday' or 'spontaneous' concepts and 'scientific' or 'schooled' concepts (Vygotsky 1987). Nevertheless, from the socio-cultural perspective, participation in *any* social practice constitutes learning. In other words, learning cannot be equated with or compartmentalised as the activities that go on in school, nor can it be restricted to the outcomes that result from adults in the school setting 'teaching' children.

From the discussion in earlier chapters, it should be clear that the practices and values inherent in the performance-driven classroom culture on the one hand, potentially conflict with those implicit in situations where the child is a self-directed learner, on the other. Obviously, this can present difficulties for those teachers who see children in the ways I have discussed in Chapters 1 and 3, as agents of their own learning, especially when the performance-driven agenda is not only predominant in their workplace, but also across the wider culture. The task is one of creating a context and a community of practice that embody the values, purposes and social relations implicit in this view of the child as an active maker of meaning, and of learning as much more than the acquisition of skills and knowledge transmitted by the teacher. The challenges, within the institutional setting and existing culture of the school may seem overwhelming. A starting point, however, is to explore the nature of these conflicts.

I have made the point, above, that when learning is analysed as situated, the child is learning as a participant in specific social practices, whatever those practices happen to be. This means that, even when the child is participating in the performance or outcomes-driven practices that I described in Chapter 2, those practices, specific to those performative contexts, *constitute* the child's learning. The child, even though they may be participating in an apparently passive way, is nevertheless an active meaning maker in those situations and their learning will be shaped by whatever practices prevail.

In this chapter and the next, I intend to unpack these issues further insofar as they relate to interaction and communication in classrooms. This will begin to reveal how these practices can limit children's learning within that culture as well as their cultural contribution (see Chapters 3 and 7). It seems that the dominant practices in English primary schools and classrooms might, on a socio-cultural analysis, actually be at odds with an accepted primary purpose of the school, which is to foster breadth of learning. Again, this might help to further demonstrate why it may be more appropriate to refer to these practices as 'schooling' rather than education, since – as I shall show – what children *are* learning to do is to participate in fact, in these rather limited and limiting activities of 'school'.

Learning in the home and what happens at school

One way of illustrating the way in which classroom communicative practices might work against and close down children's opportunities to extend their learning is to contrast them with those in other contexts in which children live their lives and learn. The seminal work of Barbara Tizard and Martin Hughes (Tizard and Hughes 1984) provides such an illustration. The fact that it was carried out some time ago highlights the long history of the differences between what goes on in the home and in the school. This research project demonstrated, quite forcibly, that children's meaning making was encouraged in the home in ways that were not experienced in the classroom. The researchers found out, for instance, that, at home, the children they studied talked freely about a wide range of topics: they initiated and sustained conversations, argued and endlessly asked questions. These conversations revealed the children as persistent and logical thinkers, puzzling to grasp new ideas, and the home to be a powerful learning environment. In contrast, the children's talk with their teachers lacked such richness, depth and variety. For instance, in school, children had far fewer conversations (10 an hour at school, 27 an hour at home) with adults and these were shorter (8 turns at school, 16 at home) (p. 185).

I am quoting these figures as they represent quite strikingly how different the experience was in the home and the school. The school context was not so much one of mutual communication: the conversations were more dominated by the adult. The most remarkable difference the researchers found was that the children didn't ask questions at school – 26 questions were asked in an hour at home, but only two in an hour of their teachers. And the questions asked at home were clearly indicative of the child's quest for meaning – two-thirds tended to be of curiosity questions or 'why?' questions. 'What's that?' 'How do you do that?' 'Why are you going upstairs?' Other questions demonstrated what Tizard and Hughes called 'intellectual search': those where the child is actively seeking new information or explanations, or is puzzling over something they don't understand or of which they are trying to make sense, with their limited knowledge of the world (p. 114). By contrast, in school, the children asked more 'business-type' questions (e.g. where is the glue?) (p. 201). '"Passages of intellectual search", in which the children raised questions, and thought through and discussed the adults' answers, did not occur at school' (p. 213). If we see children as active in their quest to construct meaning in the social contexts of their lives, it seems, from this evidence, that the home environment possibly afforded more scope for learning than the school. The research, in fact, presented quite a negative picture of what children might be experiencing when they went to school.

A pressing question arises: how can this be explained? One possible explanation for the discontinuity between the pre-school experience at home and what happens at school, observed by Tizard and Hughes, may, for instance, have been a lack of understanding of children's learning – as active meaning making – on the part of the individual adults in the school context. The children's teachers may have been failing to see the centrality of participation to the children's learning; that interaction and collaborative activity is key to both how and what children learn. They may not have seen that the kinds of sustained communication, in relation to everyday purposeful activities with which children engage in the home environment and where they play a part in deciding what to do, constitute the constructive context for their meaning making and, potentially, provide a model for patterns of participation in the school in the kinds of intellectually challenging and worthwhile activities it is meant to offer.

There is another possible explanation that is perhaps a more likely one. Arguably, the differences between home and school may simply have reflected the insurmountable difficulties of providing for the learning of individual children in a busy classroom. As many teachers will attest, contradictions can exist between their actual practice and the theories and values to which they feel they are committed, because of the practicalities and pressures of their situation. In practical terms, the obligation to engage with children's activities and to make careful observations to find out about the individual learner's current thinking is a demanding one. The need to be 'contingently responsive' (Wells and Chang-Wells 1992, see Chapter 3) to children's preoccupations, concerns and questions has to be set against the large numbers of children in a typical classroom. It may simply not be practicable or achievable for teachers to act consistently on what they understand about learning. The child might be receiving very focused support and more or less individual attention from adults in the home or out-of-school setting, but clearly this is very difficult, if not impossible, to sustain in a class of 30. It may be more feasible for a parent to accommodate children's choices in out of school environments than it is for the teacher of a large class. Even when teachers are well-intentioned, the school situation can work against them. In fact, it may well be the teacher's commitment to democratic principles of equal treatment and respect for all children that limits the possibility of responding to, and engaging with each child adequately. As Galton (2007) has pointed out, it has been a consistent feature of primary classrooms that teachers are concerned to provide 'fair shares' of attention and response to children resulting, inevitably, in restricted interaction between child and teacher, in terms of its quality as well as its extent.

Either way, the effect is that discontinuity may exist between home and school environments. It may seem that there are differences in terms of how children are valued, if not in the values held by parents or carers and teachers, then in what individual children themselves experience in the different settings. It appears that, in Tizard and Hughes' account, the use of language would indicate that the adults in the home were receptive to the children and encouraged their participation, even if they did not necessarily perceive their activities as 'learning'. In school, however, whatever good intentions teachers might have had to respond to and engage with children, the practices described by the researchers told a different story.

It may be true that the disparity should not be overplayed, for as Alexander says – though he is careful to point out that cultural differences should not be defined as in terms of deficits – 'children's access to opportunities for talk outside the school vary considerably, as do the quality and potency of the talk they encounter' (Alexander 2008 p. 18). Nevertheless, it does seem that in Tizard and Hughes' (1984) research, the children were getting messages that taking part in activities within the community of the school was a very different experience from doing so within the family or in other non-formal situations. They were finding a very different culture. For instance, as the researchers suggested, teachers were, if only unintentionally, communicating to children that it is their pupils' role to answer questions, but not to ask them.

From the perspective of socio-cultural theory, as I have tried to show, these differences in the forms of interaction can be seen in terms of differences in social contexts. As Lave and Wenger (1991) and Wenger (1998) explained (see Introduction), when the ways in which language is used in the home and in the more formal setting of the school are analysed as being situated in particular social contexts, they can be seen as being specific to different communities of practice. Barton and Hamilton (1998 p. 9) have referred to this as differences in practices within different 'domains of life' or 'domains of activity'. I have already discussed how children's actions (Chapter 3) are motivated and intentional, shaped by the patterns of activity of the cultural context, and how children learn to use the mediational means within those contexts. Though Barton's and Hamilton's work is concerned with literacy, verbal interactions can be seen in very much the same way, as 'purposeful and embedded in broader social goals and cultural practices' (p. 7). Different forms of interaction are used within the differently 'structured, patterned contexts' (p. 10) that they describe as different domains of life. 'Talk' in school has goals and purposes that are structured by the social and cultural practices of the institution of 'school' as these have been shaped culturally and historically. On this kind of analysis, in the domain of the home, the child's intentional and purposeful actions are motivated within the patterns of everyday activity that they experience within it and with which they engage. When the child goes to school, they encounter a quite different culture that presents a different range of practices in which to participate. In the domain of the school, people relate to each other differently and the child must make sense of that, negotiating the new social relations.

A paradox

The situation, described by Tizard and Hughes, then, presents evidence of the kind of paradox I mentioned earlier. The kinds of practices that the child encountered in the school appeared to be less in tune with the child's activities, as a self-directed active meaning maker, than those in the home. As I pointed out, this may seem strange, and antithetical to the very idea of school, given that it is an institution specifically intended to be a context for learning. 'School', it seems, might be a setting that presents barriers to participation in the kind of activities that it is meant to promote. On the other hand, to return to the argument I have already introduced – and to risk labouring the point – it cannot be concluded from the kind of evidence presented by Tizard's and Hughes' research that learning is going on in the home, but *not* in the school. As I have noted (if we follow Lave and Wenger), although it would be misguided to identify learning only with specific 'educational' environments such as the school, learning is nevertheless going on in the school, as it is in any other social context. To reiterate, this is because learning is *integral* to *all* social contexts. It may be worth elaborating on this. When seen in the broader social context, 'the instructional environment' (Lave and Wenger 1991, see above) provides resources for learning like any other community of practice. From a socio-cultural perspective, sense making is going on in both the child's everyday world of the home and family and the institutional world of the school, but the practices the children take part in are different in these different communities. In the community of the home and family the child is engaging in and learning within their everyday and self-chosen activities. At school, the child is making sense of a different world, participating in its distinctive social practices. To put it another way, when home and school are analysed as different domains (Barton and Hamilton 1998) or as different communities of practice (Lave and Wenger 1991) in which participation and learning are integrally interrelated, each setting is to be viewed as a context for learning. Children will construct meaning within the specific communities that they are part of, each with its own particular social practices. So, from the socio-cultural perspective, participation in the unfamiliar ways of interacting in this strange community of the school constitutes the children's learning. As it happens, the communicative practices of this institution called 'school' are peculiar, in both senses of the word.

Through participation in this new community of the school, the child both learns *to* interact in new ways, and learns *from* these new communicative practices. In effect, when the child encounters the instructional, didactic use of language in the school, this is a 'new linguistic practice' (Lave and Wenger 1991 p. 108) specific to this particular context. Whatever this talk is supposed to be *about*, whatever else they are intended to learn from it, 'newcomers' will be participating in, and learning about, this different use of language – this different discourse; this new form of interaction – as a new social practice (pp. 52–3).

In the process, they learn new identities as members of this community: they become 'pupils'. They begin to understand that they go to school 'to learn' and as they participate in the new patterns of interaction within the school culture, they learn that these are what 'learning' is all about. Helping children to 'learn how to learn' is often cited as an educational aim. (I shall say more about this later.) Perhaps a critical question to ask, bearing in mind what Tizard and Hughes discovered, is: how are children coming to understand learning from participating in the culture of learning and teaching as they experience it in schools and how does that relate to what they have already learned about learning from their everyday activities?

Power and schooling

From the socio-cultural point of view, the privileged position of the school as a site for learning can be seen in terms of the relative importance of the different contexts, rather than in terms of its inherent characteristics. In other words, it is not privileged over the home because it is *the* situation where learning occurs, but because of its cultural significance. From the socio-cultural perspective, clearly issues of power and control are unavoidable. Educational institutions are socially powerful contexts through which certain practices become dominant. As Barton and Hamilton put it (1998. p. 10): 'These dominant practices can be seen as part of whole discourse formations, institutionalised configurations of power and knowledge which are embodied in social relationships.'

What seems evident, in the children's experiences and responses in the research carried out by Tizard and Hughes, is the difference in the balance of power between children and adults in the home situation and in school. Moreover, there is this further dimension of difference in the way that the practices in these different contexts are valued. In other words, not only is the child faced with a new set of social relationships when they begin school, in which they arguably have less power in relation to the adults than they had at home; they are also faced with a new, institutionalised context, where the patterns of interaction are seen to have generally more significance than those in the domain of the home. This double shift in the balance of power on the inter-personal level between child and adult *within* these different domains and also *between* the different domains themselves is reflected in the dominance of the adult's voice over the child's and the dominance of the school's activities and purposes over those of the child's out-of-school worlds. Children come to understand that they do not hold power in the school situation, the teachers do, and that school is more important to their learning than their everyday activities.

How are practices changing – early years

Bearing in mind that Tizard and Hughes did their research over twenty years ago, it is reasonable to ask whether it has any relevance today. Howe and Mercer

(2007), in one of the interim reports for the *Cambridge Review* (Alexander 2010), illustrated the extent of the research over the past 30 years, over and above the seminal work of Tizard and Hughes, that has shown the range and richness of language use by children in non-formal or out-of-school contexts. Reviewing the research in relation to non-formal, pre-school contexts they say: 'observational studies, this time in homes and in nurseries and playgroups, have demonstrated that even pre-school children will justify opinions, suggest alternatives and reach compromises during free play with their siblings or peers (see, for example Dunn and Kendrick 1982; Eisenberg and Garvey 1981; Genishi and Di Paolo 1982; Howe and McWilliam 2001; Orsolini 1993)' (Howe and Mercer 2007 p. 9).

Is children's experience in more formal school settings still very different from the non-formal? In the period of time since Tizard and Hughes made their observations, practices in early years settings have certainly changed. In recent years, in particular, early years education has received a great deal of attention through Labour government policies such as Sure Start and the introduction of the Foundation Stage and the Early Years Foundation Stage (EYFS) Framework (DCSF 2008). Government guidance and initiatives were acknowledging the learning that goes on in the home and increasingly emphasised the role of play in children's learning. The EYFS, for instance, has an explicit focus on the Unique Child, which 'recognises that every child is a competent learner from birth' (p. 9) and it pays attention to 'coherence of learning and development across different settings and related to the child's experience at home' (p. 10).

A clear step forward is that the EYFS Curriculum ensured that the new practices in early years extended into the first year of the Primary School – the reception year. In particular, there has been a new focus on 'child-initiated' activities. Changes in practice have begun to reflect the growing awareness of the role in children's learning of their self-directed activity. The REPEY research (*Researching Effective Pedagogy in the Early Years*), for example, carried out by Siraj-Blatchford and colleagues after the dissemination of the government's Curriculum Guidance for the Foundation Stage (Siraj-Blatchford et al. 2002) and before the introduction of the EYFS Framework, had shown that in the most effective settings children were encouraged to initiate activities and did so as often as the adults in the setting.

With regard to adult–child verbal interaction these researchers were clearly endorsing a social constructivist account of children's learning. In their report of the research they wrote:

> If learning comes from a process of cognitive construction that is only achieved when the child is motivated and involved, we have argued that it is entirely consistent to treat the part played by the effective educator in the same way. The cognitive construction in this case is mutual, where each party engages with the understanding of the other and learning is achieved through a process of reflexive 'co-construction'.

> A necessary condition is that both parties are involved, and, for the resultant learning to be worthwhile, that the content should be in some way instructive. Our analyses of the qualitative and quantitative data have substantiated this model and our research has also shown that adult–child interactions that involve some element of 'sustained shared thinking' or what Bruner has termed 'joint involvement episodes' may be especially valuable in terms of children's learning.
>
> (p. 10)

Their notion of sustained shared thinking is a Vygotskian one, and reflects the kind of interactions that had been observed by Tizard and Hughes:

> An episode in which two or more individuals 'work together' in an intellectual way to solve a problem, clarify a concept, evaluate activities, extend a narrative etc. Both parties must contribute to the thinking and it must develop and extend.
>
> (Siraj Blatchford et al. 2002 p.8)

The REPEY project, then, demonstrated the importance of adult involvement in extending thinking in child-initiated activities. It showed that, whether through sustained shared thinking, modelling or open questioning, it provided a source of meaningful intellectual challenge. Arguably, research projects such as REPEY – and also EPPE (*Effective Provision of Pre-School Education*, Sylva et al. 2008) – have been very influential in helping to develop understanding of pedagogy in the early years, revealing and disseminating the kind of practices that are the most conducive to children's active meaning making.

The research also highlighted, however, the limited extent to which such practices had been adopted in early years settings at the time the research was undertaken. For instance, although the researchers found that sustained shared thinking was encouraged in the most effective settings they also found that 'this does not happen very frequently' (Siraj Blatchford et al. 2002 p.10), even though, where it did occur, it led to 'better cognitive achievement'. Similarly, 'open-ended questions made up only 5.1% of the questioning used' (p.11).

The lack of evidence of such approaches seems to suggest, then, continuation of the historical disparity between the home and some school settings, according to the observations in that major study in 2002.

The Primary Phase – dominant interactive practices and their long history

Even greater disparity seems to exist between the culture of the early years and the later phases of primary education. After the transition from home to school, via the Reception year, children experience a further shift in terms of their diminishing agency when they enter Year 1 (age 5/6). The experience for five-year-olds has not been helped by policymakers' attitudes. Even though early years research has been extensive and convincing, the Labour government, in 2010, rejected the recommendations of the *Cambridge Review* (Alexander 2010), that formal education should not begin until the age of six. Again there are issues of relative power, in this case, between the domains of early years and the later phases of primary schooling. This is one illustration of the resistance to ideas for reform that originate in the early years, and is a clear example of the dominance of the practices, and culture, of later phases over the earlier years (p. 163).

So, what kind of practices exist for children between the ages of five and eleven (in England, this is Key Stage 1 and Key Stage 2)? What is the nature of the communicative practices in which the child participates in school? It seems that these practices do not always reflect a view of the child as an active meaning maker in collaborative social contexts, despite what has been learned about learning from early years research.

Recent evidence of the disparity that exists between experiences in the home and the school for this age group was provided by children who participated in the Children Decide project (Cox et al. 2006). This was research (funded by CfBT) carried out by a team consisting of nine teachers and their classes of children in six Norfolk schools and two researchers (Anna Robinson-Pant and myself) at the University of East Anglia, to explore children's decision making. In this project, the children – in all years of the primary age range – found that they made more decisions at home than at school, and that at school they made more decisions in personal and informal situations, such as mealtimes and playtimes, than in lessons. When, for instance, they constructed timelines of their day, making drawings of their activities and adding counters to show where, when and to what extent they made decisions for themselves, this was clearly apparent. A Year 4 teacher, Kirsty Nudd, reported:

> Through the timeline activity, the children . . . could establish within their groups at which time of day they made the most or least decisions. Most said that they made more decisions during break or lunchtime within the school day and overall they made more decisions after school or before school.
>
> (Nudd 2006 p. 137)

One of the children in this class said 'You can choose homework or TV but in school you have to be told what to do.'

A class of Year 6 students made a graph to represent where they made decisions and how often. As one child commented: 'It shows that I make decisions in all three areas [in class; at school; at home] but I have more opportunities at home than at school' (Cox et al. 2006 p. 114).

In addition, there is evidence that schools do not necessarily foster children's inclination to engage in constructive dialogue that is evident in their everyday communicative activities. The shortcomings in classroom interaction, as Howe and Mercer point out, however, are 'unlikely to reflect a basic incapacity on the part of primary school children to engage in lively dialogue' (Howe and Mercer 2007 p. 9). They refer to research by Maybin (2006) regarding children's non-formal interaction or 'off-task' talk in school, noting that it showed 'that they use many varied language forms to discuss issues that concern them, to support their views, to report on events and generally make sense of the world . . .' (Howe and Mercer 2007 p.9).

By contrast, pedagogical practices in school seem to be dominated by other sorts of interaction. That these seem to have endured over a very long period of time is clear. David Wood, some time ago, identified the 'special characteristics' of teacher–pupil interaction in school and their enduring nature. In his discussion of the way in which adults scaffold children's learning, he noted how, again in contrast to adults in the home, teachers 'initiate and sustain interactions not by showing and telling but by demanding and asking' (Wood 1991 p. 113), which are forms of control, and he referred to the high frequency of teacher questions throughout children's schooling. He argues that the more teachers ask questions, the less likely they are to find out what the children know. Conversely, the children say less. He cited the extensive research, available at the time he was writing, that showed that questions were 'often specific, demanding a narrow range of possible "right answers" (e.g. Maclure and French 1981; Tizard et al. 1976; Wood et al. 1980)' (Wood 1991 p. 113). He argued that there were too many of these closed questions that 'lead children to search for specific right answers rather than into processes of reasoning and weighing evidence' (p.115). He also suggested that

> teachers tend to leave relatively short pauses after their questions before taking back control of the interaction. When they are helped to extend these pauses (from one to three seconds), the frequency and level of student response increase (Rowe 1974; Swift and Gooding 1983). It seems that pupils usually need more time to think about their answers than teachers normally allow.
>
> (p. 115)

Children were learning that when adults in school ask them questions, it can be with a very different purpose from when their parents ask them. As Wood noted (p. 113): 'Teachers often know the answers to the questions they ask, and children, by four years of age, possess the ability to recognise this fact, in some contexts at least (Wood and Cooper 1980).' Similar sorts of issues were raised in a significant evaluation of primary teaching in Leeds carried out by Alexander (1992).

This state of affairs was not peculiar to Britain. For instance, writing in 1990 and drawing on various research studies, Gallimore and Tharp (1990 p. 175) claimed that there was little 'serious interactive teaching' in schools in the United States at that time and that for 'over a hundred years, there has been ample evidence that recitation, not teaching, is the predominant experience of American school children'. 'Recitation', for these authors, is 'directing and assessing' and is contrasted with alternative, interactive approaches based on Vygotskyan ideas, such as 'instructional conversation'. Gallimore and Tharp, too, comment on the fact that this latter kind of discourse can be found in the home, taking place between caregivers and their children, where the 'communicative intentions' of the youngest of children, are taken seriously even before they are able to speak:

> Instructional conversational exchanges among parents and children, and in a few classrooms, are fundamentally different from the recitation script. To *converse* is to assume that the learner may have something to say beyond the 'answers' already known by the teacher. To grasp a child's communicative intent requires careful listening, a willingness to guess about the meaning of the intended communication and responsive adjustments to assist the child's efforts.
>
> (p. 197)

Recent initiatives and policy changes and dominant interactive practices

As long ago as 1990, then, these researchers were reflecting on what might be called the long-standing traditions of one-way teaching. Since the research referred to above was published, arguably the educational community has become much more familiar with Vygotsky's ideas. Yet, what has been observed in classrooms over the years seems to suggest that promoting collaborative activity has yet to become established as a guiding principle for practice.

In particular, what seems to have been lacking is what Douglas Barnes (1976) referred to as 'exploratory talk'. He used this term to describe the 'groping towards meaning' (p. 28) that he observed as children 'think aloud' interactively with others. When such exchanges occur between children, there are 'frequent hesitations, re-phrasings, false starts and changes of direction', see also Chapter 3. As Barnes observes in his discussion of one such instance:

> exploratory talk is marked also by hypothetical expressions: 'she *could have* gone out', 'she *probably* felt', '*you'd think* . . .', '*might have to* . . .'.

> It is as if the girls were perpetually reminding themselves that they were only putting up a hypothetical explanation and that every statement was open to modification.

Teachers in school tend not to share in this kind of collaborative communication. Barnes notes that in their communication with adults in school, it is 'all too possible for a teacher to be so intent on his [sic] own interpretation that it never comes into significant relationship to those of his pupils' (p. 23).

As Howe and Mercer (2007 p. 8) have claimed more recently 'one of the strongest messages to emerge from work surveying classroom activity is that, at least in British primary schools, exploratory talk seldom occurs'. These authors declare, almost despairingly, that 'the impoverished nature of classroom interaction can be taken for granted' (p. 9).To recap then, it seems that, although this situation is far from ideal, there is a substantial amount of evidence that suggests practices have changed little over many years. The institutionally dominant forms of teacher-dominated interaction have proved to be remarkably resistant.

The demands that have been made on teachers in recent years to maintain the 'pace' of their lessons have not been helpful. The 'race track' interpretation of pace (Alexander 2010 p. 295), established through the National Strategies and enforced by Ofsted, might appear to contradict what has been learned from the research about the benefits of providing thinking time. A recent Ofsted report (2009) does indeed acknowledge the need for 'thinking time', but, paradoxically, suggests that good teaching is characterised by lessons that provide 'pace' as well. Teachers might be forgiven for finding that, in practice, it is difficult to achieve both simultaneously.

Furthermore, little seems to have been gained by 'whole-class interactive teaching', which became part of the national agenda in the UK in the early 1990s, in the period following the publication of the government commissioned report of Alexander, Rose and Woodhead (1992). The whole-class interactive approach, that was heavily promoted by the secretary of state for education, and became established as orthodox practice, was clearly *intended* to lead to improved, more educationally productive forms of interaction with more children – albeit geared to the specific agenda of 'raising standards'. The introduction of the National Literacy and Numeracy Strategies, in the late 1990s, was a further endorsement of this new orthodoxy. The recommended three-part format of the literacy and numeracy 'hours' included an 'introduction' at the start and a 'plenary' at the end as the standard structure of a lesson. In these, the teacher addressed the whole class, often with children 'sitting on the carpet' or at their desks.

For the teaching to be interactive, much depended, clearly, on the nature of the exchanges between teacher and children. If the teacher did *all* the talking, this would hardly qualify – although it has to be acknowledged that even when children are 'only' listening, this is not in itself an indication of non-interactive teaching: they can actively participate in the activity of listening, after all. The intention was, however, that interactive whole-class teaching would engage children in other ways too. Teachers' questions were meant to challenge children's thinking and questioning was to be differentiated and targeted for individual children to meet their needs and take their learning forward.

The approach might be viewed as a well-intentioned response to the difficulties teachers faced in trying to manage the individual needs of a whole class of children. At least it may have provided, in theory at least, a better chance for the teacher to be able to work within the zone of proximal development, and to scaffold children's learning, than might otherwise be practically achievable. Research has shown, however, that the use of the whole-class interactive teaching strategy, in itself, did not necessarily improve the quality of interaction in the classroom and could not, therefore, guarantee improvements in children's learning. Smith et al. (2004), for example, whose research followed up on the implementation of the National Literacy and Numeracy Strategies, showed how little things had changed. The 'recitation' pattern of interaction – of teacher question, pupil response and teacher evaluation – continued to dominate. This is sometimes referred to as IRF (initiation, response, follow up – Wells and Arauz 2006) or, as Alexander (2008 p. 22) describes it, as 'test' questioning.

Smith and her colleagues reported that 'teacher-directed interrogation' of children was the most common form of interaction, focused mainly on 'recall and clarification of information' (Smith et al. p. 407).

It is worth quoting at some length from these researchers, to give a picture of what they were finding:

> In the whole-class section of literacy and numeracy lessons, teachers spent the majority of their time either explaining or using highly structured question and answer sequences. Far from encouraging and extending pupil contributions to promote higher levels of interaction and cognitive engagement, most of the questions asked were of a low cognitive level designed to funnel pupils' response towards a required answer. Open questions made up 10% of the questioning exchanges and 15% of the sample did not ask any such questions. Probing by the teacher, where the teacher stayed with the same child to ask further questions to encourage sustained and extended dialogue, occurred in just over 11% of the questioning exchanges. Uptake questions occurred in only 4% of the teaching exchanges and 43% of the teachers did not use any such moves. Only rarely were teachers' questions used to assist pupils to more complete or elaborated ideas. Most of the pupils' exchanges were very short, with answers lasting on average 5 seconds,

and were limited to three words or fewer for 70% of the time. It was also very rare for pupils to initiate the questioning.

(Smith et al. 2004 p. 408)

Children learned to play along in whole-class sessions, however. Hazel Denvir and Mike Askew suggested, as a result of their research into the Numeracy Strategy, that in the whole-class interaction part of the numeracy hour children were not, in reality, engaging with the mathematics, but they had nevertheless developed clever strategies that would give their teacher the impression that they were. Interpreting their observations of one child, for instance, they note the following:

> It seems that Meg is not trying to explain her method but only striving to take part in the 'game' of providing an explanation. Time and again, we have observed Meg produce post hoc explanations which do not match what she did but are sometimes not even mathematically correct (add on 9 by adding on 10 and taking off 6). She can do it with great conviction, and even present it in a way that covers up the nonsense.
>
> (Denvir and Askew 2001 p. 28)

Improved interaction or merely organisational change

Maurice Galton and his colleagues investigated classroom interaction through the ORACLE project in the UK and showed the extent to which, in 1980, forms of interaction that would lead to 'higher order' thinking were generally lacking in primary classrooms (Galton et al. 1980). Galton's research led him to conclude that this kind of thinking could not be achieved by making changes to what he referred to as surface features. He argued that interaction between children and teachers could not be improved simply by making organisational changes or coming up with new policy directives.

For example, it became clear, from the research, that to improve the level of talk between children, it was not enough merely to move from the individualised interaction that had been the norm at the time, to organising children into groups. The researchers found that sitting together did not necessarily mean that children worked as a group on joint projects with shared purposes. These findings have been widely corroborated by researchers, for example in the observations and analysis of group work in the SLANT (Spoken Language and New Technology) project, described by Wegerif and Scrimshaw (1997). Similarly, the introduction of government-mandated policy of whole-class interactive teaching would not in itself bring about change.

Galton and his team were able to clearly demonstrate this when they replicated their earlier study 20 years later in the 1990s. They showed how

child–teacher interaction continued to exhibit some of the specific characteristics they had previously identified in the 1970s (Galton et al. 1999). They
found that while, as a result of the policy-level recommendations and new
initiatives, there was a considerable increase in interaction with the whole
class, the nature and quality of interaction remained unchanged: when
the characteristics of the interactions themselves were examined, there were
significant similarities in the sets of data from the two investigations. For
instance, Galton pointed out that the ratio of statements to questions had
barely altered:

> Whereas in 1976–77 teachers used 3.7 times as many statements as
> questions, by 1996–7, this ratio had only marginally been reduced to
> 3.6. Teachers therefore talked mainly at rather than with their pupils . . .
>
> (Galton 2007 p. 11)

It would seem that the move to whole-class teaching had done little to coun-
teract the dominance of teaching as transmission. In reality, it had achieved
the opposite.

Similarly, Alexander has been critical of the government's tendency to
conflate 'whole-class interactive teaching' with 'dialogue' between teachers
and children. Like Galton, he sees it as mistaken to equate an organisational
arrangement with particular approaches to interaction:

> the *organisational* component of whole-class teaching – the teacher
> talking to the class as a whole – is less significant for children's learning
> than the *discourse* and *values* with which this organisational arrange-
> ment is – or most commonly is not – associated.
>
> (Alexander 2008 p. 22)

Sylva et al. (2008) also found in the recent major study (EPPE) mentioned
earlier, that teachers are engaging in more 'interactive whole-class teaching'.
Again, however, it seems that the researchers used the phrase to refer to a
common arrangement, or organisational strategy rather than to high levels of
interactivity, as the study's findings reveal that 'interactive whole-class
teaching' did not necessarily imply increased interactivity in practice. Rather,
there was evidence of 'uneven quality' of classroom practices, especially in
areas such as problem solving and higher-order thinking skills. In classrooms
where these practices were occurring, interaction had specific characteristics:
'"thought provoking" reciprocal discussions, children using hypotheses to
experiment with a range of ways of tackling a problem and teachers modelling
problem solving' (p. 58).

In around 30% of the Year 5 classes in their sample, these researchers
found little or no evidence of pedagogical practice around skills such as

'"higher order" critical thinking skills of analysis, inference, application, interpretation, problem solving, and planning.' (p. 58). This all adds weight to the conclusion that even though there might have been a general adoption of the 'whole-class interactive teaching' approach, this could not in itself guarantee that interaction to promote higher-order thinking would become the norm.

In Galton's review of the research around the implementation of the Literacy and Numeracy Strategies (Galton 2007), he too notes that, although researchers might have seen changes, the Strategies did not necessarily improve the *quality* of interaction. Although he acknowledges that Hargreaves, for instance, found that the implementation of the Strategies led to a proportionate increase in questions as compared to statements (Hargreaves et al. 2003), Galton draws attention to Hargreaves' own conclusions, noting that

> the teaching which took place during the literacy hour was only interactive in a surface sense because the initial questions rarely extended pupils in ways that required them to provide a sustained interaction in which they elaborated their initial answers.
>
> (Galton 2007 p. 25)

His analysis of several sources – the official evaluation of the Strategies (Earl et al. 2003) of Ofsted's reports (2002a; 2002b) and of conclusions reached by Webb and Vulliamy (2006) – reveals that perceived changes in pedagogy as a result of the Strategies are, again, in reality 'changes in organisational practice rather than to the nature of the interaction taking place during classroom talk' (Galton 2007 p. 25).

Where Galton (2007) reviewed the range of research at a more detailed level, looking at the kinds of questions asked, again he showed that the quality of interaction had changed remarkably little over the last three decades. He reviewed the empirical evidence of the proportion of open and closed questioning, across five different research studies carried out over the period between the late 1970s and 2005. To summarise Galton's findings, he showed that there was a consistently much higher percentage of closed questions than open questions throughout the whole 30-year period. If open questions open up dialogue, give children more control of its direction and are more likely to encourage children to extend and challenge their thinking, the limited use of such questions might indicate that teachers do not prioritise these aims. The continued emphasis on the teacher–pupil–teacher pattern of closed questions in classroom discourse suggests that teachers' dominant role in classroom interaction has, by and large, remained unchanged.

When Galton compared the different kinds of *statements* teachers used in a range of studies, again over the same 30-year period, he noted that 'ideas' are the least used form. By contrast, factual statements have doubled. Again, these observations tend to confirm the view that classroom interaction over the years has been characterised by 'transmission'. They certainly seem to suggest a renewed emphasis on the dissemination of factual information – from teachers to children – that coincides with the rise of the performative agenda (see Chapter 2) and which, it seems, may be given yet more emphasis in the current government's reforms.

The teacher's voice

It seems, then, that changes in organisation and policy, including the movement towards group work and whole-class teaching, have achieved little in changing the communicative practices in classrooms. The classroom has remained a place where the teacher's voice tends to be dominant, reflecting existing institutional and societal norms and expectations. This same phenomenon was encountered and explored in the Children Decide project (Cox et al. 2006; Cox and Robinson-Pant 2008). The project revealed that both teachers' and children's understandings and relationships were embedded in the unequal, 'transmission' approach, shaped by the wider culture. Though the teachers' starting point in the project was their commitment to 'promoting genuine participation, communication and decision making by children in the classroom' (Cox et al. 2006 p. 29) they were only too aware of the constraints. (See also Chapter 6.) To an extent they saw these as related to their duties of care as adults, but insofar as they were linked to their perceived responsibilities as teachers, they realised that 'their own agenda or their concern to get things done within the time constraints could mean that children did not have the time and space to develop their own insights, abilities and directions' (p. 29). Sometimes they felt their own motivation and actions were directly curtailed or compromised by the institutional restrictions of both school level and centrally prescribed policies and expectations. One teacher in the project put this explicitly in the context of the 'school culture'. She

> described this in terms of the 'school culture thing': '[it] is a really important issue because it depends on how the school is managed, in terms of how much the children, the class teacher is going to be allowed to initiate change, and I think that this is one of the major issues in a lot of our schools. Then some of us are talking about tight constraints . . . this is what I am choosing to do, I don't suppose I'll go against the National Curriculum unnecessarily, but I do believe that children ought to have more freedom and time to be able to complete work effectively and efficiently . . . They don't have time to reflect upon it . . .' [Workshop transcript 18.3.05].
>
> (p. 30)

What the children themselves had learned from participating in the institutional culture was also clear. Their ideas about who makes decisions showed their perceptions of hierarchy and power:

> *Teacher*: Who helps the teacher decide what to teach?
> *Sam*: Mr. Baker [the head teacher].
> *Louise*: The board of governors help decide.
> *Megan*: The Prime Minister.
> *Ryan*: The Queen.
> [Class observation notes 17.5.05]

(p. 30)

By Year 1/2, they had already learned to defer to adults and to see their teachers' contributions as superior to their own:

> [One teacher] commented that during the class discussion about football problems, the children 'came to the wonderful conclusion . . . that they didn't want to make decisions at all, that they weren't old enough – I was older, brainier was the word they came up with . . .'.
> [meeting notes 20.5.05]

(p. 31)

Similar conclusions are suggested by a further source of evidence. The children in the project carried out 'institutional diagramming' – an activity to research their ideas around which individuals or groups they felt made the most decisions in their school or the most important ones. It entailed cutting out different-sized circles to represent, for example, the importance of the decisions made by particular people and placing them in positions relative to each other to show how they were linked or whose decisions were more central. Invariably the children's visual representations showed, clearly, how unimportant they felt their own decisions to be and how little influence they had. Sometimes the children did not even include themselves as decision makers at all.

Two Year 4 children who wrote a report of the project stated: 'We found out that our head teacher made the most decisions and that we made the least decisions' (p.160).

A Year 4 teacher wrote:

> all the finished diagrams showed that the children saw themselves as having relatively very little decision-making power. They had put themselves in a small circle far away from the larger circles containing the names of the school Head and Deputy.

(p. 168)

This reflected the situation we had observed in an earlier project where we had worked with school councils in some of the same schools (Cox and Robinson-Pant et al. 2003). The aim of that project was to explore how interaction between children, their peers and adults in the school might be developed through the use of visual approaches to communication rather than the more usual oral and written practices.

As the project was carried out in the context of school councils, there was potentially scope for children to be in control of activities and decision making and to use the visual strategies to extend their participation and ownership of school council meetings and decisions. Teachers found that they would sometimes override children's decisions or not take them seriously and that, on occasion, the children could be marginalised by the sometimes inaccessible literacy practices that they, as adults, tended to favour. The difficulties in overcoming these challenges could again be explained by the wider cultural context of teachers' practices:

> Through our workshops with the teachers, it became apparent that though the teachers wanted to encourage participation on a local level within their schools, they themselves were working in an institutional paradigm of accountability.
>
> (Cox and Robinson-Pant 2005a p.59)

It became clear that:

> Neither the context of the school council itself, with its potential for participation, nor the [visual] methods could challenge the dominant communicative practices of the school. These were shaped by the 'currently privileged' educational discourse.
>
> (p. 61)

Concluding reflections

It is clear that one enduring feature of classroom practice – at least in the later phases of primary education – as it has been described by researchers, is that interactions are largely initiated by the teacher, as the authority, are controlled by them, and follow the direction determined by the learning objectives selected by them. The empirical evidence seems to show that teachers' and children's talk in the classroom is, as a social practice, still structured in favour of the teacher. The conclusions drawn from research seem to point in the same direction: 'in most of the dialogue between teachers and pupils it is rare for pupils to ask the teacher questions, and even less common for pupils to challenge explanations or interpretations of events that are offered by teachers' (Mercer 2002 p. 148). The implicit model is the simple one of transmission of information from those who know more to those who know less. To the extent that the teacher uses questioning, it continues to be appropriated and controlled by the teacher, with children being given little opportunity to initiate exchanges. Even today, it seems the situation remains as Wood (1991 p. 116) described it: 'the implicit theory of learning is one in which the teacher knows all the answers and the child's task is simply to find them'. Similarly, children perceive that it is the teacher who ultimately has the say in decision making in the classroom, and this is sometimes difficult to change, even in the context of the children's own decision-making forum of the school council.

Children are nonetheless active meaning makers participating in whatever is going on around them. But what they come up against and what they must make sense of in the school and the classroom are practices that seem not to be consistent with and do not seem to encourage what characterises them as learners – their motivated, constructive engagement with the activities and practices of the world around them. In short, in the context of formal schooling, they learn that what they have to say matters less than their teachers' agenda.

In earlier chapters, I attempted to show that when teachers consider how their work is framed by the practices and culture of the school – and by the wider social practices of politicians and policy makers – a different way of *thinking* about what they do might begin to emerge. Again, it also raises the possibility of thinking about what they might *do* differently. The socio-cultural perspective signals a different way in which teaching can be configured, that can be transformative for teachers who are open to changing their patterns of communication and action, as I hope to show in the next chapter.

Issues for teachers

- To what extent is there continuity between children's everyday worlds beyond the school and their experiences in your classroom? How would you describe their experiences in these different domains?
- How do your own interactions in your classroom reflect a responsive approach to children as active meaning makers?
- To what extent do the communicative practices in your classroom promote child-initiated exchanges, questions and decisions?

- Reflecting on your interaction with the children in your class, to what extent do you think it challenges children's thinking? To what extent does it embrace exploratory talk?
- To what extent do you prioritise participation and collaboration?
- Reflecting on any organisational changes you have made in your classroom and teaching, or any particular organisational arrangements you use, to what extent in themselves do they achieve higher-quality interaction?
- How do you think the children in your classroom see themselves?
- How do you think they understand learning?

5 Achieving change in classroom communication and interaction

Chapter overview

In this chapter, I consider what kinds of interaction might be introduced into classrooms to support children's meaning making and challenge their thinking. I discuss how, rather than identifying specific kinds of interactive strategies, it is more a question of looking at the specific situations in which language is used and for what purposes. I develop the argument from earlier chapters that this reveals the nature of the learning in classrooms. The long-standing, familiar communicative practices have tended to reflect the goals and purposes of teachers. When purposes are shared collaboratively between children and teachers and exploratory and dialogic communicative practices develop, learning can be of a different order. I discuss exploratory and dialogic practices and consider whether they should be a part of a wider repertoire of strategies as some educationalists suggest. My argument is that there is a need for a shift in understanding of learning to ensure that such practices become embedded in classrooms. I acknowledge again how the practices of the wider culture can work against the kinds of changes that teachers might make in their classrooms.

Enduring cultures

Galton (2007 p. 27) concludes that the continued lack of improvement in the quality of classroom interaction suggests that recommendations for change and policy changes are not enough. He has consistently made the point, over the years, that changes in organisational practices, or what he refers to as the conditions in which learning takes place, do not in themselves lead to pedagogical change (Galton 1999). Whatever policy prescriptions achieve in terms of changes in organisational arrangements, they cannot alone effect changes in learning and teaching. This is a view shared by Howe and Mercer (2007) and by Alexander (2008; 2010). Alexander endorses Galton's conclusions:

> although the layout and organisation of English primary classrooms and teaching practices have changed considerably since the mid 1990s, as has the structure of lessons, such change is more superficial than it may seem or than its architects may wish to acknowledge.
>
> (Alexander 2010 p. 298)

It might be a mistake to assume, however, that some sorts of interactive strategy are *necessarily* more productive of higher-order critical thinking than others (and, indeed, Galton does not make this assumption). Mercer makes this case (see, for example, Mercer 1995). From his point of view, what is at issue is not so much the forms of interaction that are being used, such as questions rather than statements and open rather than closed questions, but the purposes for which they are being used. This focuses attention on the specific context in which teacher–pupil interaction takes place and on what the participants in that particular situation want to achieve. He has reservations about the research that focuses on questioning itself, or on categorising questions. He criticises Wood (1986) and Brown and Wragg (1993) (cited by Mercer 1995) who have argued that particular forms of exchange, such as questioning, or specific sorts of questioning, limit children's learning. Mercer (1995 p. 32) does acknowledge that it can be useful to research patterns of interaction, to identify those that may seem 'unnecessarily narrow' and to suggest alternatives that might encourage children to elaborate on their own ideas, invite the children to disagree with the teacher or to ask questions. In the end, however, for him this still begs the question of what the strategy is intended to achieve (p. 30). 'The techniques are neither good nor bad in themselves, because it depends on how, when and why they are used' (p. 38).

It is more a matter of 'what teachers actually say and do with language' (p. 29) that determines what kind of interaction it is. From this point of view, it is the purposes of the people concerned that shape the form of the language, rather than the other way round. Mercer's argument endorses the view that the use of language is always bound by the context in which it takes place:

> conversations have a history and a future and take place between particular people in a specific place and time. Direct questioning might sometimes be appropriate and sometimes not. Talk is always situated.
>
> (p. 30)

He goes on to explain that 'the same kind of question, or even the same words, can be used by teachers to very different effect on different occasions' (p. 31). In the end teachers' pedagogical choices can only be made with knowledge of the context and what the goals and purposes of the different participants are. For Mercer, like Dewey (1916) before him, it is the *purposes* inherent in children's enquiring and investigative activities that generate productive dialogue (Mercer and Littleton 2007; Mercer and Hodgkinson 2008).

The evidence presented in Chapter 4, similarly, suggested that it is the goals and purposes of *teachers* that have defined the nature and quality of classroom interaction and that the culture of the school, thereby created, has remained intractable and resistant to change. Wood (1991), Gallimore and Tharp (1991), Galton (2007), Howe and Mercer (2007) and Alexander (2008; 2010) all comment on its enduring nature. It has persisted despite changes in policy and political discourses. Howe and Mercer, for instance, suggest that the culture of learning and teaching has not changed for a long time:

> Over twenty years ago, Wells (1986) drew attention to difficulties with the overall *climate* of British primary schools, arguing that the *normative environment* for talk in most classrooms is not compatible with children's active and extended engagement in using language to construct knowledge. This characterisation of the classroom environment for talk is also one that emerges from the more recent work by Alexander (2006).
> (Howe and Mercer 2007 p.11)

In the *Cambridge Review*, Alexander suggests that 'basic interactive habits are highly resilient, for they are deeply embedded, historically and culturally' (Alexander 2010 p. 298). He notes – like Gallimore and Tharp (1990) did 20 years ago – the resilience of

> recitation as the default pattern of exchange – closed 'test' questions, competitive or strategic bidding for teacher attention, brief recall answers, minimal feedback, talk for replaying the teacher's thinking rather than enabling children to think for themselves even in the ostensibly novel context of 'interactive' whole-class plenaries.
> (Alexander 2010 p.306)

Galton notes, moreover, that the observations of teacher–pupil interaction that have revealed little development over time have occurred in apparently very different eras: they 'go back to the 1970s in a period where there was considerable freedom for teachers to conduct lessons how and as they wished' (Galton 2007. p. 27) in contrast to the situation today.

It is particularly interesting that the culture that shapes teacher–pupil interaction has persisted despite the apparent differences between the

Plowden-influenced 1980s and the more assessment- and curriculum-led policy context of the twenty-first century. The established patterns seem to stretch back well before the post-1988 era of teacher accountability. Although they are now shored up by the wider performative culture at the ideological and policy levels, practices in the classroom context seem not only to be a response to those wider cultural shifts, but seem to reflect deeper, long-standing traditions.

Making changes

If the social, interactive practices of the school are so deep-rooted, it is perhaps unsurprising that they are not easily transformed by policy initiatives and prescribed changes to the ways that classrooms and teaching are organised, such as interactive whole-class teaching. Clearly something more is needed. Galton (2007 p. 27) suggests that a shift can only be achieved 'if the principles governing the changes are clearly articulated and understood'. As I suggested in the Introduction, the clarification of the principles that guide teachers' own decisions and actions in the classroom are paramount. Alexander (2010 p. 308), similarly, argues for right action framed by 'well-grounded principles'. These arguments echo those to which I referred in Chapter 4, that emerged from the projects with Norfolk schools around children as decision makers, that change requires a principled approach (Cox et al. 2003; Cox and Robinson-Pant 2006; Cox et al. 2006). As we observed, in the context of current educational practice in the UK, 'curriculum innovations are often "packaged" and promoted as off-the-shelf "activities", rather than as approaches to be critiqued and developed.' (Cox and Robinson-Pant 2005a). As we found, unless a critical approach towards initiatives is adopted, the imported changes can remain inert in classrooms, adapted to existing, entrenched ways of acting. Given that teachers have control of their day-to-day, classroom-based pedagogical decisions, developing a principled and critical approach to what they do may be a way of achieving new, shared practices that challenge the existing status quo and ultimately achieve the shift in classroom and school culture that is needed.

The established practices arguably derive from the conception that learning and teaching are simply a person-to-person matter. So, the grounding of such principles in a different, socio-cultural, participative understanding of learning may be what is required at the classroom level, to help teachers break with the traditional habits of communication and interaction. To return to the arguments I have already introduced, when learning is 'not construed as a purely interpersonal phenomenon' but is, instead, 'understood with respect to a practice as a whole, with its multiplicity of relations – both within the community and with the world at large' (Lave and Wenger 1991 p. 114), a different understanding of what is going on in classrooms and between learners and teachers emerges, clearing the way for a different understanding of teaching and new pedagogical principles.

To illustrate this we can revisit the example of Meg in the discussion of Denvir and Askew's research in the previous chapter. It is clear, if the situation is viewed from this different perspective, that the child is making her own sense of how to participate in the specific activities in the situations in which she finds herself – in this case in a 'whole-class interactive' teaching episode. Again, taking Lave and Wenger's analysis, she is indeed learning from her participation, but what she is learning is not the mathematics that the teachers may think they are imparting. The example demonstrates that when a teacher fails to ground the interaction in the child's own sense making, if they fail to engage with the child's contributions, then their own reasoning and the child's reasoning may fail to connect – the dialogue has failed, as Mercer puts it, to 'keep minds mutually attuned' (Mercer 2001 p.143). The child will be participating in the particular patterns of activity in her own terms, unable to engage with her teacher's understandings. For Meg, the activities – and hence her learning – revolve, instead, around the rituals and routines of the teacher's modus operandi. The child will construct her own meanings around the situation and around what is required of her as a pupil.

To look at this example another way, it may well appear that the child is taking a passive, rather than a truly interactive role in this 'whole-class interactive teaching' session. This might imply that the teacher has indeed retained a 'teacher-directed' approach and a 'one-sided' (Rogoff 1994) or 'one-way' (Bruner 1996) view of learning – expecting that they will simply transmit what they know to the child who does not know; that the child will assimilate the information; that she will absorb whatever she is told. The critique of the transmission approach might, on the face of it, suggest that the child is not actually learning. This fails to acknowledge, however, the deeper issue which I have highlighted in preceding chapters. From a socio-cultural perspective, it is not that the child is *not* learning, but that they are engaged in activities in ways that their teacher may not have anticipated. It is their participation in these activities that constitute the children's learning.

If the teacher adopts this alternative perspective and becomes more critically aware of the situation itself, what it is presenting for children's learning and what sense a child is making within it, as they participate in it, they can get a clearer picture of their pupils' *actual* learning and the ways they might change the communicative practices in their classroom.

The same analysis can be applied to the findings from the Empowering Children project (Cox et al. 2003). The children were, in some instances, learning how to play the game of being a participant in the decision-making body of the school council. As their 'real' decision-making power was actually quite limited, their learning about decision making was similarly restricted to what they could learn in this role-playing situation. Their teachers may have theorised that they were imparting neutral skills – for instance, the adult literacy practices for meetings – such as agendas and minutes.

> 'We've got class council and we write things down in a book and then you go down to school council with our books and then we just talk about it to school council then it's OK.' 'They write the stuff down on paper and they bring it back and say what is good.' [Children talking about school council]
>
> (Cox and Robinson-Pant 2003 p. 18)

In reality, these were literacy practices favoured by the teachers in the context of the need to raise standards in reading and writing. Although the teachers were also concerned to teach knowledge and skills for citizenship around democratic processes, the focus on imparting knowledge and skills potentially set up a distraction from the primary purpose of making decisions and 'sometimes hindered genuine participation and decision making on the part of children themselves' (Cox and Robinson-Pant 2005a p. 50). (I shall say more about the authenticity of decision making in the next chapter.) The different context and purpose would yield learning of a subtly but significantly different kind.

The more powerful learning for the children may have been that 'they had limited ownership over the process of decision making and the decisions made as they became increasingly aware of the power of the key decision makers beyond the school council' (p. 51). In addition, they may have learned that they needed to gain the teacher's permission and that there was often little room for negotiation – for example (p. 55):

The children were discussing ideas for the playground at school council meeting.

Teacher: . . . we mentioned it in my class and [headteacher] mentioned it in assembly. No balls are to be brought into the playground. What other toys would be useful to bring?
Isobel: Skipping ropes.
Ross: Hoops?
Teacher: If we say no to balls, any other toys could be misused too. We want to get some equipment . . .
Child: Could bring marbles.
Nina: Tennis things.
Teacher: That would be balls again . . .

The children obligingly followed the teacher's line of thought, learning from the exchange that this is what is appropriate to do, and also, that in the end the teacher's intentions will carry more weight.

Socio-cultural understandings, then, on the part of teachers, of what is actually going on, of how their actions are embedded in the culture of the school and its communicative practices and how these practices constitute children's learning, focus attention on the learning in the classroom context. If children are participating and learning, even in situations where interaction is 'non-participatory', it is a question of what the children are participating in. It is clear that the more opportunities are afforded for truly participating in cognitively challenging discourses, the more opportunities there are for making meaning through those discourses; the level and quality of participation and the quality of the interactive practices are crucial to the depth and range of children's learning.

It follows that this is how children learn about learning (see also Chapter 7). If the interactive and communicative practices are different, within and outside the community of 'school', then Meg, in the example above, will learn that 'school learning' has distinctive characteristics. These school activities may not actually serve her as well, with regard to what she learns about learning, as the activities of her everyday life. Moreover, if within the classroom context it is clear to children that adults are in control – that what teachers have to say is more important than their own questions and meaning making, and that their own concerns, purposes and goals count for less than those of their teachers – then this will constitute, too, what children are learning about values.

Awareness on the part of the teacher of the nature of their pupils' participation, and of the nature of the communicative practices in which they are taking part, provides them with a more comprehensive picture of the learning that is going on than a superficial focus on what they are teaching.

Extending exploratory talk; developing dialogic teaching

If the school is to build on what may already be happening in other social contexts such as the home, then, as Moll (1990) argued (see Chapter 3), it must afford opportunities for children to participate, in 'qualitatively new collaborative activities' (p. 13) maintaining a constant emphasis on creating meaning.

> The focus, therefore, is not on transferring skills, as such, from those who know more to those who know less but on the collaborative use of mediational means to create, obtain, and communicate meaning . . . The role of the adult is not necessarily to provide structured cues, but, through exploratory talk and other social mediations such as importing everyday activities into the classrooms, to assist children in appropriating or taking control of their own learning.
>
> (p. 13)

In Chapter 3, I discussed Moll's analysis of the Vygtoskyan view that the child's thinking develops through interaction with others in social situations using mediational means including spoken language (see also Chapter 1 and 3). It is helpful to revisit Moll's critique, which shows that care needs to be taken by teachers in how they interpret and respond to Vygotsky's ideas. Moll questions the common characterisation of Vygotsky's ZPD as individual change – being able to 'do something independently today that [they] could do only with assistance yesterday' (Moll 1990 p. 12). Construed too simplistically in this way, Vygotsky's ideas may be used to justify practices that, in fact, do simply rely on 'structured cues' – referred to in the quotation above – for instance, to prompt children towards desired responses (recitation). This is a misrepresentation. According to Moll, the

> essence of the zone of proximal development concept . . . is the qualitatively different perspective one gets by contrasting students' performance alone with their performance in collaborative activity . . . Vygotsky . . . viewed thinking as a characteristic not of the child only but of the child-in-social-activities with others (Minick 1985).
>
> (p. 12)

This establishes a clear distinction between recitation and exploratory talk (see Chapter 4). Ideas around Barnes' conception of exploratory talk have been developed extensively by Neil Mercer in particular (for example, Mercer 1995; 2000; Mercer and Littleton 2007; Mercer and Dawes 2008; Mercer and Hodgkinson 2008). Building on the work of Barnes (1976), which I introduced in the previous chapter, and Barnes and Todd (1977; 1995), he has developed the idea that to extend the educational value of classroom talk children should 'engage critically but constructively with each other's ideas' (Mercer and Littleton 2007 p. 59). The process involves challenge and counter-challenge, with points of view justified and alternative hypotheses offered. 'Partners all actively participate, and opinions are sought and considered, before decisions are jointly made' (p. 59). In this way children make their reasoning more visible. It 'represents a joint, co-ordinated form of co-reasoning in language, with speakers sharing knowledge, challenging ideas, evaluating evidence and considering options in a reasoned and equitable way' (p. 62). Mercer's and his team's concern with the promotion of reasoning through talk (p. 74) led him to devise an approach to teaching they called 'Thinking Together'. As he points out, this is an attempt to put socio-cultural theories of learning into practice:

> To do so, it places special emphasis on the role of the teacher as a guide and model for language use, who fosters an inclusive climate for discussion while also enabling children to understand better how language can be used as a tool for thinking. It supports children

in learning to talk as well as in providing them with opportunities for talking to learn. Through the systematic integration of both teacher-led interaction and group-based discussion, children are helped to understand that aims for group activity and the use of spoken language are as much to do with high quality educationally effective talk and joint reasoning as with curriculum learning. The processes by which children learn how to learn are directly addressed rather than being ignored or left to chance.

(p. 69)

Like Moll (1990) and like Lave and Wenger (1991), Mercer emphasises the interconnectedness of individual cognition and discursive activity. Again, he makes the point that how children participate and the activities they partici- pate in are all important. Like Moll, and like Barnes (1976), Mercer shows that how talk is conceived and used by teachers is crucial. We see again that 'talk is not just the mediating means for supporting individual development, but rather that ways of thinking are embedded in ways of using language' (Mercer and Littleton 2007 p. 29). This takes us back to the issue raised by Moll. Mercer and Littleton, again reflecting Moll's analysis, explicitly call into question the sort of practices that might be misinterpreting Vygotskyan ideas about the collaborative nature of learning. To make their point, they draw on the idea that in exploratory talk, knowledge and understandings are negotiated 'inter-subjectively' through a process of 'inter-thinking'. These features are all-important in any attempt to implement Vygotsky's ideas through 'scaffolding' children's learning, for example. For Mercer and Littleton, the emphasis on collectivity and dialogue

> redresses the emphasis in some neo-Vygotskyan research on the trans- mission of skills and knowledge from adult to child. Some applica- tions of the metaphor of scaffolding arguably neglect the child's own contribution to her development – conveying an image of a child's learning as being propped up by an omniscient adult who invariably directs and controls the interaction. The allocation of such a passive role to the child oversimplifies the nature of teaching and learning interactions which are exercises in collectivity, involving both the child and the adult in processes of negotiation, disagreement, the exchange and sharing of information, judgement, decision making and evaluation of one another's contributions (Hoogsteder et al. 1998).

(Mercer and Littleton 2007 p. 22)

Once again this highlights the need for teachers to look closely and critically at what is actually occurring in classrooms. Attempts to challenge the status quo by invoking the practice of 'scaffolding' may in reality be a travesty – the result of a cursory take on what it might entail and a superficial view of social-constructivist theories of learning. They might serve only to further entrench interactive practices that preserve the existing patterns of interaction – just as in the situation where children can be organised into groups and apparently be engaged in joint activities but where no collaboration is actually going on.

To ensure that interactional practice in educational settings can fully benefit from socio-cultural insights, Mercer and Littleton link their own ideas to those developed by Alexander around 'dialogic teaching' (Alexander 2008) which they describe as

> that in which both teachers and pupils make substantial and significant contributions and through which children's thinking on a given idea or theme is helped to move forward. It is intended to highlight ways that teachers can encourage students to participate actively and so enable them to articulate, reflect upon and modify their own understanding.
>
> (Mercer and Littleton 2007 p. 41)

For Alexander, as for Barnes, dialogue is not just a feature of learning, but 'one of its most essential tools' (Alexander 2008 p. 25).

Alexander acknowledges that his conceptualisation of dialogic teaching resonates with the work of others. He cites Wells' (1999) ideas around dialogic enquiry; Bruner's (1996) 'mutualist and dialectic pedagogy; Mercer's (2000) 'inter-thinking'; Palinscar and Brown's 'reciprocal teaching' (Brown and Palinscar 1989); Barnes and Todd's (1995) 'joint enquiry'; Resnick's (1999) 'accountable talk'; Nystrand's (1997) 'dialogic instruction' and, the linguistic theories of Bakhtin (1986). Like many of these educationalists, Alexander's dialogic teaching is firmly grounded in socio-cultural theory and the Vygotskyan view of the close relationship between children's cognitive development and the 'forms and contexts of language which they have encountered and used' (Alexander 2008 p.10) – in other words, the idea that children 'talk to learn'. The implications for practice in classrooms are clear:

> if we want children to talk to learn – as well as learn to talk – then what they say probably matters more than what teachers say. So it is the qualities of extension and cumulation which transform classroom talk from the familiar closed question/answer/feedback routine into purposeful and productive dialogue where questions, answers and feedback progressively build into coherent and expanding chains of enquiry and understanding.
>
> (p. 26)

'Cumulation' is one of the key features of dialogic teaching (Alexander 2008; Wells and Arauz 2006) – the process of teachers and children building on their own and each other's ideas (Alexander 2008 p. 28). Like Mercer's 'thinking together' the implication is that what children say needs to be 'reflected upon, discussed, even argued about, and the dialogic element lies partly in getting pupils themselves to do this' (p. 27). One of Wells' and Arauz's (2006 p. 414) findings was the importance of asking 'questions to which there are multiple possible answers and then to encourage the students who wish to answer to respond to, and build upon, each other's contributions'.

The notion of 'repertoire' – some implications

Alexander advocates dialogic teaching as the 'most cognitively potent' (2008 p. 31) of a 'repertoire' of teaching talk (Alexander, Rose and Woodhead 1992). Such a repertoire is wide. Perhaps controversially, Alexander (2008 p. 30) includes teaching by rote: 'the drilling of facts, ideas and routines through constant repetition' – as well as 'recitation' and expository teaching. This may seem contentious, given that I have suggested that such strategies might be associated with a 'transmission' approach to teaching and I would urge caution. I will turn again to the arguments I have been presenting. When understood from the socio-cultural perspective, any teaching strategy is seen as a specific practice within the social context of the classroom, and as such constitutes part of children's learning. It is therefore also part of what children will learn about schooling and learning. From this perspective, then, teachers must consider all classroom interactions as sources of learning; when children participate in any kind of exchange they are learning to engage in specific ways of going about things; they are learning what different sorts of interaction entail. This means that it is important for teachers to be aware of the learning that is implicit in different sorts of interaction: when children participate in dialogic talk they are learning to talk dialogically; they are learning in ways that are consistent with their activities as meaning makers and are learning that this is what learning is all about. When a teacher, on the other hand, teaches by rote and recitation, children will learn to listen to, and repeat, what the teacher says. They will learn to do what is expected and to interpret the teacher's cues in order to deduce the answer the teacher is looking for. They will, as I have pointed out before, learn that *this*, perhaps unfamiliar activity, is what 'learning' is about.

This is not to deny that there may be occasions when these kinds of strategies might seem appropriate. Sometimes, in a teacher's judgement, children need to be told and to listen. Alexander's premise is that the teacher may select them from their repertoire, when they make a judgement that it fits their purpose. It may, for instance, seem useful for children to learn some information in this 'monologic' (Wertsch 1991) way so they have it ready and available to reflect upon later. Nevertheless, in itself, the material will remain inert and of limited use unless children engage with it dialogically to make sense of it and to develop their own perspectives on it. Wells and Arauz argue that, while monologic instruction may be necessary, it is not sufficient. At school:

> there is much that students need to take over from previous genera-
> tions, and monologic, direct instruction is sometimes the best way of
> providing the necessary opportunity for such learning (Wells, 1998).
> But . . . monologic instruction alone is not sufficient. Not only do
> children not always understand what they are told and so need to
> engage in clarifying dialogue to reach the desired intersubjectivity,
> but frequently they also have alternative perspectives on a topic that
> need to be brought into the arena of communication and explored in
> more symmetric dialogue in which there is reciprocity in the roles of
> speaker and listener, and equally, an attempt by each to understand
> the perspective of the other.
>
> (2006 p. 387)

The point I want to make is that the availability of the repertoire in itself may be insufficient to ensure that dialogic methods become embedded in the class-room. Instead, this will very much depend on how the teacher understands learning. If, say, a particular teacher holds the traditional cultural assumptions – that knowledge can be directly imparted from one person to another – then they will believe that this is indeed what happens as a result of their teaching by rote or recitation. These assumptions, however, are inconsistent with the socio-cultural understandings underlying dialogic teaching. This is a differ-ence in principle that will set up a tension between the different methods and arguably result in the continued overvaluing of monologic methods. What is actually needed is not so much an available repertoire, but a paradigm shift (see Chapter 7) in the understanding of learning. If this teacher came to under-stand learning, instead, from a socio-cultural perspective, the limitations of the monologic approach would become clear. Such a view of learning, as I have been arguing, would reveal that the consequences of the teacher's actions for children's learning cannot be isolated from those actions; that those actions themselves are not the invisible vehicle that delivers the learning but are inte-gral to the learning. Again, whatever the monologic teaching was about, the teacher with this socio-cultural understanding of learning would be aware that the child's learning would extend beyond that to encompass features of these pedagogic practices and the context as a whole. These may, as I have suggested, carry less than positive messages to children about their learning, their agency and how they themselves are valued.

An example of dialogic practice

In the Empowering Children project (Cox and Robinson-Pant 2003) one of the schools had a well-established dialogic approach within the school council's meetings. The interactive strategies differed from the dominant practices:

> there was a clear intention on the part of teachers to take their place as an equal member of the council, allowing children to take control. The children were familiar with the practice of teachers putting their hands up along with everyone else.
>
> (p. 23)

From these practices, the children were learning that they could take control:

> *Nick* (child chairperson): Anything else on the agenda, Miss C.? [Miss C. has her hand up.]
>
> (ibid.)

The dialogic engagement of the children in this particular school was based on a well-established respect for children's contributions, from their teachers and each other. They were encouraged to voice their opinions, qualified with their reasoning. The practice was to state when they agreed or disagreed with a point of view, following this up with 'because . . .' and giving their reason.

The children's sense of their identity as school council members in this school went beyond a perception of themselves as traditional 'pupils'. They felt that they could initiate dialogue, rather than being on the receiving end of the teacher's talk, for example:

> *Jamie*: School Council is fun because you get to ask lots of questions (Tuckswood Community First School project report).
>
> (Cox and Robinson-Pant 2003 p. 47)

The interaction is clearly dialogic: children are recognising through this 'opportunity to participate in the cumulative construction of community problem solving . . . that their contributions are consequential for the decision that is jointly constructed over successive turns' (Wells and Arauz 2006 p. 415).

The visual approaches to interaction introduced to children in all the project schools to use in their school council meetings helped to extend these practices. As an alternative to the dominant literacy strategies that relied on children being able to use written forms of communication, visual strategies made the processes of decision making more transparent and accessible to the children, enhancing their participation in interactions between peers and also in the process of decision making. Such strategies as visually representing their ideas and physically sorting and ranking these collectively; using objects to represent people and ideas; constructing visual agenda where items were represented with pictures; using drawings and map making; comparing alternatives by voting with beans or counters; building a matrix to compare alternatives against criteria and 'pair-wise ranking', comparing two alternatives on a grid were all used by the children. Here the interaction becomes multi-modal (Kress 1997), and as I pointed out in Chapter 3, communication in all its forms can be exploratory (Barnes 1976).

The following comment illustrates the way the strategies changed the way one teacher perceived the children's contributions:

> I feel through our mapping and timeline and things like that, I'm really better at understanding an awareness of what children can actually come up with in their ideas. They just really amaze me with some of the things they've wanted to talk about that I wouldn't have known. If we'd just said, 'Put your hand up if you want to make a suggestion' if they're actually given a bit of paper they all come up with something rather than just the few 5 or 6 who always say things. And especially the younger children. I really feel it has benefited the younger children (Emily Millner, Hillside Avenue Primary School).
>
> (Cox and Robinson Pant 2003 p. 32)

Wider constraints and teachers' actions

So far in this chapter, I have focused mainly on practices at the classroom level to explore how long-standing traditions might be challenged. Although I have suggested that these traditional practices have survived despite the changing ideological and policy contexts, nevertheless this wider framework, which encompasses the institution of the 'school', is ever present. In the Empowering Children and Children Decide projects, we were constantly reminded of how the teachers' decisions and strategies were constrained by the framework of expectations of the culture of performativity. I have argued that if teachers have resisted the possibilities for change through 'interactive whole-class teaching', and, instead have perpetuated the established routines of classroom interaction, this, in part, can be explained by how learning and teaching have been conventionally understood. Questions remain about the nature of the institution that we call 'school' and how it shapes those understandings. As Wood (1991 p. 118) has written:

> If we find ourselves dissatisfied with the interactions that take place in such institutions, measured against what we take to be the optimum

contexts for learning, then we must question not simply the teacher's 'skills' but the form of the institution within which we expect these to be deployed.

As I have been suggesting, when what goes on in schools between children and teachers is seen as embedded in the wider historical and cultural context, it is easier to see how the status quo has been maintained into the present century. If the immediate interactions are seen in the broader context that shapes and is shaped by them (Lave and Wenger 1991 p. 55) this can add a further dimension to teachers' understanding of how habitual interactive strategies and communicative actions are being sustained. It can draw attention to the values inherent in discourses and practices within the wider world, including those of political and education policymaking – in particular, how the relationship between the community of the school and the community of politicians and policy makers can be characterised by unequal power. This might help to highlight the entrenched power relations *within* the school; it can help to show how the existing culture of learning and teaching sustains unequal relations between children and adults.

Arguably, this broader framework inhibits changes to the communicative practices of the classroom that teachers might otherwise achieve and which would create a better learning experience for children. While the patterns of interaction that seem to typify the culture of the school have not necessarily been the product of only the last couple of decades, seen in the wider context it is clear that the imposed expectations of this recent period may have helped to maintain them. Conversely, the compliance demanded of teachers in recent years, would not come easily to responsive teachers who take children's meaning making seriously and whose teaching is grounded in dialogue with children and in children's participation. It does not sit well with dialogic teaching (Alexander 2010).

From the socio-cultural perspective, it is also clear that teachers' own learning about learning is embedded within a particular culture. A culture that drives teachers to be 'effective', defined in the narrow, instrumental terms I have already described (Chapter 2), does not encourage reflection or the development of alternative approaches. The world of teacher development has its own implicit power dynamics. Gallimore and Tharp (1990) suggested 20 years ago that one explanation for teacher-dominated interaction might be that teachers do not know how to conduct 'instructional conversations' for the reason that they themselves have not learned through these means. Given the current top-down culture of compliance and performance, this may still apply today. In effect, the culture of the school, the patterns of interaction adopted within it, and also, the institutional power relations, are as unhelpful for teachers' learning as they are for that of the children. If learning is interpreted in Vygotskyan terms, then the need for 'instructional conversations' – or what

David Hargreaves (2006), more recently, has referred to as 'learning conversations' – exists for all learners, including teachers. Again, in the performative culture, it is hardly surprising if this is not part of teachers' professional lives. Instead, they attend training sessions where they are told what to do by the powers-that-be. Their own professional development has been typified by 'transmission'. A way forward might be to prioritise communities of practice in which participants can engage in dialogue about their decision making and the principles that inform it. Ironically, this monograph might seem to come into a similar monologic category – but I would hope instead that it is seen as a resource in the reflective activities of these communities of educators.

Concluding reflections

The evidence reviewed in Chapter 4 suggests that communicative practices in schools may leave much to be desired. It also suggests that they bear little relation to what is understood about children's everyday learning as active meaning makers. To change this situation, it is not, however, a matter simply of altering the forms of organisation or the particular type of interactive strategies the teacher employs.

Much depends on how learning is understood; what theory of learning underlies the teaching. If it is seen in socio-cultural terms, the teacher needs to be critically aware of what they are doing and the interactive strategies they are using if they are also to be aware of what is constituting the children's learning.

Where learning and teaching are seen differently, from a socio-cultural perspective, there is the potential for doing things differently. The articulation of principles for pedagogical decision making and action within school settings, grounded in this view of learning, provide an alternative to the de-contextualised prescription for teacher behaviours that has been a major factor in shaping teachers current interactive practices, and has not achieved the desired effects. These principles would need to prioritise children's participation and also the quality and purposes of the communicative practices in which they participate. They would also need to confront the power imbalances within the classroom – issues of equality, rights and respect.

The kind of principles that are being developed through research into exploratory talk in classrooms, dialogic teaching, children as decision makers and other kinds of participatory approaches embody these kinds of socio-cultural insights and could help transform teachers' interaction with children in the classroom. Again, to the extent that teachers have control of their decision making, teachers' day-to-day actions, within the classroom community of practice – informed by such principles – could contribute to a transformational shift in classroom and school culture.

The need for change further strengthens the case for professional, reflective communities of practice in which participants can engage in alternative ways of talking about educational practices with a view to bringing about changes in the classroom climate and in children's learning. Teachers, however, do not act as an autonomous group. They, themselves, are bound by wider cultural practices and may still be struggling to be heard within the wider political and educational community. If the performative structures and expectations imposed on schools limit the development of principled discursive practices in the way they seem to – not only in classrooms, but for the professional community of teachers – then reasons to challenge them are even more compelling.

Issues for teachers

- How might you become more critically aware of the culture in your classroom – of what is going on, of the relationships and of the communicative practices?
- Looking critically at your own interactions with children in your classroom, whose goals and purposes do they reflect?
- How could you make changes so that activities are more collaborative?
- How might you develop exploratory talk and dialogic teaching?
- How is your understanding of learning changing and how is this changing your view of interaction and communication in your classroom?
- Where do you think changes need to be made beyond your classroom? How might you contribute to these?

6 Communities for learning

Chapter overview

In this chapter, I develop the discussion around children's active participation in their communities in relation to their agency as learners and,
also, their agency as citizens, with a voice, having a say in the real-life
community of the school. I discuss the home and the school, to raise
some of the issues around how these different domains are interlinked,
with regard to children's learning, and how relationships between them
might be developed. I discuss how practices in schools might limit or
extend opportunities for children's agency as participants in the school
community; I consider how the social practices of the school can work
against their agency, not only as learners but also as fully participating
citizens in a democratic community. I discuss what children learn about
what it is to participate, as a consequence of how they participate in the
community of the school and its practices.

The community and learning

If children's self-directed, purposeful activity, and the dialogue that is a part of
it, are so central to their learning, it may seem surprising that the community
of the school which is specifically intended to foster learning seems, in some
cases at least, to be lacking in these features.

A number of important considerations have emerged from the discussion
in the previous chapters. First, what the child experiences as a member of a
community is integral to their learning. What they learn – the meanings that

they make and the ways they come to understand their experience – is insepa-rable from the ways they actively participate in their worlds and their encoun-ters with the meaning making of others in those worlds. When the child enters the school, they are entering a new world – a new community with its own ways of doing things, its own codes and meanings and its own patterns for participation. This much seems very obvious on one level, but it should now be clear, in the context of the socio-cultural approach, that this is more than simply saying that the child goes to school with an autonomous identity as a learner and that school merely offers new experiences that will enable the child to develop. Rather, the child's actions and their interactions – their communicative actions – within the new community of the school are consti-tutive of that development. They are integral to what gives rise to individual cognition: to the way the child thinks; to their developing mind. They also contribute to the collective activities and thinking within that community, helping to make it what it is. As Mercer (2002 p. 145) puts it: 'A socio-cultural perspective helps us to appreciate the reciprocal relationship between indi-vidual thinking and the collective intellectual activities of groups.'

This kind of framework gives theoretical importance to the notion of 'voice'. The use of this term from a socio-cultural perspective 'serves as a constant reminder that mental functioning in the individual originates in social, communicative processes' (Wertsch 1991 p. 13). Conceptualising learning in a socio-cultural way means that children's voice is closely aligned to the participation that is central to learning. The notion of 'voice' here is a broad one, developed by Bakhtin (1981; 1986): the 'speaking subject's perspec-tive, conceptual horizon, intention, and world view' (Wertsch 1991 p. 51).

Second – and this follows from the first point – whatever programme of learning or curriculum content the mature members of the school community might intentionally wish to impart to its new members, this cannot be seen in isolation from the ways that individuals act and interact within the school community. (I shall discuss this further in Chapter 7.) In a sense, it is impos-sible to disentangle content and context. Again, it is not a case of the indi-vidual arriving at school as the potential recipient of the programme of learning. They arrive as an active meaning maker, encountering a new social situation that will shape their activities, and therefore, their learning, in new ways. It became clear in the previous chapter that *how* children participate as a member of the school community, and the communicative practices that characterise it, are central to the learning that occurs.

Moving into the world of the school

I showed in Chapters 4 and 5 that there has been a long history of children in England engaging in very different kinds of communicative practices in schools from those in their home and out-of-school environments. As we saw, 'exploratory talk' (Barnes 1976; 1992; 2008; Mercer 1995; 2000; Mercer and Littleton 2007; Mercer and Dawes 2008; Mercer and Hodgkinson 2008) or 'intellectual search' (Tizard and Hughes 1984; 1987) can be less in evidence in formal situations at school. In the Foundation Stage, practice has increasingly developed more continuity with children's out-of-school experience, especially with respect to such features as self-initiated activity, play and responsive, 'contingent' adult support. Even so, this is not always found to be the case, as the REPEY study has shown (see Chapter 4). In relation to the move from home to a formal school setting, Siraj-Blatchford et al., the authors of the REPEY report, noted that

> there are still major concerns. The issues relate to transition from the nursery to the school reception class and also at the end of reception, from the foundation stage to year 1 of the National Curriculum.

The majority of the settings in their case studies

> made provision for transition by attempting to make children more familiar with school (through visits etc) and/or by making the nursery practice a little more like school in the latter months (whole class activities, etc.).
>
> (Siraj-Blatchford et al. 2002 p. 14)

As I mentioned in Chapter 4, practices in the Foundation Stage were being shaped by those in the later years.

Similarly, in a significant study carried out in 2005 by Dawn Sanders and colleagues (Sanders et al. 2005) there remained signs that 'greater structure' – more typical of the Key Stage 1 classroom – was being introduced in some Reception (Foundation Stage) classrooms to prepare children for the transition to Year 1. For Sanders:

> The reference to 'greater structure' was shorthand for placing a greater emphasis on adult-led, whole-class sessions, especially in literacy and numeracy, encouraging the children to remain still for longer periods of time (e.g. getting used to them sitting on the carpet for longer periods) and reducing the amount of time devoted to free choice and play-based activity.
>
> (p. 75)

I suggested in the previous chapters that when children move beyond the Foundation Stage, participation is managed and controlled in ways that represent key characteristics of the culture of schooling that, historically, have existed over many years. The focus shifts from the child's active quest for meaning from the everyday or naturalistic contexts of their own lives to making sense of the new 'contrived' (Wood 1991) world of the school. Parents are aware of the 'formality' of classrooms beyond the early years. As Sanders (2005 et al. p. 60) found:

> some parents had concerns about their child's transition to Year 1. The biggest concern for this group of parents was related to the work required in Year 1 and the loss of activities that their child enjoyed. This included the worry that their child might not be able to play any more, or have the opportunity to choose activities, but would have to sit at a desk and do work.

Participation and democratic communities: the home and school

The child learns, by being a member of this community, what their place is within it: children learn about being a pupil and what to do in that role. In practice, the children are legitimate participants in – in relation to the overt activities of the school as a site for learning – the predominantly non-participatory culture of the classroom. Non-participatory, that is, in the sense of a lack of opportunity to exercise agency (see also Chapter 5).

The forms of participation and the patterns of interaction in the school are conventionally structured, it seems, in ways which, as well as devaluing the agency of the child in their learning, also model relationships that are unequal in terms of power. The child is learning within a community that represents a rather undemocratic way of life. Their teacher represents the authority to which they must defer. In this sense, children's participation and voice in the community of the school have significance not only in relation to how their thinking develops, but also in terms of how children learn to be participants. *By* participating, children learn *what it is* to participate. How their overt participation, or agency, is facilitated or limited in particular ways, is one element of what they learn in the communities of practice of their classroom and school. How they learn to be a citizen in a democratic society will thus be influenced to some degree, by the ways in which and the extent to which their agency is encouraged in those communities.

It is interesting that, in the report of the *Cambridge Review of Primary Education*, the evidence from practitioners suggested that 'children should take the initiative in learning, that their creativity should be harnessed and fostered, that schools should listen to children' (Alexander 2010 p. 64). This might appear to reflect teachers' awareness of the importance of children's participation to their learning and the role that they, as mature members of the community can play in guiding participation (see Chapter 3); it might also reflect their conception of the classroom as a community that can model the values of a democratic society. What these practitioners say, however, does seem to contradict the evidence, discussed in the previous chapters, which suggests, on the contrary, that it is adults who have control and that when they are interacting with children, teachers do not always engage with children's thinking or encourage them to explore or develop their ideas. It is interesting that the children who contributed to the *Cambridge Review* saw themselves as active agents and were in favour of their own active participation. Significantly, however, this perception arises out of their participation in the home and family situations rather than the school: 'Their experience of interactive engagement with other people at home was the backdrop for their advocacy, in the Review's soundings, for interactive learning at school too' (p. 64).

The studies reviewed in previous chapters show how in their everyday worlds, the child's learning is focused around their own intentions and purposes, which are mediated by the tools available in the environment, including the activities and purposes of other children and adults. The intuitive responses of their parents, for instance, can scaffold the child's learning, firmly grounded in its real-life contexts. They are contingent on what the child is currently doing and saying and help the child to achieve their own goals. Where this occurs, parents and carers are already supporting the child's learning within their ZPD. This means, of course, that when the child arrives at school, they come with ways of acting and ways of understanding their world that are specific to a very different kind of community, with different sorts of relationships and activities.

Awareness, on the part of teachers and the school community, of what the child brings with them when they come to school, and the need to take account of it, is of course, not new. There has long been considerable interest in the need to improve links between home and school, for instance, to enhance children's learning. This has often been seen, however, from the school's point of view, with the home environment deemed somewhat deficient. Again, this reflects the imbalance of power – the possible hegemony of the school.

Hughes and his colleagues at the University of Bristol, together with other researchers and the Local Authorities of Bristol and Cardiff, were particularly aware of this tendency and deliberately set out to address it through their work on The Home School Knowledge Exchange project (Hughes et al. 2005; Hughes and Greenhough 2006) by trying to bring together the two separate domains of home and school, valuing existing learning practices in the home and the children's own 'knowledge'. One way that this was achieved in practice was for children to bring into school shoeboxes of artefacts that were important to them; another was giving disposable cameras to the children to record aspects of their own lives of their own choosing. It is interesting that both teachers and parents initially found it difficult to accept the idea of the 'transfer of knowledge' from the home to the school, reflecting the established balance of power, and there remained, for the researchers, a concern around the possibility that the school was appropriating the children's out-of-school knowledge for the school's own ends – that 'the artefacts that children bring to school because of their importance in their out-of-school lives become transformed into props which help the teachers deliver the school curriculum' (Hughes et al. 2005 p. 11).

Children and teachers' experience of their agency in the school community

The differences between children's experiences as learners as they move from one context to the next has not escaped the notice of children themselves. This was again highlighted by Sanders and her co-researchers (Sanders et al. 2005) in the investigation referred to above. In Reception classes, it was clear that the children had opportunities for play and for self-initiated, free-choice activity. There was more adult support too. These researchers gained evidence directly from the children, through their drawings and through interviews which were very revealing of the children's own perceptions. In relation to the transition from Reception classes to Year 1, the children seemed well aware of differences. The findings showed that the children were conscious of the different structures and expectations in the two settings: for instance, they noted the decrease in opportunities for play and the increase in the time spent sitting on the carpet in Year 1. The researchers report on the key messages emerging from the children's views (p.54):

- Children's comments focused on notions of work and play in both Reception and Year 1.
- Children who experienced Year 1 classes where staff were providing play-based, practical learning opportunities in Year 1, tended not to use the phrase 'hard work' to describe their experiences.
- In the majority of schools in our sample the children noticed the loss of particular activities in Year 1, especially role-play and construction.
- Children had a negative view of the ways in which the carpet area was used in Year 1.
- Some children in our study were sad at the loss of choice in their Year 1 curriculum.

There was clear evidence of the children's dislike of the more teacher-directed sessions that they experienced in Year 1.

When asked whether there was anything they did not like about school, a common issue in children's responses was a concern with sitting on the carpet. This was an activity in which they were required to sit still and listen to their teacher (especially during the whole-class activities within the literacy hour and daily mathematics lesson). Here is an extract from an interview with two children at [one school]:

> *Researcher*: 'Is there anything you don't like about being in Year 1?'
> *First boy*: 'Being on the carpet for a long time.'
> *Second boy*: 'Neither do I because it's very boring.'
> *First boy*: 'And it wastes our time playing.'
> *Second boy*: 'It wastes your life.'
>
> (p. 50)

These exchanges seem to suggest the children's own recognition of their loss of agency. They might indicate that the opportunities to initiate their own activities and pursue their own lines of enquiry and meaning making, which the children had previously experienced, are being curbed by the teacher and replaced with the adult's agenda. The fact that the children do not respond well to this could, perhaps, be explained in terms of the period of adjustment they might need to get used to the new setting. But this explanation implies inevitability in the way things are, inviting acceptance of the different environment; of the predominant patterns of interaction that are possibly habitual and impoverished – patterns that have tended to marginalise the child's own intentions and their purposeful activity and undervalue exploratory talk. It reflects a conception of school as the ultimate authority in determining the direction of the children's learning, overlooking the fact that until this point the child has assumed this responsibility.

By way of an alternative, school might be seen as a community that fosters the kind of active, self-directed, dialogic participation the child has previously experienced, one that itself adapts to the activities and priorities which the child has already been developing in their everyday, out-of-school environments. Observing that the features of exploratory talk are found to occur in children's play activities, in particular during symbolic and construction play, Howe and Mercer tentatively suggest that play activity might have continuing value as the child moves through the school, given its contribution to the quality of dialogue in the early years:

> when activity is a factor that teachers could, in principle at least, influence, it is worth asking about its [play activity's] relevance to primary school interaction, as well as to pre-school. The activities that children engage in shift from play to more formal tasks at primary level, and they are less focused upon children's needs and wishes. Yet, when

> the form of activity has been found to exert such a significant influence at pre-school level, it seems possible that this is one reason for the impoverished dialogue in primary schools.
>
> (Howe and Mercer 2007 p. 10)

If, from the kind of socio-cultural, participative perspective adopted, for example, by Hughes and his team (see above), there are grounds for challenging the entrenched position of schools and teachers as the arbiters of knowledge and action, then such changes might seem the obvious path to follow. Howe and Mercer's suggestion, quoted above, that teachers can 'in principle at least' influence the nature of classroom activities, is consistent with the arguments I have been presenting. But again, it needs to be seen in relation to the broader issues of power and control that extend beyond the child–teacher relationship. It must be borne in mind that teachers' vision of the kind of practices they might wish to establish in their classroom community may yet be constrained by the power relationships within that wider context and the limits to their power imposed by the performative culture (see Chapters 2 and 5). The restrictions on their own activities that teachers experienced were revealed explicitly in Sander's study:

> This teacher reported that she felt constrained by the curriculum for Year 1: 'We have a lot to get through in Year 1 and just have to get on with it.'
>
> Another teacher expressed concern about the appropriateness of the Year 1 curriculum and approach, but she had not taken any action as she did not feel it was something she had control over: 'We haven't got enough of the practical activities for the children [in Year 1] and it all moves on too quickly . . . the pace is too fast . . . nothing is being consolidated. We should all have role-play situations for these children for things like teaching money but we don't because they have to start recording [in Year 1].'
>
> (Sanders et al. 2005 p. 97)

Children as decision makers?

These are the sorts of comments I have heard time and again, as a tutor working with student teachers. They illustrate the sorts of constraint that were similarly evident in the Children Decide project. As an action research project, it directly involved the children in the nine classrooms in the process not only of researching the decisions they made as members of their class and school communities (see Chapter 4) but also focused on bringing about change. Children themselves were to take the lead, as researchers, in investigating both their present level of decision making and, beyond this, what they might want to change about the situation. This was to lead into a later phase where the children and their teachers, and in some cases the wider school community, were actually implementing changes resulting from the children's own decisions that were of consequence to their lives in school. It became clear that the teachers involved in the project were comfortable with the first phase of the action research: they were happy to develop participatory approaches to investigate the range of decisions the children already made (see Chapter 4), and to encourage them to take the lead on this. They were also supportive of children collaboratively investigating the kinds of changes that they would like to bring about, with a view to making decisions for action.

All this arguably came within the existing parameters of classroom activities that were based on established relationships and approaches to learning. To be clear, the adult researchers in the team had never expected that all decision making could be simply handed over to the children. The team (Cox et al. 2006 p. 12) had acknowledged from the start 'the non-negotiable constraints which limit their power (e.g. statutory curriculum, legal governance of schools)' but were interested, nevertheless, in 'the potential for questioning these'. The project was intended to give the children the opportunity to investigate 'the potential for renegotiating the limits to their power with teachers, other children and other parties'.

When it actually came to negotiating possible changes, however, the teachers found it more difficult. The barriers the teachers seemed to encounter could possibly be seen in relation to perceptions of risk (Cox and Robinson Pant 2010). On the one hand, it seemed that some teachers' perceptions of 'childhood' itself meant that they felt they were putting children at risk by exposing them to the 'adult' responsibilities of making and acting on their own decisions. Their values, as caring teachers, shaped their ideas of children as in need of protection, which meant that they were concerned to maintain some of the accepted boundaries between adult and child. On the other hand, the teachers' perceptions of risk may have been linked to the established culture and practices of the school, in particular the obligations to teach the curriculum and the predominant requirement to reach pre-set targets for children's achievements. It was risky to engage with children's decisions in a context where they, as teachers, must implement the agenda and meet the expectations of authorities beyond their classroom and school. They were working, after all, within a system in which they remained fully accountable for their own actions and the outcomes. 'From the teacher's perspective – working in a world where curriculum and attainment targets must be met, time is short and colleagues may have differing ideas about "pupil participation" – there were compelling reasons for staying in charge of decision making' (p. 145).

Moreover, as I have suggested already, the existing structures within the classroom are not only sustained by the adults, working within the wider performative culture, but by the children themselves. I suggested earlier that children become 'pupils' on entering school and discussed how their actions and responses can become routinised. Children act out their identities as pupils – members of the school community who have limited agency with respect to directing their learning activities. They find ways of acting that conform to prevailing classroom practices. The children in the Children Decide project were no exception. I noted in Chapter 4 that children deferred to their teacher. In addition, at the beginning of the project the adults noted that they tended to focus on what appeared to be rather trivial decisions:

> we noticed that from an adult perspective the decisions seemed to be surrounding quite trivial issues. We were unsure whether the children regarded them as such and perhaps underestimated the importance of the decisions the children were making. These 'trivial' decisions largely involved the physical aspect of the classroom, for example, which pen they chose, where they sat on the carpet, and who they played with. We noticed that the children rarely reported making decisions that directly affected their learning and [they] felt that this was the teacher's responsibility.
>
> (Cox et al. 2006 p. 49)

Although we needed to be mindful that triviality was being judged by the adults, there was a sense in which the children were demonstrating their tacit recognition of the areas over which they might have expected to have some control. These perceptions of their restricted influence endorsed the findings of the Empowering Children project (see also Chapter 4), where we found that children's decision making in their school councils rarely touched on matters of learning and teaching (Cox et al. 2003; Cox and Robinson Pant 2005a; 2005b; 2006). We had already noted that this reflected the findings of other researchers too (for example Fielding 2001a; Wyse 2001). This situation has persisted: more recently, Whitty and Wisby (2007) have found that, even though there has been an increase in the number of schools with school councils, the majority of the decision making in which they are involved tends to be around environment and facilities. Only 7% have any input into decisions around teaching and learning. And all this is nothing new. Thirty-five years ago Barnes maintained: 'the expectations set up in a classroom, and more generally in a school, constrain – though in a greater or lesser degree – the pupils' participation in the shaping of learning' (1976 p. 32).

As the Children Decide project progressed, there was some opening up of possibilities for new forms of agency and power. By the end of the project, 'some classes reported that the decisions their children were now making were impacting upon their learning to a greater degree' (Cox et al. 2006 p. 49) and teachers were seeing how they could face the risks and relinquish some of their control:

> I very quickly realised that the sheer quantity of everyday decisions and my justifications were largely inaccessible to the children. In opening up this process it became very apparent that the children could easily understand, partake in, succeed in and benefit from making their own effective decisions.
>
> (White 2006 p. 172)

The children, too, were challenging their own assumptions. A striking example of this was provided in a Year 2 class when the teacher and the class were discussing whether they thought she always made fair decisions. The children saw they could question the power of their teacher:

> [They] commented that teachers usually made fair decisions and that sometimes it would be 'rude' to object even if they disagreed with a decision. However, they could see that they could override the teacher, as Robbie commented: 'If you make bad decisions, like torture us, we'll phone the police.' [Class observation notes, 14/6/05]
>
> (Cox et al. 2006 p. 31)

This was a particularly interesting incident. As the adults present at the time observed, the rest of the conversation, the tone of Robbie's comment and the reactions of the other children suggested that it was something of a revelation to the children. It might have represented both recognition of their potential power and a possible threat to the stability of the established culture of the classroom, the relationships and responsibilities within it. The children might themselves have sensed the possible risks in making decisions and in sharing or even challenging the teacher's authority.

Nevertheless, this example illustrates that the project may have opened up a space for the children to bring their everyday knowledge to the classroom situation – in this case, that even their teacher is subject to what the children know, as citizens in the wider world, to be right and fair. Learning is situated, but this does not mean the children's learning is specific only to the present context they find themselves in. It is not 'simply a matter of becoming acculturated into existing practices. . . learners move between settings and need to learn how to navigate them and reformulate their prior understandings so that they can act knowledgably in a different setting' (Edwards 2009 p. 159). A situated view of learning does not mean that learning is fixed by the local setting. The relevance of what is learned as a participant in one setting is not irrelevant to another situation. Identities emerge as participants move from one setting to another: 'what participants learn in both settings becomes part of their identities, and is thus carried into other parts of their lives' (Wenger 1998 p. 268). These children were crossing the boundaries between the domain beyond the school and the domain of the school itself. In coming to see, metacognitively, how their teacher holds power and how that might be challenged, on the basis of what they have learned from their relations in other social settings, and seeing the possibility of a different relationship with their teacher, the children open up the possibility of taking action in the classroom community in ways that can change it.

Collaboration or compliance and competition?

Underlying the research I have discussed here are questions around what kinds of community both children and teachers want. Do they value a more collaborative form of practice? Research evidence has suggested that this is something that children appreciate:

> Our recent interviews with pupils in primary and secondary schools across the country (see Rudduck and Flutter, 1998; Flutter et al., 1998) confirm that pupils are interested in changing structures that cast them in a marginal role and limit their agency. Pupils of all ages ask for more autonomy, they want school to be fair and they want pupils, as individuals and as an institutional group, to be important members of the school community.
>
> (Rudduck and Flutter 2000)

I have been building the case for pursuing these aims. I have suggested, on the one hand, that there are reasons for increasing children's participation and control: this is the key to creating a context where children can follow their own lines of enquiry in their quest for meaning. The level of cognitive challenge that can be provided through responsive scaffolding – or, rather, guided participation – has the potential to support children's development in ways that far outreach the conventional approaches of transmission: 'monologic' teaching and the 'recitation script' (Alexander 2008). I discussed what can happen when an adult-prescribed task is mismatched with the child's prior understanding (Drummond's example of Jason, Chapter 2) and when interactions with children are misinterpreted by the teacher in a large group, as was illustrated by the example of Meg in Chapter 4.

I have discussed the fact that within the framework of a top-down, target-driven agenda, there is a danger that the classroom ends up as a community of practice where teachers and children simply comply. Teachers feel obliged to 'cover' dis-embedded, de-contextualised material, even when they are already aware that what they teach in this way will not be what the children learn. Even committed teachers have arguably been driven to adopt practices which do not reflect their beliefs. This seemed to be the case for teachers in the Children Decide team: they reported that the project had 'given them back' their values (Cox et al. 2006 p. 50). In the Introduction I raised the likelihood that some teachers might even have come to accept that there *is* an unproblematic relationship between input and outcomes and, as a result, do not question their compliance: such is the possible hegemony of the 'performance model' of learning and teaching, that teachers might have come to take its assumptions for granted (Pollard 2001).

There is a great deal to overcome, then. All may seem driven in directions that run counter to what is potentially realisable. It seems that both children and teachers are trying to act out or 'perform' what they think is required of them by those more powerful than themselves. Children are finding ways of acting and presenting themselves that are consistent with what is expected of them as 'pupils'. They are doing their best to bring their existing knowledge to bear on teacher-initiated tasks, even when they make little sense, or they are learning to appear competent in meeting the demands of the situations they find themselves in. Some children may give up altogether, motivated – by their fear of failure – to find strategies for avoiding any tasks presented to them by adults. Teachers are trying their best to improve children's outcomes in the SATs and to implement the latest government recommendations, which, as I showed in Chapter 2, can lead to teaching to the test.

They may be geared towards satisfying the Ofsted inspector, securing a high place in the league tables, gaining promotion or some other indicator of performance (see Chapter 2). In the performative context, the actions of all members of the classroom community tend to be instrumental to achieving some other goal than high-quality learning and teaching. As one of the teachers in the Children Decide project commented:

> As teachers we have become inhibited by the expectations of the establishment. Ofsted inspections, SATs and certain government initiatives (such as the literacy strategy) have steadily eroded our professional judgement and self-confidence. To conform to their authority and, in order to avoid sanction, we tend to structure learning in very conservative ways.
>
> (Taylor 2006 p. 99)

The stakes are high and consequences can be punitive on both a professional and personal level: teachers become 'non-compliant' at their peril. As for children, their self-esteem may depend on securing the good opinion of their teacher or peers by going through the motions of being a good, compliant pupil, or hiding their perceived inadequacies with attention-seeking behaviour or withdrawal, in a situation which is predominantly competitive rather than collaborative.

Collaboration between home and school?

In this climate, parents' primary role is to be consumers of education. Since schools are ranked on their performance and an educational market place has been created (as I discussed in earlier chapters), parents have been encouraged to make comparisons and to endeavour to secure the best educational product for their children from what is on offer, and to expect satisfaction. This state of affairs, which was foreshadowed by the reforms in 1988, received further official endorsement through the Parent's Charter in 1992. But, as Andrew Pollard (1996 p. 308) pointed out, the Parents Charter

> missed the real educational point . . . the notion of parents as consumers does not recognise the vital role that mothers and fathers play in supporting children's identities, self-confidence and learning. The danger is that it can create detachment and division.

His study, with Ann Filer, of children's learning in the context of all aspects of their social worlds, represented a very different point of view. It demonstrated how important it is to see children's development in the full complexity of their relationships in the home, the school and the playground. He, along with others at the time (for example Bastiani 1987; Vincent 1996), was arguing strongly for the development of collaborative parent–teacher relationships, that are on more equal terms and where parents are *partners* rather than customers.

Pollard observed that the educational potential of parent–teacher partnerships had not, at that time, been fully realised. Later, it came to feature much more prominently in official policy under the Labour government – in *Every Child Matters* (DfES 2004) and then in *The Children's Plan* (DCSF 2007b) and in *Every Parent Matters* of the same year (DfES 2007) where it was a 'unifying theme'. The Primary Strategy and The Early Years Foundation Stage curriculum both acknowledged the importance of parents to children's education. The bid to develop partnership with parents remained firmly within the agenda of raising standards, but it was also driven by the need to address inequality. As the evidence about the effects on educational achievement of the child's early experiences at home and school, including living in poverty, became more apparent (as has recently been confirmed by Sylva et al. 2008), so the need to engage with parents was recognised. The emphasis has clearly shifted, then, since Pollard was writing. The role that parents play in children's learning and development was clearly stated in *The Children's Plan*: 'Working in partnership with parents will be vital at each stage of children's development' (DCSF 2007b p. 56). *The Children's Plan* also explicitly recognised that children's educational achievements depend on their experiences in the home as well as the school and that parents are the child's first educators. There was a movement, too, in talk of 'involvement', to the idea of 'engagement': 'Our vision of twenty-first-century children's services is that they should engage parents in all aspects of their children's development' (p. 57). This was not intended to be based on one-way communication from school to home: 'The school actively engages and listens to parents, makes sure their views shape school policies, and works with them as partners in their child's learning and development (p. 145).

Clearly, in policy terms, it was becoming important to fully acknowledge what goes on in the home, rather than only encouraging parents to take part in school activities (Alexander 2010 p. 86). Hughes et al. (2005) and Alexander (2010) have noted that there was also, official recognition of the need to take account of the 'funds of knowledge' (Moll and Greenberg 1990) that children bring from outside school. It is significant, however, that Hughes and his team, who made use of the term 'funds of knowledge' in their Home School Knowledge Exchange project, later raised doubts about it. They were concerned that, as a metaphor it explicitly endorses the conceptualisation of knowledge as a 'commodity' (Hughes et al. 2005). It is the kind of language that can perpetuate the deficit view of what is learned in the home that they themselves set out to challenge. 'Funds' are quantifiable and can be found wanting. The terminology seems to sustain the consumerist orientation. It perhaps sits quite comfortably, however, with the underlying central policy agenda, which remained, under the Labour Government, firmly focused on measurable achievements and may continue to do so under the Coalition government. It is of interest too, that the evidence submitted to the *Cambridge Review* (Alexander 2010) illustrated the continued pervasiveness of the 'deficit' view of children's home lives. It was apparent, for instance, amongst some teachers and teaching assistants, who referred to 'poor' or 'pushy' parenting (p. 80). It may be perceptions such as these that motivate teachers in their bid to improve children's life chances. It is, however, a compensatory approach – making up for what are seen to be the inadequacies of the home – and implicitly suggests judgemental rather than collaborative relationships. It can lead to parents feeling that their agency is not respected and the home–school relationship remains one where the school sets the agenda and, through its increasing invasion of the private space of the home, even imposes its own values and practices on the family community. To the extent that these kinds of relationships and practices maintain the balance of power in favour of the school, they can perpetuate the kinds of divisions to which Pollard (1996) and, also, Vincent (1996) referred. They can work against the achievement of shared support for children's learning in its different settings.

Learning in democratic classrooms

It can make a difference if teachers acknowledge children's agency in their own learning. If teachers recognise that children's voices, and children's participation in dialogue are, as I have been arguing, constitutive of their learning, they have reason to actively foster communicative practices that provide a responsive, interactive environment to support children's meaning making. If they do so, they can also achieve a more democratic context for children's learning, as I suggested in the opening section to this chapter. Teachers who encourage participation in the classroom – that allows the development of children's meaning making in ways that fully acknowledge their agency and identities in their lives as a whole, rather than only their lives at school – are valuing children as people, not only as pupils. They are embracing a shift in relationships and practices that creates a different kind of community within the classroom – one that encompasses the children's worlds beyond the classroom and offers more potential for authentic participation inside it. In allowing that children come to the classroom with their own voices as members of communities of practice outside the school, both within the home and beyond it, with their own perspectives, conceptualisations, intentions, purposes and values, as well as with their own rights to be heard as members of a democratic society, this kind of shift gives a different emphasis to children's participation in the classroom as a community and a different dimension to their learning. As I pointed out earlier, by participating, children learn what it is to participate. By actively participating in a practising democratic community, they learn what it is to be a citizen.

Within a more restricted school community, by contrast, where children's agency in their own learning and in their communities is unrecognised or only partially acknowledged, or where children's role in decision making is limited to matters that have no significant impact on those areas that are traditionally under the sole control of adults, it is clear, from a socio-cultural perspective, that children's learning will be around these restricted forms of participation. They will learn about being 'minimal', rather than 'maximal' citizens: learning to be a full participant will be deferred to adulthood (Holdsworth cited in Rudduck 2003). They will be learning 'about' citizenship in preparation for their future rather than being actively engaged in democratic practices and enacting identities as democratic citizens in the here and now (Rudduck 2003; Cox and Robinson-Pant 2006; Fielding and Rudduck 2006). Children's rights to be heard were enshrined in the UN Convention on Children's Rights 20 years ago (United Nations 1989) and the movement to increase children's involvement in decisions around matters that affect their lives has gathered pace over recent years.

Even where schools have taken this on board, however, teachers need to be wary. The performative culture of schooling may possibly distort the way the new agenda is implemented. Student participation, adopted in official policy documents including the Children's Plan, is now monitored by Ofsted. There have been concerns for some time that schools' adoption of student participation has either been seen as a means of acquiring data for the managers' purposes or of meeting the schools' performance objectives (ticking the box for student participation) rather than promoting children's democratic agency (Fielding 2001a; 2001b; 2009). The children may have been consulted, but the more radical aim of achieving their full contribution to the transformation of their educational communities through active participation (Cox et al. 2010; Fielding 2004; 2009) may have been eclipsed by the more immediate, extrinsic ends.

Concluding reflections

I have tried to show that children's learning about democratic participation in schools is grounded in the practices in the classroom and school communities. As things stand, given the predominant culture of schooling this can be different from their learning as members of other communities outside the institution of school. Practices in school might be better adapted to build on that non-institutional, non-formal learning, so that children continue to engage in the kind of exploratory play and exploratory talk they pursue in their self-chosen activities and developing interests within their everyday worlds. They might also be more focused on promoting respect and children's rights to be heard so their voices influence decisions that affect them in the here and now of their lives in school, and in turn, have greater significance in the wider world.

Again, change has to be achieved in the context of existing power relations across all communities: between local communities beyond the school, the institution of the school and the wider educational community, including policy makers. To repeat, teachers are faced by the constraints on their actions and decision making, presented by their accountability within these power structures. Nevertheless, if they are prepared to take some risks, there are grounds for believing that teachers who understand learning as integral to communities might begin to initiate those changes in their own classrooms, avoiding tokenistic involvement and instead creating more authentically democratic communities that foster children's participation in genuine decision making. Learning *to* participate and exercise agency entails very different sorts of practices than simply learning *about* participation. What teachers do, in this regard, is central.

Issues for teachers

- What kind of adjustments do you think young children must make when they enter your school? How is Year 1, and beyond, different from Foundation Stage?
- How do the children themselves see this? How might you find out?
- How do you see relationships between the home and the school?
- What do you think the children in your classroom are learning about participation from the practices within your classroom community?
- Taking account of everyday activities in the family community and other out-of-school contexts, and of how children participate in them, how might you change the activities and the ways children participate in your classroom?
- To what extent would you describe your classroom as a democratic community?
- To what extent do you actively prioritise collaboration in your classroom and children's participation, voice, agency and decision making? To what extent do you prioritise compliance and competition? What are your reasons?

7 Co-constructing the curriculum

Chapter overview

In this chapter I relate the arguments I have been developing to the curriculum. The discussion so far has shown how learning is integral to all social contexts in which children live their lives and how children face particular sorts of activity and participation in school. Here, I discuss how the school, as a specific social context is distinctive because of its curriculum and I consider what that means for children's learning. I explore the implications of the socio-cultural perspective for both what is taught and how it is taught, discussing how 'subjects', when they are seen as enquiring practices and discourses, can extend learning beyond what is available to children in their everyday worlds. I make the case for children using the curriculum toolkit to realise negotiated and shared purposes in the context of the activities of their own lives, as children. I suggest that children (and teachers) make their own contribution to the culture. I discuss throughout how teachers can contribute collaboratively to this, again showing that transforming children's learning calls for a different understanding of learning.

Conceptions of curriculum

I have been developing the discussion around the boundaries that exist between the community of practice of the school and the social contexts beyond the school in which children live their lives. I have been arguing that the kinds of practices, and thus the kinds of learning, that are characteristic of 'school' are not necessarily consistent with children's activities and learning in other contexts: the culture of 'school learning' embodies specific ideas about what it is to learn, so that school life and learning become a world apart – one which children and their parents can 'buy into' in the commodity sense, to achieve the advantages that the product on offer may provide, but one which seems, also, to work against children's learning, rather than fostering it.

I have yet to fully address the issue of the school curriculum. One of the specific features of the school that does indeed set it apart from other social contexts, and with good reasons, is the fact that, through its curriculum, school introduces children to experiences and activities that they might not other-wise encounter – and with that, to opportunities to engage with knowledge, understandings and skills that might not otherwise be available to them to learn.

Paradoxically, it is this characteristic of 'school' that has helped to create the kind of performativity that I have been attempting to challenge throughout this book. The specific activities and experiences that make up the school curriculum are selected from those available within cultures, usually by those who are assigned to undertake the task on behalf of the wider community and using whatever means are considered appropriate within our democratic society. The public at large needs to be assured that the curriculum is being taught, that public funds are being properly spent and that the school's obli-gations to society are being met. The system that has been developed to ensure that schools are held accountable is that of 'measuring' how well they are doing in teaching that curriculum. On the assumption that there is some pre-existing body of knowledge that teachers should teach and children should learn, a curriculum is laid down and these measures are taken to ensure that it is taught. The idea is that a prescribed curriculum will standardise the process, to ensure equality of entitlement for children, but also, when a market model is introduced, so that comparisons can be made (see Introduction and Chapter 2).

From the performative perspective, 'learning' itself may become identified with 'school' and with its formal curriculum. As I discussed in earlier chapters, school can be seen by children – and also by adults – as 'where you go to learn', as if learning is limited to school settings. I have attempted to challenge this view, from the socio-cultural perspective. As Lave and Wenger (1991 p. 113), for instance, point out learning 'is not necessarily or directly dependent on pedagogical goals and official agenda'. When learning is seen as situated in social practices, it is not only the official school curriculum that constitutes learning. As I hope I have shown, even within the school, development is not construed only in terms of intentional teaching, but in relation to children's participation in all the practices of the institution.

When the curriculum is brought into the frame, however, it is easy to see how this can lead to a conception of learning as a process that specifically involves schools and teachers. This is because what is to be learned seems to be in the hands of experts. In turn, this helps to further explain the assumption that learning entails the 'transmission of knowledge' from knowledgeable teacher to uninformed pupil: the content of the curriculum has to be passed on to children. It is the responsibility of the school – to use the current terminology – merely to 'deliver' it. From this view is derived the apparently simple, linear model, which, I have explained, underlies current practice in the performative culture, with its emphasis on pre-determined objectives for children's learning and summative assessments in the form of SATs.

What should be taught in schools?

The idea of a pre-determined curriculum, though apparently straightforward, nevertheless begs a range of questions. One of these concerns the nature and origins of what is taught in schools. The structure and also the content of the formal curriculum – the actual subject matter – have been determined in different ways at different times in history and in different settings. (For an account of this, see, for example, White 2007.) Whatever decisions have been made have reflected ideas about what children *ought* to learn. In other words, values and aims have been implicit, even if they have not been openly acknowledged. Sometimes decisions have been based on the thinking of educational philosophers, or they have involved other experts and elites within society, elected governments, the institution of the school and even teachers themselves. The Coalition government, in power in the UK at the time of writing, has suggested – under their 'free school' proposals (DfE 2010c) that parents and other interested parties should be able to determine the curriculum.

It is easy to take the traditional curriculum subjects for granted, as what should be taught in school and what there is to 'learn', but where do they come from? As I have mentioned, Paul Hirst (1973), practising the Liberal Humanist educational philosophy of the London School in the 1970s, presented an epistemological account, related to the aims of liberal education. He argued that there was a limited number of distinctive 'forms of knowledge', identified through an analysis of the nature of knowledge itself. These were presented as necessary forms, through which humans categorise and organise their thought, each employing distinctive concepts and processes for establishing the truth of their propositions. So, for example, science, focusing predominantly on physical phenomena, would employ concepts such as 'cause and effect'. History would be more concerned with motives than causes, as it is focused on the actions of human beings. A scientific claim would be tested for truth empirically through observation and experimentation, whereas historical truth would be established through, for example, the interpretation of artefacts and documentary evidence. On Hirst's argument, the knowledge produced is always contestable, but the aim is to seek out the truth, through these different processes of rational enquiry.

Hirst's analysis at least served to highlight that curriculum subjects are not collections of inert factual information. Rather, what is known has been arrived at through a variety of processes – of exploration, investigation, evidence gathering, interpretation and analysis – and would change and develop as new knowledge is acquired. Learners who were 'initiated' (Peters 1966) into these forms of knowledge or disciplines would eventually contribute to the sum of human knowledge through this knowledge-getting process. Hirst's ideas went further, however. His arguments implied that these were forms of rational enquiry necessary to human thought; the 'forms of knowledge' were fixed and limited to those that could be identified through epistemological analysis of the kind he had carried out, as the essential components of human rationality. Their value was also timeless and universal: in seeking justification one would employ the very processes of rational thought that one would be seeking to justify. Since it would thus be irrational to dispute the value of rational thought, no further justification was necessary. They were, as the basis of rational thought, necessarily or intrinsically worthwhile – in other words, they were worth pursuing for their own sake. The aims of education were thus conceived as the development of minds, which was construed in terms of these forms of knowledge and understanding. Education was valuable in and for itself.

It was these claims to universality and this kind of 'transcendental justification' that were challenged by the socio-cultural analysis.

The curriculum from a socio-cultural perspective

To clarify the view from the socio-cultural perspective, first, the domain of the school does not have any precedence over any other as a context for learning, apart from its social and cultural significance as an institution expressly created for learning. Once it is recognised that school is just one context amongst all the others in the social world, its characteristics as a site *specifically* designated for learning can be contrasted with those of any other setting. This arose in the last chapter, where I used Wood's (1991) terms, referring to the 'contrived' world of the school to contrast it with 'naturalistic' or everyday situations. Lave and Wenger (1991) refer to the 'teaching curriculum' in contrast to the 'learning curriculum'. Vygotsky (1987) distinguished between 'everyday' and 'scientific' concepts. Mercer (1995 p. 83) refers to the specific 'educational discourse' that teachers, in schools, use to guide children into 'educated discourse'. From the point of view of all these theorists, all these concepts mark out the setting of the school as a particular kind of situation, with social practices that shape learning in particular ways.

Perhaps the distinction between the learning and teaching curriculum, that Lave and Wenger make, will illustrate this, (even though they do not suggest that a 'teaching curriculum' is only to be found in schools):

> A learning curriculum is a field of learning resources in everyday practice *viewed from the perspective of learners*. A teaching curriculum, by contrast, is constructed for the instruction of newcomers. When a teaching curriculum supplies – and thereby limits – structuring resources for learning, the meaning of what is learned (and control of access to it . . .) is mediated through an instructor's participation, by an external view of what knowing is about.
>
> (1991 p. 97)

As I indicated in the introductory section above, one of the reasons it is deemed important for children to be able to go to school is to learn what is valued within the wider culture and, in Lave's and Wenger's view, this would make up a teaching curriculum.

Second, given that one of the school's defining characteristics that sets it apart from other social contexts is its curriculum, the socio-cultural perspective provides alternative approaches to how it might be taught. I have already explained how, from this perspective, children's learning occurs through joint action, with more experienced others, in 'communities of practice' (Wenger 1998). The child learns, whether in school or outside it, through participation in the communities' social practices. In school, then, children are encountering the specific practices of the 'teaching curriculum' or the 'educational discourses' which the teacher has a designated responsibility to teach. From this perspective, the curriculum might be construed as the social practices that have cultural significance in generating knowledge.

These social practices, through which human beings make sense of their experience, are the ways of understanding and knowing that have been shaped and developed over time. The processes are collaborative: the practices are shaped through discourse and in the context of people getting things done together – as Bruner argued, 'domains of knowledge are made, not found' (Bruner 1996 p. 119). For both Bruner and Vygotsky, ways of representing experience and constructing meaning have been developed in these ways, historically and culturally, in social contexts. They have become part of the shared toolkit of the culture; as Bruner (1996 p. 168) says, 'culturally devised ways of thinking' are as much a part of human tool using and tool making as digging sticks and stone choppers.

It follows that, unlike Hirst's forms, these practices are not static, fixed, or even necessarily discrete. Their value does not rest on the kind of justification that transcends their social and historical context. Furthermore, they are not taken to be the means of pursuing, or ultimately arriving at the 'truth' about reality. I discussed in Chapter 3 how knowledge that is produced in any community of practice in a particular time and place is seen as bounded by its cultural context, whether that is a local or broader cultural frame. The way it is valued reflects the purposes and interests of the community and culture. Those who actively participate in these modes of enquiry construct and re-construct them in their particular cultural and historical contexts: new ways of making meaning are constantly being created. The way in which explanatory frameworks can change for example, was explored by Thomas Kuhn (1996) in his account of 'paradigm shifts' in relation to science. If sense was to be made of new evidence that could not be explained within existing theoretical constructs, Newtonian physics to take an example, then completely new ways of thinking were required – such as those that were created by Einstein's theory of relativity. These are new paradigms.

To see knowledge as constructed in this way, through social practices – or discourses – is to provide a different way of seeing the origins of the 'knowledge' on which curriculum designers draw when deciding what to include in a school curriculum. It is very different from Hirst's rationalist view, although it is significant that Hirst himself revised his original thesis and came round to the idea that 'We must shift from seeing education as primarily concerned with knowledge to seeing it as primarily concerned with social practices' (1993 p. 184). In itself, Hirst's change of mind illustrates how ways of thinking are continually being transformed.

From the socio-cultural perspective, there is no blueprint for the content of the curriculum. As the product of collaborative, joint activity and meaning making through history and across cultures, knowledge is ever-changing and multi-faceted, the result of human beings' joint endeavours in communities of enquiry. New ways of making meaning can be generated, as new practices, or as adaptations or extensions of those already in use, or as paradigm shifts.

The cultural origins of these ways of making meaning have sometimes been seen, by educationalists as well as cultural theorists, in terms of 'narratives' that shape the way we live and make sense of our experiences. Bruner (1986; 1996), for instance, has taken this line of thinking. He notes the crucial change in people's thinking in the first part of the twentieth century which he refers to as the 'interpretive turn'.

> The object of interpretation is understanding, not explanation; its instrument is the analysis of text. Understanding is the outcome of organising and contextualising essentially contestable, incompletely verifiable propositions in a disciplined way. One of our principle means of doing so is through narrative: by telling a story of what something is 'about'.
>
> (1996 p. 90)

There are echoes of Kuhn's thinking when Bruner relates narrative explicitly to science – which, of all the possible ways of creating knowledge in our Western culture, is arguably the one least likely to be accounted for in terms of narrative invention:

> the focus of attention shifts from an exclusive concern with 'nature-out-there' to a concern with the *search* for nature – how we construct our model of nature. It is that shift that turns the discussion from dead science to live science *making*. And once we do that, we are able to invoke criteria like conceivability, verisimilitude, and other criteria of good stories.
>
> (Bruner 1996 p. 126)

The culture of schooling and the school curriculum

From the point of view of teachers in classrooms, working within the performative culture, these accounts of the curriculum may seem remote and irrelevant to what happens in their classrooms, where they are focused on the immediate need to 'cover' the given curriculum content, to prepare children for tests that measure a specific range of outcomes and to reach targets. They may feel that their statutory duties oblige them to make sure they 'get through' the National Curriculum. This intensively content-driven approach was possibly most recently strengthened at the turn of the present century which saw the introduction of the QCA 'schemes of work'. (See Introduction.)

The QCA schemes of work were devised only to provide exemplars of curriculum planning and were non-statutory, but their widespread adoption by schools, and the timing of their dissemination, may have led to the perception, on the part of some teachers, that these *were* the National Curriculum. They came on top of the Literacy and Numeracy Strategies (DfEE 1998; 1999b), which, as I have already discussed in earlier chapters, were also very detailed programmes that stipulated teaching methods and prescribed how lessons should be structured as well as specifying numerous learning objectives. The level of prescription at this point was particularly burdensome to teachers. The Strategies were also, in fact, non-statutory and there was some relaxation of the requirement to teach the whole of the National Curriculum, as long as 'breadth and balance' were maintained. Regulatory systems, however, such as the inspection process and the requirements for initial teacher training, made them more or less mandatory.

All this no doubt contributed to teachers' perceptions of excessive amounts of content in the curriculum. As I mentioned in the Introduction, that they found the curriculum to be too crowded and over-prescriptive was overwhelmingly clear in the evidence gathered for both *The Independent Review of the Primary Curriculum* (DCSF 2009a) and the *Cambridge Review* (Alexander 2010). Teachers reported that, as a result, their teaching was superficial in some subject areas and it was difficult to achieve 'breadth and balance' across the curriculum as a whole. The study by Boyle and Bragg (2006) shows the significant effect of government policy on breadth and balance. The increased emphasis on literacy and numeracy through the National Strategies had led to more pressure on the remaining core subject of Science. The Foundation Subjects of Art and Design, Music, History, Geography, Physical Education, Design and Technology and Religious Education also suffered (see for example, the case of Art and Design, Cox 1998b and Herne 2000). Over and above these areas there were the non-compulsory subjects of Citizenship, Personal and Social Education and Modern Foreign Languages, as well as the cross-curricular elements of spiritual, moral, social and cultural development; key skills; thinking skills; financial capability, enterprise education and education for sustainable development. From a teacher's perspective, it might well have seemed that the best, or only, way of achieving – at least some – 'coverage' of the weight of material in all these subjects might be through the transmission approach. The practical pressures of limited classroom time, with half of it taken up with Literacy and Numeracy, and the demands to raise the attainment level of all the children in the class in terms of measured outcomes in the core subjects, along with Ofsted's insistence on fast-paced lessons, were almost inevitably going to push teachers in that direction.

The tendency of teachers to use the pressures of the National Curriculum to account for didactic approaches to their teaching makes sense within the existing performance-led values and practices of the educational system (Galton 2007). These pressures alone, however, cannot entirely account for the dominance of the transmission mode of teaching (see Chapters 4 and 5). In its detail, the National Curriculum focuses on developing skills of enquiry – not only knowledge – which cannot be simply imparted by transmission. Furthermore, as Galton argued, the National Curriculum and other programmes could not explain why such approaches had been consistently in evidence for such a long period of time – before teachers were subjected to such levels of prescription (see Chapters 4 and 5). For Galton, the reasons are more complex and deep-rooted in the culture of teaching and learning. As I have been suggesting, these practices are in part shaped by the culture of 'schooling' and the institutional commitment of the school community to the delivery of pre-packaged, pre-ordained knowledge, but they are also constructed by teachers in their classroom contexts. A cultural shift recognising the centrality of pedagogy in schools is yet to be achieved (Simon 1983; Alexander 2004).

A different vision: practices; discourses; dialogue

Returning to the different view that the socio-cultural perspective provides, where the curriculum is conceived in terms of the practices through which knowledge is generated, and learning is understood as participation in communities of practice, a different picture of teaching the curriculum emerges that holds the potential for teachers in their classrooms to challenge the existing practices and help to re-shape that culture of 'schooling'. As with classroom interaction and communication, the emphasis on participatory activity is the key. Learning in 'science', 'history' or 'art' implies participating in those collaborative practices and discourses; entering into the community of those who practise those modes of enquiry. It means actively *becoming* a scientist, a historian or an artist, engaging in the processes of enquiry and making meanings in the ways that members of those communities do. In this way, children learn what it is to *be* a scientist: they 'learn how' to carry out experiments – how to make sure their tests are fair, for instance. They might learn how to find out the best conditions for growing plants, say, and as a consequence they may 'learn that' plants need water, sunlight, air and nutrients to grow. So,

> what, for example, makes a person a scientist is not a unique way of thinking (as a traditional approach implies) but the person's participation in a scientific community (recognised as such by other members of the community and by people outside the community) (Latour 1987).
>
> (Matusov and Hayes 2002 p. 242)

Similarly, children can learn what it is to *be* a practising historian, or artist, or geographer, or mathematician. To provide some examples, a class taught by Jenny Houssart (1999) were given a collection of letters and other documents – at the time, only recently uncovered and never examined before by historians – from a Jewish family who lived in Austria and other European countries during the Second World War. This opportunity to piece together stories, from original evidence, may have been unusual in the scope it offered the children to be 'real' historians and to learn how to carry out historical enquiry; but children can also learn what it is to be a historian working with other sorts of evidence that is already in the public domain, for example, in the environment, in museums, or in educational collections. Similarly, children in a history project in Bermondsey worked with older people who had experienced the Second World War first hand, to construct their own interpretation of events using oral sources of evidence (Cox 1998a). To be clear, the practices of science, history and art – or any other way of knowing – are not just the 'practical' activities that are central to it. I have been using the term 'discourse' to emphasise this. It is the whole 'discourse' of the subject in which those practical activities have meaning – the shared understanding of what makes sense within it; the language and concepts it employs, the kinds of questions and avenues of enquiry that it is concerned with; the ways of interpreting evidence and theorising its uses and its forms of reasoning – that are the 'practice'. I have already discussed the range of tools – the languages, or forms of representation – that make possible the collaborative generation of meanings and knowledge that constitute these discourses. I have emphasised the centrality of verbal language to learning and its place in classrooms. For Mercer, Wells and Alexander (see Chapter 4 and 5), amongst others, engagement in 'collaborative and collective talk' (Mercer 2002), in dialogue, is the key to learning in classrooms. Furthermore – as I have also shown (Chapter 3) – communicative practices are not restricted to verbal language. People's actions, and their thinking, are mediated by a whole range of artefacts, gestures, sounds and images that are given meaning as semiotic systems within the culture.

Children enter a world that has been given meaning by others through these kinds of joint activity and, as I have argued, it is these activities that give rise to learning. In giving meaning to their experiences, as part of their learning they encounter the different specific modes of enquiry that human beings have developed; different ways of interpreting the world and knowing it through symbolic or semiotic systems that have already been invented. These are the practices that constitute the cultures that children are born into. Active participation across the range of different communities of enquiry and discourses that are used and valued in the culture provides children with access to the wide range of the resources and tools for making meaning and generating knowledge that is available; in participating, they enter into worlds of meaning of which they might otherwise be unaware. Through the curriculum, schools and teachers can offer children activities that complement children's own worlds – the epistemic activities of enquiry and reasoning beyond children's everyday lives, through which meanings can be made and knowledge constructed. Learners are inducted into 'the culture's ways of making sense of experience – its modes of classification, its understanding of means–ends relationships, and its aesthetic and moral values' (Wells and Claxton 2002 p. 4). As these researchers suggest: 'it is particularly by learning to use these semiotic tools in discourse with others that humans appropriate the culture's dominant ways of thinking, reasoning and valuing.' (p. 4).

These sorts of activity are different in kind to those that would be typical of a classroom where the teacher adopted a purely content-driven model of the curriculum, and a 'delivery' or 'transmission' mode of teaching. As Barnes (1976 p. 22) put it:

> It is misleading to see learning as the adding of new blocks of knowledge to an existing pile of blocks. Cognitive psychologists such as

Piaget and Bruner have given us the metaphor of knowledge as a series of systems for interpreting the world. From this point of view, learning is a matter of changing the system by which interpretation is carried out.

What do children actually learn in school?

As I discussed in earlier chapters the new social setting of the school can disrupt the self-directed pattern of activity in children's everyday lives, in some ways placing limits on their scope to act in and on their worlds, restricting them to the narrow range of practices prescribed by the school. I have suggested that this can be particularly so in a teacher-centred classroom, where the teacher determines the activities. In such classrooms, communication can follow an unfamiliar pattern: it is initiated by the teacher and certain formalised responses are required of the child. There are new forms of activity with purposes that may not be matched with those of the child. This might be further illustrated (see also Chapter 4) by the example of Rachel, who at five years old was given a worksheet of simple flower shapes – circles of petals – printed on white paper. She was asked by the teacher to go to her table and to colour in six of them. Rachel took a few seconds to put a yellow dot in the centres of six flowers and returned to the teacher. Distressingly, for Rachel, the teacher was not impressed. 'Miss' was even less pleased when Rachel explained that she had coloured them as daisies – six yellow dots at their centres, leaving the petals white (personal communication: Kath Green).

Rachel had brought her existing knowledge of counting to the task and she had even followed the teacher's instructions, but her interpretation of the task did not, it seemed, coincide with that of her teacher, which remained a mystery to her. Arguably, the teacher had wanted to keep Rachel occupied for as long as possible – colouring in – and to make sure she learned how to do as an adult says. If these were the underlying goals, they might even have overridden the educational intentions the teacher may have had – to give Rachel some experience of counting, perhaps; to apply what she already knew about number or to assess what she knew and what she could do. Rachel, on the other hand, did indeed know how to count and, given that the paper was white, confidently used her prior knowledge to deduce that here was a picture of daisies and that she was to mark out six of them. Or, perhaps she surmised that she could promptly accomplish the task the teacher was asking her to do if she turned the anonymous flowers into daisies. Either way, she would have quickly learned that, in this strange new world of the school, she had failed to please her teacher and did not know why. Her actions, and her knowledge and thinking, were not appreciated in the way she might have hoped. She also learned, as the teacher asserted her own view, that she was not expected to question the teacher – she had little power in this new situation. What this story illustrates is that the meanings that Rachel had constructed in her everyday world, which she brought to school, were not so very different to the teacher's. The social situation of the school, however, its ways of doing things and its expectations and relationships, created new, dissonant meanings.

To reiterate the arguments I have been presenting, from a socio-cultural perspective, where it is the social nature of situations that accounts for learning and learning is understood as integral to the social situation, it is clear that learning is going on whether or not there is any teaching involved. When 'learning' is uncoupled from its traditional association with 'school' and from the specific instructional intentions of teachers, there are significant implications. This way of looking at learning – as being situated in all social practices, rather than being dependent on the specific agenda of the school or the teacher – not only challenges the assumption that the formal curriculum, delivered by teachers, is the necessary source of learning. As learning is conceived as integral to social situations in their entirety, not only as a response to what is specifically taught person to person, this view also draws attention to what is actually going on from the vantage point of different participants, and to what they may be learning. Clearly, what children learn may be different from what teachers set out to teach.

These arguments highlight the need for teachers, especially when they are focused on the curriculum, to be particularly mindful of where their purposes and intentions may conflict with those of the children and where children are bringing different meanings to a situation and constructing possibly unpredictable interpretations within the context as a whole. As Lave and Wenger (1991 p. 114) point out:

> Dissociating learning from pedagogical intentions opens up the possibility of mismatch or conflict among practitioners' viewpoints in situations where learning is going on. These differences often must become constitutive of the content of learning.

Where teachers are unaware of these complexities, they can be inadvertently placing the onus on their pupils to decode what is, to the children, an unfamiliar world of 'curriculum content' – to make sense of these mismatches of viewpoint and conception, which is to ask too much of the child. As Pollard has said: 'Pupils need to be sufficiently confident of their identities and abilities to be able to work with ambiguity within classrooms – but most are not' (1996 p. 311). The lack of engagement by teachers with the thinking of their pupils can result in impoverished educational provision, such as tasks that are easily achieved. An example might be the use of low-level, repetitive worksheets. As Pollard went on to say:

> Unfortunately then, both parties [teachers and pupils] cope by nego-
> tiating a reduction in cognitive challenge and task ambiguity, thus
> tending over time to create routinisation, drift and lower expectations
> than are probably justified.
>
> (p. 311)

Similarly, in assuming that learning results from a simplistic transfer of knowledge from themselves to their pupils, teachers can be unaware that they are
simply loading onto children the burden of adapting to the strangeness of the
activities of the school and its curriculum. Anxious to 'cover the curriculum'
and to demonstrate their delivery of 'subject knowledge' they can overlook
what the children might be making of it all. They might, for instance, ritualisti-
cally oblige them to sit uncomprehendingly through their well-intentioned
expositions. Pre-service teachers, for example, can often assume that this is
what is required, as was illustrated by a student teacher with whom I worked.
In response to being observed in the classroom she reverted to the security of
an ingrained idea of teaching, and delivered a long lecture full of complicated
scientific ideas and vocabulary, even though the children were only five years
old and despite everything she had learned on her university teacher education course. This illustrates how the default approach of 'delivery' can seem to
be woven into the fabric of school life and culture and is already familiar to
those entering the school community as new teachers, because they themselves have been pupils. The children, well trained in their classroom routines,
and already accepting of such school specific behaviour, obligingly tolerated
her mystifying monologue.

Once again, care needs to be taken not to assume that if children are on
the receiving end of transmission modes of teaching, they are simply, by definition, not participating and therefore not learning. Children are, nonetheless, participants in the practices of the classroom even when they sit at their
tables or on the carpet listening to, say, scientific facts imparted by the teacher.
Clearly, though, in such circumstances, they are not participating in 'doing
science', for instance, as scientists would – through investigation, experimentation and observation, for example – so are not 'learning how' this community of practitioners goes about its activities and generates knowledge. On the
contrary, from their participation as an audience to their teacher, they might
learn that the way to learn science is by listening to what others have to say
about the subject. As a result they might come to know *about* science. They
may also construct meaning from the propositional knowledge ('learning
that') that the teacher imparts – the knowledge that scientists have arrived at
through *their* activities as scientists. In this way, the children may learn some
scientific facts. This is not to deny that if the teacher carefully scaffolds the
learning, then this learning can be meaningful to children and that it may also
have its place (see also Chapter 5). From what the teacher tells them, they may

even be able to make some sense of scientific activities such as carrying out experiments, if they can relate this to what they have already learned in other contexts.

But this learning is situated outside not only their everyday experience but also outside the practice of science itself. By not engaging with the subject as 'scientists', they are denied the benefits of immersing themselves in this social practice in its full complexity, with all its opportunities for learning: of understanding the way that problems are identified, thought about, addressed and solved, in context. This leads back to the point that if it is included in the designated teaching curriculum that children should be learning *science*, then it seems, from a socio-cultural perspective, that learning must be situated in a context where they are *doing* science and acting as scientists.

To summarise: where the learner is seen as an active meaning maker, constructing new knowledge by making sense of new information in terms of what they already know, and where knowledge is seen as socially constructed, then a transmission-of-content model of curriculum seems headed in a misguided direction. While transmission may be able to achieve *some* learning about a 'subject', if it is not contextualised within the practice and discourse itself, it is at the very least more of a challenge for the children to understand the mode of enquiry.

As with patterns of interaction, it does seem, however, that the belief that knowledge comes pre-packaged and ready to deliver is hard to shake. In 1992, Wells and Chang-Wells (1992 p. 95) discussed this in a way that may be as relevant today:

> Unfortunately, as is illustrated by one authoritative pronouncement after another, the methodologies of teaching at all levels of education are still to a large extent based on implicit beliefs in the absolute nature of this knowledge and in the feasibility of the transmission of knowledge from expert to novice. Such methodologies, furthermore, accord little significance to the active, constructive nature of learning or to the role of social interaction in the processes whereby each individual comes to know.

Children's everyday activities and purposes

Rachel's story illustrates that it would be mistaken to assume that children do not come to school already partaking in ways of knowing about their worlds – the enquiring practices – that the school curriculum offers. As valued cultural tools, these are shared in different ways across different communities of practice and are used in out-of-school, everyday contexts. This is evident when a parent, who is cooking with their child, uses the mathematical language of quantity and capacity. ('Let's put in a bit more milk.' 'How many eggs go in?' 'Add another spoonful.') Similarly, they might use the scientific language of cause and effect. ('It's burnt – we must have left it in the oven too long.') This happens in the course of activities and conversations, without the parent or carer having any specific intention of teaching these 'subjects'. They are engaging with the child in the discourses of mathematics and science in the context of achieving practical goals: the learning is embedded within the real purposes of everyday life. Rachel's learning about counting may well have not come about as the result of a specific instructional exchange between herself and her parent. It is more likely to have arisen in the context of a purposeful activity that she was engaged in. Yet, as I have shown, when children go to school, especially when they leave the Foundation Stage classroom, the nature of the activities usually changes: purposes are appropriated by the teacher and children must adjust to this. The point of what they are expected to do is framed within the overarching purpose of school activity, which is to 'learn'. In a linear teacher-directed 'lesson', the main point of the activities is to achieve the given learning objective.

Hughes et al. (2005 p. 10) were aware of this when they noted that their data

> support what other researchers have said about the way in which much out-of-school learning of literacy and numeracy is embedded in authentic everyday practices such as cooking, shopping, playing games (Baker et al. 2003; Hannon 1995). Such activities are usually purposeful, but the purposes are not primarily to acquire literacy and/or numeracy – rather they are to produce a cake, to buy some clothes or to pass some time in an enjoyable way. In contrast, the main purpose of school literacy and numeracy activities is to acquire specific literacy and numeracy skills or knowledge, with little or no obvious purpose beyond this.

Regarding the curriculum, a tension seems to exist between the child engaging in these formalised activities, which adults value as a means of enriching the child's learning, and the child pursuing their self-directed activities, which are meaningful within the context of their own world and which they, themselves, value. For some children, the values and practices of their lives outside school are very different from those of the school. To them, the activities of the school curriculum might seem even more puzzling and 'contrived' than they did to Rachel, who lived in an economically advantaged home, where the values were more likely to coincide with those of the school. Teachers need to be aware that the curriculum of the school may be very far removed from the social practices of the everyday lives of children living in poverty, for instance.

In all cases, however, the social worlds of children as children are, arguably, very different to those of adults, making it challenging for any child to build the connections and negotiate the boundaries between the different worlds. Given that, ostensibly at least, school offers a 'teaching curriculum' (Lave and Wenger 1991) and exists to extend children's everyday worlds, teachers' activities will inevitably embody pedagogical intentions in one way or another. But the potential for mismatch with children's concerns, in a context of adult-led, inauthentic, dis-embedded, performative programmes, with preconceived content and objectives, and transmission modes of 'delivery', should give teachers pause for thought. It demands careful reappraisal of what those pedagogical intentions should be.

Children's participation in communities of enquiry across the curriculum and beyond their present worlds

If many children, to a greater or lesser extent, already have a foothold in the ways of making meaning and of knowing that are traditionally used and valued in the culture and if educators can extend children's learning in these ways of thinking, then schools have a clear educational role in ensuring that children come to see their use and value. Rather than re-interpreting the point and purpose of these practices in terms extrinsic to them – where the reasons for engaging in them might be to achieve the learning objectives; to pass a test; to comply with the teachers' wishes; to please the teacher or to become a 'pupil' – the school should make sure that children appreciate their worth in terms of what is intrinsic to them as meaning-making practices; as activities that both create practical purposes in life and pride means of achieving them. If children are to participate in these activities – to join in with practitioners in these communities of enquiry – schools and teachers need to ensure they are carried out in ways that embody purposes that are authentic to those practices. In other words, as I have indicated, the activities need to reflect the genuine purposes and practices of scientists, artists and historians.

Children cannot, however, be expected to enter worlds that are entirely alien to their own. While the context for their learning must be genuine participation in these enquiring practices, to be able to act as scientists, artists or historians, children must do so in ways that are meaningful to them. This implies collaborative activity where purposes are shared. As children take their place alongside more experienced practitioners in a community of enquiry, they learn what the aims of it are and give their own meanings to what they are doing, through the guidance of the teacher. In the context of joint activity, teachers can share with children, for instance, what the point of a scientific investigation is; how people can communicate their ideas through artistic media; how mathematics helps to solve practical problems; or why it is useful to find out what life in a particular period in the past might have been like. Clearly, that 'shared activity' is not merely a case of the teacher imposing their own purposes on the child – with all the potential for mismatch that this can bring. It is not a one-way process of the child 'joining in' with the teacher. To build a community of enquiry in the classroom (Wells 1999; Wells and Arauz 2006), the teacher must take account of and respond to the child's existing intentional activities and purposes – what they want to do and what practical problems they need to address.

Imaginative and responsive teachers are well placed to build on the kinds of activities that children themselves already find interesting and purposeful in their everyday worlds, while keeping in their sights the important pedagogical purposes of the 'teaching curriculum' – of introducing children to new worlds of practice and meaning making that are valued cultural resources. So, for instance, an investigation into the children's local environment, already familiar to the children, might replicate the kinds of enquiry that geographers would carry out. It could be initiated by the kinds of questions that geographers would ask but that children themselves might also pose in their 'intellectual searches'. These are questions that are, indeed, built into the National Curriculum. For instance the programme of study at Key Stage 1 requires children to undertake geographical enquiry through which they would ask geographical questions (for example, 'What is it like to live in this place?') and at Key Stage 2 such questions as 'What is this landscape like?', 'What do I think about it?' (DfEE 1999a). By engaging in these genuine kinds of investigation, children begin to participate in the activities of the community of geographers.

The programme of study for Key Stage 2 Science has a central focus on scientific enquiry where children engage in the same sort of practices as scientists: 'planning'; 'obtaining evidence' and 'considering evidence and evaluating'. For instance, in learning to plan it is stipulated that they should learn to 'ask questions that can be investigated scientifically and decide how to find answers' and how to 'make a fair test or comparison by changing one factor and observing or measuring the effect while keeping other factors the same'. With their teacher's support, they can learn to ask questions and put forward hypotheses about the phenomena that they encounter in their immediate experience and to test them, in the way that scientists do. What makes the difference to the speed of the toy cars when they are rolled down a ramp? What changes will occur when their clay sculpture is heated up in the kiln? To take a specific example, a student teacher with a Year 1 class, had frozen some plastic insects in large blocks of ice. Initially she was intending that the children should learn about the properties of materials and the changes when they were heated and cooled (Key Stage 1: Science programme of study Sc3 2a – DfEE 1999a). The child began to bash the block of ice with a wooden spoon, however, and then set off to search for a better tool, saying 'I should be able to get this out.' The student teacher soon became aware that he was already hypothesising about physical processes. She realised that she could join in with *his* activities and support him in testing his hypothesis, before jointly considering other possible ways of solving the problem.

Similarly, in the domain of history, children can be encouraged to act as historians, making links with their everyday lives by investigating the past through the memories of their grandparents and the artefacts in their homes, for example, or by experiencing historical artefacts, first hand. Teachers will be aware of children's inclination to spontaneously engage in drawing activities; it is clear that they are already motivated to represent their world visually, through whatever means are available, making meaning in similar ways to artists. Teachers can introduce them to the wider range of media and strategies used by other artists, to help them to develop and fulfil the ideas that arise in their own everyday representational activities.

Transforming learning

Children, then, can be taken by their teachers into avenues of enquiry that lead them beyond their present worlds (Dewey 1938). The differences that can be made to children's learning by helping them to transform what they do in their everyday lives into the more disciplined activities of practitioners in different modes of enquiry, and how this occurs, are well illustrated by Eberbach and Crowely (2009). Their focus was observation in biological science. As they point out, observation in science is not the simple, everyday activity that it might appear to be. In a context where students and teachers were observing birds, they noted the problems with identification and counting that emerged:

> Students could not identify birds in flight, nor could they distinguish between individual birds, making it impossible to generate accurate population counts. As trained observers, ornithologists know what features to observe when identifying kinds of birds and to look for field marks to identify individual birds in flight. Lacking this special-ized knowledge and practice, students were unable to make scientifi-cally meaningful observations.

(p. 40)

Acknowledging the tendency of young children to notice only surface features rather than underlying relationships and to attend to isolated instances rather than all the available evidence, they argue that this is linked to their lack of 'domain knowledge' rather than to their stage of development. Without this knowledge, the phenomena are too complex to explain:

> When children are cast into an activity with inadequate knowledge and instructional support, observation becomes a weak method for collecting data rather than a powerful method for reasoning scientifically. In short, everyday observers fail to notice the right things. Instead, they notice many irrelevant features and behaviours that fail to forge connections or to support deeper understanding of complex phenomena. Disciplinary knowledge, however, can filter, focus, and foster understanding.
>
> (p. 50)

They refer to evidence that shows that children as young as five years old could grasp abstract concepts around form and function as their knowledge developed. Reflecting a socio-cultural perspective they argue that

> The transition from noticing phenomena through one's own 'conceptual spectacles' to observing scientifically principally occurs through participation in shared practices and importantly, shared conversation. Children learn to coordinate expectations and observational evidence when they start to think about, talk about, and publicly organize their observations and knowledge in ways that are consistent with a disciplinary learning community.
>
> (p. 57)

This is a convincing example of how, through joining in with this kind of disciplined and knowledgeable community of enquiry children learn to use tools and resources they might not otherwise encounter. They can be taken beyond familiar territory in other ways too, by introducing them to new environments – to 'distant places', for example, through an international school link, or to castles, museums, beaches and planetariums. All the while their teachers can ensure that the children are fully participating in those ways of asking questions, investigating and interpreting evidence and in the ways that practitioners in the different modes of enquiry do, to help them construct meanings and expand knowledge.

Learning how to learn

In these ways, as teacher and child engage in activities together and the teacher supports the child's participation in the discourses through which knowledge is constructed, the child begins to share, with their teachers, a 'meta-level' of thinking – building understanding of the activities, constructing meaning and developing insight around central principles and concepts. As they construct this meta-level of understanding, children are learning how to learn, again as members of the communities that engage in these enquiring practices in the wider world. This is rather different from learning how to learn in the narrow sense of being a pupil at school and conforming to the practices which that entails. From this perspective it becomes clearer how educational practices are distinct from those of schooling. It provides the tools for what Bruner referred to as 'going beyond the information given'. If children learn how to use the curriculum toolkit – its enquiring practices and ways of knowing – they have the means, potentially, to learn independently of the teacher by applying what they know in new situations.

This brings back into view the idea that the key to this kind of learning how to learn – and 'thinking about how we think' – is talking, or dialogue, in the context of collaborative practices. Through the conscious articulation of what is going on and how things are being done, the child learns not only the words and terminology, but what is appropriate to say and how to say it; what kinds of reasoning help to construct meanings within a particular community of practice and enquiry.

This kind of meta-level thinking tends to be lacking in classrooms, as Mercer has observed: 'the use of language as a toolkit for collective reasoning is not a common topic in classroom talk, nor does it figure explicitly in any school curriculum' (2001 p. 147).

He argues that it can best be achieved by making explicit the 'ground rules' for talking together. (Mercer 1995; 2002; Mercer and Littleton 2007). Children are often left to 'work out the "ground rules" of effective discussion for themselves' (Mercer 2002 p.148). For Mercer, it is a crucial role for teachers in classrooms to teach children more explicitly about the ways in which language is used, by engaging them in the appropriate practices in thinking and reasoning, shared through talk. In this way, through scaffolding they can support the child, initially, in doing what they could not do on their own, to establish the understanding and skills to be able to do it independently and to progressively broaden and deepen their learning. It is at this level that teachers can begin to engage children in the 'higher-order thinking' that Galton found to be missing in classroom interaction (see Chapter 4). But again, the scaffolding must be of an appropriate kind (see Chapters 3 and 5), otherwise, as Mercer says, it is not scaffolding – just 'help' (Mercer 1995 p. 74). It is perhaps better construed as 'guided participation' (see Chapter 3).

Transforming the practices that generate knowledge

To fulfil the role of guide, teachers must, then, be able to support their students as they construct meaning, creatively, in different ways to expand the breadth and depth of their learning. I have been intimating that to be able to induct children into these 'educational discourses' – these important ways of making meaning and creating knowledge that are available in the wider culture – teachers must, themselves, have an understanding of these cultural resources for constructing knowledge. To have sufficient familiarity with and insight into the principles and practices of specific modes of enquiry, they must themselves be participants in these communities of practice – mature members of them or 'elders' (Wells and Claxton 2002). They need to not only 'know' the factual information that those practices might have generated, but to have an understanding of how that knowledge was arrived at. Their knowledge and understanding of the form of enquiry should, moreover, be communicable to children. This might be what Shulman (1987) calls 'pedagogical content knowledge'.

I have been referring to the familiar curriculum areas such as history, science and maths. There might be an inclination, in thinking in terms of a familiar list of distinctive disciplines or discourses, to revert to the view that the knowledge that teachers need pre-exists as some kind of reified knowledge that they 'acquire' and then pass on to their pupils as a body of content. I will re-emphasise here, however, the socio-cultural view of the nature of knowledge as the product of human social activity and that different modes of enquiry, even when they are characterised as disciplines through which new knowledge can be generated, are not seen as 'given', immutable or 'necessary forms' (as, for example, Hirst's original account implied). It is clearly important for primary teachers to know how to engage children in the practices of different forms of enquiry, to actively represent and model those practices with the children they are teaching. At the same time, from a socio-cultural perspective they would need to recognise that the knowledge generated by these practices is continually under construction and re-construction by all those who participate in their making – in other words, by *all* learners. This goes for the way the different disciplines or modes of enquiry are identified and how they are classified as distinctive as well. The 'list' of different disciplines, referred to in accounts of the curriculum, or in its design, is forever subject to being extended, re-framed or re-conceptualised. Ways of knowledge making, as well as the knowledge made are always in a continual state of flux – of formation and re-formation. Practices that have been valued in the past may not necessarily serve the purposes of the present or the future. Others proliferate and might take priority. In presenting a socio-cultural view of the curriculum I have not intended to identify exactly the way in which the 'valued cultural practices' should be selected or classified.

The discussion of collaborative, enquiry-based teaching leads back to the idea of both teachers' and children's activities as generative of knowledge (see Chapter 3). Children not only learn the language of the subject, but their part in shaping it is acknowledged. With their own powers of meaning making and invention – through actively participating in these practices themselves – they not only construct their own meanings but also contribute to the continued, collective shaping and re-shaping of these practices and of cultures. In other words, as they participate in these areas of human activity, through their reasoning they can create new interpretations and meanings, contributing to the construction and re-construction of knowledge and knowledge making practices. As Bruner has argued (1986; 1996), this is a process not only of using cultural resources to construct meaning within the culture but also of transforming the culture itself.

This may sound too abstract or improbable, but when meanings and knowledge are understood as being generated through social practices, the activities of all participants play their part. When teachers recognise learning as participation and collaboration, they may take a different view of a young child's art work, for instance, where the child has used the practices of drawing to invent their own way of representing an idea, or, their writing, where they have used the conventions of narrative to construct their own story. They may respond differently to what children say about a historical event; what they notice when they carry out an experiment; or the patterns they observe in a mathematical investigation. They will acknowledge children's creative contribution. They may take a more responsive view of children's subversion of the way things are traditionally done, for example, or of their supposed 'misconceptions'. The teacher who understands learning from this perspective, who connects with children as co-constructors of knowledge may see new ways of using familiar tools and, as a result, may arrive at new understandings themselves (see also Chapter 8). They too, are learners.

Children as participants: which communities of practice; whose purposes?

The argument that collaborative activities must have authentically shared purposes that build on what children are already learning through their own, purposeful activities might well suggest that the curriculum should be built entirely around the immediate concerns and activities of children. In the days of child-centred education, philosophers of education often debated whether 'disciplines' or 'interests' should form the basis of the curriculum, and whether teachers should be concerned with what was 'in the interests' of the child or with what the child was interested in (Wilson 1971; Dearden 1968; Pring 1976).

A point that was raised by such writers was that the apparent dichotomy here was actually a false one, since children's interests are, in any case, learned. This clearly still applies on the socio-cultural analysis: activities that children participate in constitute their learning and new activities at school will introduce new learning. This is the case for traditional curriculum activities as well as for any others. New interests and motivations to engage in the activities of mathematicians and scientists, for example, can develop. While some teachers will see this simply as introducing children to what goes on in school, others will see it as providing young people with the opportunity to share their own passion. As children join in with the activities of these adult communities, new avenues for their curiosity will open up and their own questions will contribute to the collective concerns of those who already committed to these practices.

As well as making available to children the communities of practice of scientists, historians, artists and designers and other traditional disciplines teachers can also open the door to the activities of communities of practice that cross the boundaries of the traditional disciplines – to other worlds such as engineering, archaeology or filmmaking, for example. In addition, they can focus on contemporary concerns that some children would love to engage with. For instance, they can help children to genuinely participate, as active researchers and decision makers (Cox et al. 2010), in the kind of current and pressing matters that face them as 'global citizens' and often preoccupy them – issues around sustainable development and the environment, for example.

Children's existing awareness of such matters, however, reminds us that children live out their lives in other contexts, in their own communities, all with their own practices: the family; the local neighbourhood; a cultural group; a peer group; an on-line group; and countless other 'communities of practice', either within or beyond these, to which a child might belong. This brings into focus the possibility of the teacher participating in these activities – in the *children's* social contexts.

The adult, bringing their knowledge as a participant in other communities of practice, can make their own contribution to children's practices. As an educator they can bring the resources and tools of the modes of enquiry and discourses (the 'teaching curriculum') to help children deepen and enrich the meanings they construct within their own contexts. As the 'newcomer' participating in the children's activities, the teacher can learn from them, and can also bring their enquiring mind set, their mathematician's and historian's (for example) toolkit and insights. Again, children's own meaning-making activities can be shaped and expanded in asking questions, interpreting evidence, representing ideas and constructing knowledge in the company of established, knowledgeable practitioners in the different disciplines or communities of enquiry, who are already familiar with them.

This would shift the emphasis away from the teaching agenda of discrete subjects such as mathematics and science, and towards the children's concerns, helping them to learn about their worlds *through* these enquiring activities. (This was a position adopted by those who advocated a developmental curriculum many years ago – see Blenkin and Kelly 1981.) This affords the possibility of genuine power sharing with the children. The prioritised activities and concerns are those of their particular communities – which are not dominated by teachers or even by scientists or historians.

That said, the teacher needs to be acutely aware that the established power relations might, nevertheless, lead to children's activities – their goals and purposes – being taken over by the adult as the children defer to their apparent authority, even though the adult is the 'newcomer' in the children's domain. There is always the possibility that children's activities might be appropriated by teachers to serve the ends that they themselves have in mind in relation to the 'teaching curriculum' and the school's priorities – say, learning maths or learning science – rather than children's own authentic purposes (see, also, Chapter 6). This awareness is essential if the activities are to be truly collaborative. The approach again calls for a shift in teachers' understanding – it is not merely a matter of making existing curriculum activities more 'interesting' or 'enjoyable'.

As Hipkins, Reid and Bull (2010 p. 115) argue, this approach for personalising the curriculum 'goes beyond the dominant rationale . . . as being about relevance and motivation (important as they are) and incorporates socio-critical understandings about power and knowledge'. Citing Zipin and Reid (2008), they suggest that the curriculum 'starts with the lived experience of students, families and their communities'. As Hughes et al. (2005) also argued (see Chapter 6), this changes the traditional deficit view of the 'cultural knowledge and skills from "disadvantaged" communities'. Instead these are seen as a benefit.

Aims of education

These choices about what should constitute the curriculum take us back to the question of what the aims of educators might be. I do not mean to imply that adults must always defer to children. As mature members of the wider community of educators they legitimately engage in decision making as to what activities may have positive value for children. But if we take account of the above, then they will be taken responsively and in negotiation with children themselves.

I have already suggested that the transcendental sort of justification for learning particular 'forms of knowledge' for their own sake no longer suffices as the basis for the aims of education. Both White (2007) and Alexander (2010) have stated that the old argument that these subjects are included in the curriculum because they are simply worth studying in their own right 'cuts no ice' in the twenty-first century. It is, rather, a case of competing justifications, which depend on how different social practices are valued. There may be those who would argue, even from within a socio-cultural perspective, that in school, children should participate, exclusively, in the communities of practice of the traditional forms of enquiry, on the grounds that these are valuable practices to learn, in and for themselves. I hope I have presented some of the limitations of this approach.

Teachers might turn, instead, to such aims as those offered in the *Cambridge Review* (Alexander 2010) of 'well-being' and 'empowerment'. These embrace the value of the contribution of disciplined modes of enquiry or educational discourses to children's meaning making in the ways I've described: children who are equipped with the 'cultural toolkit' they provide will certainly be empowered. They also legitimise specific kinds of influence that teachers might bring to bear on the selection of activities in which they and the children might engage in school, to ensure that they promote well-being and empowerment and do not have any damaging or disempowering consequences. This does not rule out the prioritisation of children's own concerns and pursuits – as long as these activities are not detrimental to the achievement of these aims.

There remains a crucial question: is the emphasis to be on the achievement of these aims 'now' or 'later'? If children's education is meant to secure their well-being and empowerment as adults, then there is an argument that their current activities in school should be focused on practising – in the sense of rehearsing – the use of tools and resources that will help them to achieve these ends in the future. This might justify giving attention in school solely to the activities and purposes prioritised by adults, since it is they who are in the position to anticipate children's future needs. If, however, educationalists are concerned with children's *present* well-being and their empowerment *now*, as children, then overriding consideration should be given to how children's and teachers' activities in school might contribute to these in their lives as they live them. To achieve these ends, teachers would be obliged to take full account of children's *current* concerns in the ways I have been suggesting and to support children in doing what they value doing in their own communities of practice in the here and now.

Again, as in the last chapter, I would argue that it is a respect for children as people, who have a contribution to make, that would impel curriculum planners, schools and teachers to ensure that children were able to use cultural tools to further their own interests and concerns, and those of their out-of-school communities. This ultimately provides the justification for a curriculum that is negotiated between children and their teachers, where children's existing concerns are taken seriously and the here and now is all-important. Their learning in the culturally valued modes of enquiry, or educational discourses – guided by adults – occurs as these contribute to the children's own purposeful activities and to the achievement of their own ends, as children.

Cross-curricular approaches

The arguments I have been developing so far suggest that when children are motivated by their own purposeful activity, where the tasks they are engaged in are meaningful to them, when, in a sense, there is a real job to be done, whether in playful activity or in 'real life', there is every opportunity for the teacher to support children's learning in directions that have point or purpose in children's terms. In ensuring that children themselves have the opportunities to have some genuine input into decisions about their own activities in school, through negotiation, the contribution of all participants is more equitably balanced. Children can bring their enthusiasms, projects and questions; and teachers contribute to the resources for learning with their knowledge of the tools, and the *range* of these tools, that will help children achieve their purposes. With their access to educational discourses and the concerns of the wider world, teachers are in a position to engage children in ways of knowing, understanding and acting that help the children to develop and achieve their own ends. Both children and teachers would join in with getting things done for reasons that had some significance in the children's 'real' lives. In other words, classroom activities would engage in the worlds of children both within and beyond the school. This provides a rationale for the renewed enthusiasm for 'cross-curricular' teaching in English primary schools.

In the wake of the Primary National Strategy (PNS) (DCSF 2003) there has been something of a sense of release from the rather rigid structures that have evolved since the inception of the National Curriculum. Subject-based timetables and whole-class teacher-led approaches had become the norm – even though the legislation did not require them. This arrangement enabled teachers to comply with the subject-driven agenda and to more easily prove they were doing so to inspectors. The PNS, however, brought in an official change of emphasis. As its title – *Excellence and Enjoyment* – suggests, it combined encouragement to foster enjoyment with the imperative to maintain performative success. In research carried out by Troman, Jeffrey and Raggl (2007) it was clear that 'cross-curricular' approaches were becoming popular once again. These researchers' quotations from headteachers' and teachers' responses in interview give a flavour of the kind of changes that they found to have been occurring:

> '. . . I don't know where this is coming from or if it's official policy but I know it's happening in a lot of schools because I've spoken to teachers about it and I know – speaking to people when you go on training courses, that what's happening, is it's beginning to move back towards the topic-based approach and linking things together and having experiences and making a little bit more fun' (Tamara, Foundation Teacher, Albert Road).
>
> (Troman, Jeffrey and Raggl 2007 p. 558)

Teachers have interpreted the policy text in their own terms and were using it to justify preferred curriculum changes:

'We are trying in this school the idea of bringing excitement back into look at our curriculum planning in school and to make the cross curricular links and to get away from the National Curriculum and Literacy and Numeracy Strategy' (Mary, Foundation, Green Common).

(p. 558)

The researchers go on to cite the headteacher of Green Common School:

'We've had Healthy Schools Week, an Arts Week, a Science Week, a Friendship Week, a History Week and a Careers Week and the teachers love it and the kids love it. In our "World of Work" we got lots of people coming in to talk about their jobs . . . It was like the joy of teaching in the 70s and 80s when you didn't have the curriculum restrictions and there was a lot of freedom. It takes you back to a situation of dressing up and painting at 9.00 in the morning. A lot of the teachers who've been through training in the 80s and 90s think you have to do the literacy hour first but I tell them it isn't true. One morning they took the children over to the Common at 9 o'clock in the frost and let them paint frosty pictures and then they wrote poems. To me that's wonderful. To me that's what they should be doing and the children loved it and . . . So the teachers are becoming freer . . .' (Christine, head teacher, Green Common).

(p. 562)

This may, on the surface, seem consistent with the arguments I have been developing. There are, however, potential pitfalls. While the opportunity to develop these practices was clearly welcomed by the teachers, the move towards more 'creative teaching' and the officially backed trend towards more liberalised approaches took place without any policy-level reappraisal of aims of education or epistemological principles. With the demise of the Rose Review and the government sidelining of the Cambridge Review this vacuum remains. Teachers may have been developing their approaches in a context of nostalgia for past 'freedoms' rather than analysis of learning and the curriculum. The extent to which 'cross-curricular' experiences comprise meaningful participation in disciplined modes of enquiry or educational discourses must therefore be addressed. Are these cultural practices being made available to children – are children in classrooms learning to pose distinctively different sorts of questions, to hypothesise and to test their hypotheses in ways relevant to these disciplined practices? Are they seeking appropriate evidence, interpreting and analysing it, conceptualising experiences and developing ideas? Are they engaged in reasoning; are they constructing arguments and critiquing and challenging them? Are they coming up with imaginative and inventive solutions, points of view and artefacts? In short, are they developing the tools on which creativity is based? There is a risk – and I simply raise this without making any assumptions about actual practices – that they might engage instead in rather unchallenging 'occupational activities' that do not make use of the valuable cultural resources that schools and teachers at their best can offer. Furthermore, does cross-curricular teaching deter teachers from becoming fully engaged, themselves, in such activities, so that they are no longer equipped to build these educational communities of enquiring practice in their classrooms?

Alternatively, cross-curricular teaching that is based on a rationale of the kind I have been proposing has the potential to provide rich educational opportunities through which children can develop and extend their own concerns and agency. For example, children who decide, in negotiation with their teachers, to conserve their local environment (as a cross-curricular project) can draw on the resources offered by historical and geographical enquiry to construct their understandings of what conservation and sustainability might mean; to use scientific investigational tools to find out how to best maintain the bio-diversity in their school grounds, say, and to decide on positive interventions. They can use the resources of art and design to improve the visual and tactile qualities of their surroundings. They can use mathematics to work out how well they are doing – not how well they are doing in maths as such, but how well they are doing with their conservation strategies. In doing this, in genuinely collaborative contexts and with the skilful guidance of their activities by their teacher, they are at the same time constructing their understandings of how they are using these tools, so they can apply them independently and appropriately in other contexts.

Concluding reflections

In the background of the discussion in Chapter 4 was the assumption that schools are institutional settings established to help children to learn, which have the specific designated purpose of teaching a curriculum. In this chapter I've developed the discussion around the school as a context that provides this 'teaching curriculum' (Lave and Wenger 1991). Until the child enters school, their 'learning curriculum' is 'the field of resources' of the 'communities of practice' in the naturalistic context of their everyday lives. Their activities – and thus their learning – have been motivated by their own purposes and intentions as active meaning makers in their home and family contexts or in the setting in which they are looked after. Their learning may have been supported through guided participation by their parents or other adults in their family, their carers or their local community and sometimes by their peers in their play. The school, in contrast, in introducing children to a 'teaching curriculum' provides access to specific resources for learning. The teacher's intentional teaching is framed by the valued cultural practices – the traditional modes of enquiry or discourses as well as other activities – through which meanings are made in the world and through which knowledge is generated. The curriculum is a representation of these practices. It provides access to areas of learning that the wider society deems important and that children may not otherwise encounter through their everyday lives. In effect, the 'learning curriculum' is now extended to the school situation with its new activities.

Through participation as newcomers in these communities of practice, children learn how to engage in these activities. In the context of joint activity, teachers can share with children how to go about a scientific investigation, for instance, or how to construct and communicate ideas in artistic media, how to tackle a mathematical problem and how to interpret a historical artefact. The teacher creates a context where children can participate in these practices and can construct new meanings through learning new ways of acting, thinking and knowing. The activities have point and purpose to those who practise them. As these are to some extent outside children's everyday experiences, the teacher has a role in guiding their participation carefully if they are to meaningfully engage in them.

As the adults who are inducting children into these practices (the 'teaching curriculum'), it does seem that it is teachers who hold the power to determine the nature and direction of the activities. It appears that the child's own purposes and intentions might be appropriated by these more expert participants. In the predominant classroom culture, the child is not in control of the direction of their own learning the way they have been in everyday settings outside school. As I pointed out in earlier chapters, in the new social setting of the school, the child must come to terms with formalised practices that call for particular kinds of responses.

The new communities of practice of the school, however, co-exist with the child's other community contexts. The disruption to the more self-directed pattern of activity in their everyday lives can seem to the child to impose limits on their scope for self-determined action, especially where the values and practices of outside-school communities are very different to those of the school, as is the case for some children. There is a tension, here, between the activities and values of school and its curriculum and those of the child. Again, these different values are inevitably influenced by power structures that exist within the wider culture which tend to prioritise the school.

If, as I have argued, through participating in these activities jointly with their teachers, children learn how to learn, to learn how to use these cultural tools, then when are children to have the opportunity to use them independently in new situations? Is their learning only a preparation for adulthood? I have tried to present the case for providing those opportunities in the here and now, when they are living their lives as children.

Lave and Wenger (1991) have shown that learning is not restricted to the pedagogical intentions of the teacher or the official curriculum. It is the situation as a whole – the classroom, the complexity of its relationships, its values and purposes, its multiplicity of activities that constitute the 'learning curriculum'. The kind of negotiated approach to the curriculum I am suggesting potentially offers a very different kind of experience for the child in terms of their developing identity as a child who matters, who has rights as well as responsibilities and who contributes more fully as a human being in a democratic society. Teaching the curriculum by providing contexts where children can actually participate as a newcomer along with their more expert teachers in its different communities of enquiry and discourses, gives them access to the culture's resources to achieve negotiated and shared purposes. This means that their learning is arguably of a different kind and quality. There is the potential for re-shaping the classroom culture, around relationships, activities and learning that are more flexible, more cohesive, more constructive and more democratic. And these need not be in conflict with achievement agendas. As Bruner (1996 p. 84), in arguing for a 'renewal and re-consideration of . . . "school culture"' and in advocating the creation of 'communities of learners' suggests:

> Indeed, on the basis of what we have learned in recent years about human learning – that it is best when it is participatory, proactive, communal, collaborative, and given over to constructing meanings rather than receiving them – we even do better at teaching science, math, and languages in such schools than in more traditional ones.

Issues for teachers

- To what extent do you feel that you are covering the curriculum and how does that affect your teaching?
- What is your conception of 'subjects' or 'curriculum areas' in your teaching and how might you see them differently?
- How does your teaching of the curriculum relate to broader aims of education? Are your visions for primary education changing?
- How is learning across the curriculum manifested in the activities in your classroom? How might this be changed?

- If you negotiated the activities around children's purposes and joined in with them collaboratively, how might you contribute to the learning as a knowledgeable adult, familiar with disciplined curricular modes of enquiry?
- If you negotiated the activities around children's purposes and joined in with them collaboratively, how might the relationships and interaction in your classroom change?
- What kind of contribution might the activities within your classroom community of practice (the children and you) make in the wider culture?
- To what extent and in what ways is your understanding of learning and the curriculum changing?

8 Making sense of learning: assessment in context

Chapter overview

In this chapter, I consider some of the implications that the dominant, performative model of teaching in English primary schools has for assessment practices, and present a contrasting view of assessment from the alternative perspectives that I have been exploring. I start by considering how the dominant approach influences the way the curriculum is implemented in classrooms – how the school's 'teaching curriculum' is actually taught – and discuss what this means for assessment. I go on to discuss the developments that have taken place in relation to formative assessment through the 'assessment for learning' approach and look at these, critically, from that alternative point of view. I show how assessment can be collaborative and can help to improve the quality of participation and, therefore, learning.

Summative and formative assessment

In a culture where the achievement of targets is paramount, the measurable outcomes of children's learning are an obvious focus for assessment. This 'summative' form of assessment, of what children know, understand and can do, are epitomised in the SATs, but summative assessment is not limited to such high stakes types of testing. It is perhaps best defined by its purpose, which is to identify what has been learned as an outcome of teaching and learning activities – for example, what has been learned as a result of any particular unit or sequence of teaching. As the assessment of outcomes, summative assessment can be used to compare one child's performance against that of another. It can be used normatively, to create benchmarks, for instance, such as the expectation that a child at the end of Key Stage 2 should be able to achieve Level 4 in their SATs. By contrast, formative assessment has a quite different purpose. It is the kind of assessment that teachers make of children's learning 'in progress'. As Black et al. (2003 p.122) define it: 'formative assessment is a process, one in which information about learning is *evoked* and then *used* to modify the teaching and learning activities in which teachers and students are engaged'. It yields the kind of insight into the child's current understanding and knowledge that teachers need if they are to take the child's learning forward. Its specific purpose is to assess 'where a child is' so that the teacher can decide what provision to make for further learning. I should point out that the language I am using here assumes that the teacher determines the direction of this learning – a position that I shall continue to question in the discussion below.

Covering content or setting objectives?

The overriding significance given in English schools to summative assessments of the 'high stakes testing' kind (see Chapter 2) may be one of the reasons why teachers feel compelled to cover the content of the curriculum (see Chapter 7). One point to be made, in any discussion of the curriculum and how it is to be taught, is that there is a difference between thinking about the material that is to be covered – the content – and thinking about what the children are intended to learn: between what the teacher is teaching and what the 'learning objectives' are. In this chapter I shall continue the discussion, begun in earlier chapters, of the possible shortcomings of a model of teaching that is driven by learning objectives. But to begin with, it is helpful to point out that the shift in focus from what is taught to what is to be learned clearly gives greater emphasis to assessment – it draws attention to what comes about as a result of the teaching – the outcomes.

As I have said, when the emphasis is on covering content the material that is taught is arguably most readily conceived as 'information' – rather than, for example, skills or attitudes. This perhaps explains why the default approach to teaching can so readily become 'transmission' (see Chapter 7) and why the simple recall of factual knowledge might seem to be the implicit approach to classroom assessment. I discussed in Chapter 4 how questioning, of a kind that focuses on eliciting this kind of response, is a very common form of interaction between teacher and child. While the recall of factual knowledge may be one kind of outcome – for example, the child is to learn that Henry VIII had six wives or that water boils when it is heated – it is clearly not the only kind. A child can learn how to use multiplication, for example, and build their understanding of mathematical concepts; how to use oil pastels or how to write a report. They can learn to value the opinions of others or learn why it might be a good idea to recycle materials. The learning objectives, then, can be seen in terms of factual knowledge or information, but they can also be identified as concepts, skills, or values and attitudes, for example.

Pre-specification is implicit in the term 'objective', as an objective is what someone *sets out* to achieve. Where a unit of teaching is intended to achieve a particular learning objective, the teacher would plan the teaching sequence specifically to that end. The basic unit of planning is often a 'lesson'. The objective would relate to a particular element of the curriculum and the teacher would need to decide what content and what teaching and learning strategies would enable the child to meet it. The overriding purpose of the teacher's and children's activities during the lesson would be to bring about the desired learning. On this approach to planning, teaching and assessment, there is a clear link between the learning objective and the outcome, with the teaching strategy designed to lead directly to the achievement of the intended learning – it is a 'linear' model (see also Chapters 2 and 3). A successful lesson, in these terms, is one where the assessment shows that the objective has been achieved. The implicit purpose of assessment at the end of the teaching sequence is summative: has the child met the objective or not?

The teacher who shifts their focus, then, from 'covering material' to thinking about objectives is implicitly giving attention to assessment, as the issue is not 'have I taught that' but 'have the children achieved the learning objectives'. The objectives-driven approach does seem to provide an explicit framework for evaluating the effectiveness or otherwise of teaching because it has this unambiguous focus on children's learning. I want to suggest, however, that this approach to curriculum and assessment, which is orientated towards goals that are predetermined by the 'teaching curriculum', is open to challenge from the social constructivist, socio-cultural perspectives. I have already noted the dominance of teaching that is driven by pre-specified objectives (see Chapters 2 and 3). The objectives-driven model of planning and assessment has become such an accepted way of thinking about teaching that younger teachers, at least, are not always aware that any alternative is conceivable. Its status as official policy has been endorsed by Ofsted inspections and by the 'Professional Standards'. For example, in order to achieve Qualified Teacher Status, one of the Standards specifies that prospective teachers must be able to 'Assess the learning needs of those they teach in order to set challenging learning objectives' (TDA 2007 p. 11).

Some difficulties with objectives-driven teaching

A closer examination of the objectives-driven approach, however, reveals some of the possible difficulties it can present for judging the success or effectiveness of teaching. First, there are issues related to how it is implemented; second there are theoretical considerations. With regard to implementation, the approach requires the teacher to select teaching strategies that will actually provide the necessary opportunities for the child to achieve the learning objective. This demands careful analysis of the strategies to ensure that they do indeed provide appropriate opportunities. To take an example: a teacher might set about planning a lesson where the objective is for the children to learn how to design a moving toy. The way the objective is conceived is important. For instance, the teacher might decide that *'learning how to'* implies that she should arrange the lesson so the children can actually build the toy. But then, consider the following scenario. The teacher decides to simply show the children how the parts of the toy are put together with the idea that the children will replicate that; she does not discuss what she is showing the children in terms of the design process but only in general practical terms ('put the split pin here, like so and then bend this piece of card round here . . .'). Imagine she does not include any explanation of how the design decisions have been made, but is only concerned that the children arrive at a finished toy that moves in the same way as her model. (This is an example of what Mercer would describe as 'help' rather than appropriate 'scaffolding' – see Chapter 7). In this case, it could be argued that the teacher has given insufficient attention to the analysis of 'learning how to *design*' the toy. The children have not been given the opportunity to actually engage with the practical and cognitive process of designing as such – only with making.

Designing a moving toy requires the designer to think about the best ways of relating the way they make the toy to how they want it to move – in other words, making decisions about its form so that it is related to its function. At the very least, for the children to fulfil the learning objective, they must engage in some 'design thinking'. To be able to say that the children have learned 'how to design' a moving toy, arguably they would need to make their own design decisions, using their own ideas and relating their decisions about how to make their toy move to what they, as designer, intend it to do. Their teacher would provide appropriate scaffolding, which may entail modelling designing activity. This is not to suggest solving the children's own design problems for them, or merely helping them. This would amount to presenting the children with the teacher's own solution, rather than engaging them in thinking through the problem and investigating solutions. Rather, the teacher should be enabling the children to see how designers (this community of practitioners) go about solving design problems. In order to articulate the principles that are involved, the teacher and children would need to engage in dialogue: the teacher would need to talk with the children about what they and the children were doing. In summary, it is collaborative activity; guided participation. If children are to develop designing *skills*, they must actually do the designing and making. For them to build their *understanding*, they would be using the various mediational means of the design activity – for example, drawing, model making, constructing artefacts – along with dialogue. Of course, what does actually count as 'designing activity' is up for debate, but I have used this example to show how what might appear to be straightforward can actually be complex.

My point here, however, is not so much about the quality of the children's learning – though of course that is central. I am making the further point about the potential for mismatch between the intended learning and the task. I am not suggesting that *no* worthwhile learning went on in my imagined scenario where the children simply replicated what the teacher had made. This may have had value in some ways. I am simply saying that this was not the learning that the teacher intended – her objective was for the children to learn how to design the toy. Unless the teacher's strategy is carefully analysed in relation to the intended learning outcome, then her attempts to assess the children's achievement of it will always be thwarted. The teacher may think the children are 'achieving the learning objective', when indeed they are not at all, because the opportunities to do so have not been made available in the teaching strategy. In the example I have given, in order to analyse the objective and to provide the relevant learning opportunities the teacher required a more in-depth knowledge and understanding of designing, as well as understanding of how to engage children in this activity and its modes of enquiry. When the 'learning curriculum' is considered it is clear that the children would not have actually learned what the teacher intended. What the children may, in fact, have learned from the situation as a whole has gone unacknowledged. In the example I gave, they may learn how to successfully follow the teacher's instructions, for instance, or how difficult it was to copy what the teacher had done.

Even when the teaching strategies and the objectives are well matched some children's learning may go unacknowledged. Some may have failed to meet the teacher's learning objective, but will, nevertheless, have been learning. Again, as this learning was not the focus of the teacher's assessment, it is likely to have been missed: when the teacher is looking for evidence that children have achieved the predetermined objective for the lesson rather than looking out for what each child is actually learning (the 'learning curriculum'), the teacher may well discount evidence of other learning. In their efforts to keep children on track (the teacher's track), they may ignore the meanings that the children themselves have constructed.

A further example will similarly illustrate the need to ensure that the teaching and learning strategies make it possible for the children to achieve the objectives. This was a situation I encountered where a student teacher was intending that six-year-old children would learn how to give change. She introduced them to the idea of the shopkeeper 'taking away' or subtracting the price of the item they were buying, from the amount of money the customer was offering. This was explained and the children spent a while practising taking away. When it came to them actually putting this into practice with goods to buy that she had prepared and coins she had provided, they were flummoxed and, though they spent some time 'shopping' and trying to apply what she had suggested, they did not learn much about how to give change. To her credit, the student teacher could see this straight away from her initial assessments. What she had failed to do was to analyse the situation from the children's point of view to see that they were not actually able to engage in the practice of 'giving change' and did not yet share her understanding of it. They needed their 'shopping' to be contextualised within the social practice of trading, or exchanging, one item for another – the goods to be bought which were worth a certain amount and the coins proffered which had a different value. Using language they already understood, they could then consider whether the exchange was fair and make up the difference so that it was. The operation was one of 'finding the difference' (comparing two amounts) rather than subtracting or taking away. The student teacher needed knowledge of both the mathematical operations and how to contextualise them, bearing in mind the extent to which children would be able to meaningfully participate in the activity. To know this, she needed insight into their existing conceptions. The situation required careful analysis of the objectives, the proposed activity itself and the children's possible conceptions, both prior to and within the lesson.

Who directs the learning?

These examples highlight a second, more theoretical point, which leads back to the issue of how children learn. The learning objectives, set by the teacher, by their nature constrain the kinds of activities that the children engage in, and therefore the kind of learning that is going on. Once again, it is evident that the children, as active meaning makers, are obliged, in these situations, to adapt their thinking, as best they can, to the context created by the teacher (see Chapter 4). The teacher's purposes are paramount; the child's self-directed activity and own intentions are, in effect, less valued than the teacher's.

To return to the distinction between summative and formative assessment, it would be wrong to assume that objectives-driven teaching necessarily, and only, makes use of summative assessment to check whether the objective has been met. Clearly, teachers whose teaching is driven by objectives may use formative assessment to inform their teaching. When the objective is preset, however, and the teacher has a particular range of evidence in mind around the intended learning, this does have implications for formative assessment practices. The fact, noted above, that the teacher is likely to be drawn towards particular responses from the child and to ignore other evidence may mean that she fails to engage with the different ways in which individual children might be making sense of what is going on. In situations where the teacher is interacting with a group of children, this may well account for the practice – noted as common in many whole-class situations (see also Chapter 4) – of the teacher focusing only on the child who provides the 'right answer'. This is the answer that the teacher already has in mind as the evidence of 'correct' understanding (Black et al. 2003). The teacher may look for this preferred answer from a child before she goes on, but once the 'correct' answer is given by a single child it is common practice for the teacher to then move on to the next step. In other words, the teacher's formative assessment is based not on the learning needs of all the children but on the teacher's need to take the lesson forward towards the objective.

As the teacher moves on to new material, those children who have not understood in the way the teacher intended, may be left to find their own coping strategies. As a result they can often engage in what has been referred to as 'off-task behaviour' – which creates its own focus for intervention (see for example Kern and Clemens 2007). Perhaps this is, in reality, 'other task' behaviour. 'Off-task' suggests deviance. The child may have diverged from the teacher's agenda because they have been unable to participate in the activities, but they have found something else to do and to learn. Sometimes, such a situation can result in, seemingly, disruptive activities on the part of the child to redeem the loss of self-esteem they experienced through their apparent failure to follow the teacher. The concept of 'off-task' behaviour in itself illustrates only too clearly that teaching is usually conceived as teacher directed and teacher controlled.

Interestingly, it is common for teachers who teach to objectives to not, in fact, keep to their original lesson plan. This will almost inevitably be a result of the teacher giving attention to formative assessment of the children during the lesson. As the lesson proceeds and as the teacher interprets the evidence of the children's responses, she may well realise that what she had planned is inappropriate. In short, the children do not understand – though what this means, looked at from a constructivist and socio-cultural perspective, is that they are not able to build their understanding in the way the teacher intended. As a result, the teacher may decide to change tack in their teaching. From the perspective of the objectives-led linear approach, this can be seen as failure on the part of the teacher. On the one hand, she may have failed to start from a clear understanding of the children's existing conceptions. As I have shown, prior assessment is a prerequisite for any planning that aspires to build formatively on children's existing understanding and knowledge. On the other hand, it can be deemed a failure because the children did not achieve the intended learning outcomes. On the linear model of planning, where the teacher sets out to achieve specific learning outcomes, a successful lesson is one where the assessment, related to the pre-specified learning objective, shows that the objective has indeed been achieved.

It may seem odd, if lessons can so often 'fail' in this sense, that the linear model remains the predominant approach to planning. The reflective teacher, mindful of the need to adapt her teaching to her assessment of the children's learning and responding to the evidence that is presented by what the children do and say, deviates from or adapts the plan despite the fact that this will result in failure to achieve the objective. It seems that the teacher, in this situation, who follows the orthodoxy of planning to objectives, but is at the same time aware of the evidence of children's conceptions, interpretations and learning, is caught in a dilemma. Do they persevere with their original plan and delude themselves and others with assumptions that the children are learning what they (the teacher) had intended, when in reality they are not, or do they act in accordance with their insights into the children's actual learning? The latter course of action seems to both do justice to children's learning and to undermine the case for objectives-driven planning.

Alternatives to goal-orientated teaching

The Assessment for Learning (AfL) initiatives that have taken hold in recent years certainly point in a direction that does justice to children's learning (Black and Wiliam 1998a; Black et al. 2003; Black et al. 2004). For instance, the strategies they advocate have helped teachers to improve their questioning, to gain insight into and to develop children's own thinking.

> This led to richer discourse, in which the teachers evoked a wealth of information from which to judge the current understanding of their students. More importantly, they had evidence on which to plan the next steps in learning so that the challenge and pace of lessons could be directed by formative assessment evidence rather than simply following some prescribed agenda.
>
> (Black et al. 2003 p. 41)

As I shall go on to suggest, however, while the AfL approach implicitly endorses the alternative account I have been developing, it seems to stop short of adopting it fully. Instead, it appears to maintain a performative goal-orientated perspective.

The AfL initiatives were a practical response to the review of the research evidence related to assessment practices, carried out by Black and Wiliam (1998b): 'This review covered a very wide range of published research and provided evidence that formative assessment raises standards and that current practices are weak' (Black et al. 2003 p. 6). The kind of shortcomings in everyday assessment practices that were identified included those that directly affected learning, such as teachers' use of tests that 'encourage rote and superficial learning' and the 'tendency to emphasise quantity and presentation of work and to neglect quality in relation to learning' (p. 11), which was apparent in primary teachers' assessment practices in particular. These difficulties all clearly suggest that teachers were concerned with outcomes and coverage rather than learning itself. Black and Wiliam had found that the learning function of assessment, and the guidance that assessment could offer on how to improve, were overridden by the giving of marks and grades, and the function of comparing children, so that children saw the purpose of assessment as 'competition rather than personal improvement' (ibid.). This led to the perception that learning is about ability rather than effort: 'assessment feedback teaches students with low attainments that they lack "ability", so they are de-motivated and not able to learn' (ibid.). The review also revealed the 'managerial' purposes of assessment – the focus on keeping records at the expense of giving attention to children's learning needs.

Responding to children

It was, therefore, the quality of learning that became the focus of the research on Assessment for Learning that Black and his colleagues went on to undertake. This work was carried out with a group of secondary teachers but what was learned is applicable in the primary context in many respects. It enabled teachers to see that assessment is integral to learning. Strategies such as questioning took on a different purpose during the project – the aim became not to elicit right answers but to explore ideas, so children's responses were seen always as a valid contribution on which to build. With a different *aim*, teachers found new ways of responding to what they had previously thought of as simply 'wrong' answers. Instead of quickly moving on to the 'more able' child, who might provide the right answer, or changing the question or answering it themselves, teachers began to value 'incorrect' responses for the insight they gave into children's thinking (as Mary Jane Drummond did in her discussion of Jason, that I referred to in Chapter 2). As one teacher pointed out, questioning should not be a matter of children finding out what is in the teacher's head but the teacher 'probing to find out what is in theirs' (Black et al. 2003 p. 88). The teachers in the study carried out by Black and his team discovered the need to formulate questions more carefully to develop children's understanding, the need to increase the time that they waited for responses – to give children the chance to think – and the need to provide opportunities for further 'meaningful interventions' (p. 42) to consolidate and develop children's learning.

The research also challenged the nature of the feedback that was given to children. The marks and grades, that had hitherto been given to them, without comments, clearly had little value in helping children to understand how they

could improve their work. General praise ('well done') gives the child no information on what has been done well. Seen from the socio-cultural perspective,
these practices will constitute at least a part of the children's learning: pupils
will learn how to please the teacher or that they have done better than their
classmates who didn't receive the compliment. This may even be the most
significant part of their learning. To scaffold the *intended* learning, children
need to be given feedback that shows them exactly what they have achieved
and how they can develop their understanding or skill. Feedback, then, needs
to be descriptive rather than evaluative. In this way, the criteria, as to what
counts as 'success' become more clear to the child.

Peer and self-assessment

To make the criteria transparent to children, teachers in the Assessment for
Learning project explored peer and self-assessment, 'so enabling them to
develop a clear overview both of the aims of their work and of what it meant
to complete it successfully' (Black et al. 2003 p. 52). The idea was that children
should work together to assess each others' work through peer assessment and
should take responsibility for their own learning through self-assessment.
Black et al. refer to the work of Sadler (1989) here, pointing out that the learner
has to acknowledge the gap between their present level of achievement and
the desired goal and then has to take steps to address that. Although the
teacher can guide the child, it is the child who must do the learning: 'The
learner first has to understand the evidence about this gap and then take action
on the basis of that evidence' (Black et al. 2003 p.14). Black and Wiliam's
review (1998a) had found research that had already shown that this kind of
self-assessment could benefit children's learning – for example White and
Frederiksen (1998) (cited in Black et al. 2003) argue that it is central to formative assessment.

Self-assessment: shortcomings of children's participation in the 'setting of objectives'

The implications of self-assessment are that the learner must understand what
it is they are trying to achieve. I would suggest that there are inherent difficulties here, however, which may, perhaps, account for some of the problems
teachers experienced in introducing self-assessment as part of AfL (Black et al.
2003 p. 49). These difficulties reflect the distortions and possibly the logical
contradictions from which AfL can suffer when the strategies are introduced
and interpreted in a top-down culture and a linear framework of teaching and
learning. It seems to me that from the linear perspective, if a learner is not yet

able to meet the criteria that define successful achievement of the 'goal', then it would be difficult for them to fully understand the criteria. Or, to put it the other way round, if a child has already grasped the criteria – then have they not already achieved the intended learning? For instance, imagine that a child sets themselves the goal of learning what is meant by 'plot' in narrative. If, in order for them to assess their own achievement of that goal (self-assessment), they must understand the criteria by which 'plot' is being identified, does this not imply that they have already reached the intended learning goal – of understanding the idea of 'plot'? It does seem that they would need some prior grasp of what their teachers mean by 'plot', if they are even to begin to set themselves the goal of identifying a 'plot' – and if a child understands these criteria, if they can already demonstrate their understanding of what consti- tutes 'plot' in a story, it seems rather to defeat the purpose of the exercise. It is not a satisfactory argument to suggest that the criteria remain somehow 'abstract' at this stage. Indeed, it is difficult to conceive how a learner can come to understand the criteria at all, unless they have at least encountered concrete examples; unless they have already looked at and identified stories with a plot.

To continue the analysis from the linear perspective, perhaps this is less of an issue when the goal is for the child to develop, or to hone, a skill: for instance, it might be the case that the learner can understand what counts as a plot but is not yet skilled enough to construct one or cannot yet construct one very well. Understanding the criteria will help them – they will know what it is they are trying to do and they can use the criteria they already understand to assess whether they are getting better at it in practice.

It may also seem less problematic when self-assessment is used in helping children to gain new knowledge using understanding or skills they have already, at least to some extent, learned. For example, a child may already have an understanding of the criteria for successfully carrying out a fair test in science. It is feasible that they could use this understanding of the experi- mental process to take their learning forward. The specific goal would be to successfully apply what they have already mastered to a new topic of investiga- tion in order to learn something new. They can self-assess their achievements in terms of how well they have met the criteria for carrying out the experi- ment. Their self-assessment in this case, however, is, in reality, assessment of their ability to apply their understanding of the scientific process rather than assessment of their new knowledge, as such. In other words, it is self-assess- ment of what they understand about 'how to learn' in this particular mode of enquiry, rather than assessment of the new knowledge they have gained. Self- assessment, in both of these examples, then, may show that the child is able to apply what they have learned about story plots or doing experiments – it may demonstrate that this learning is becoming embedded – but in itself is not self- assessment of *new* concepts or skills.

Black and his co-authors do emphasise that self-assessment is not something that children can be expected to do without learning how (Black et al. 2003 p. 52). Teachers need to focus explicitly on children learning how to assess their own work. I would argue that how this is construed, however, is crucial if confusion and difficulties discussed above are to be avoided. As Black and his team suggest, concrete examples can be used as models to develop children's understanding of what they are trying to achieve and so can help them with their self-assessment of whether they have achieved it. Being given detailed descriptive feedback on what they say, do and make also helps children to develop their understanding of the criteria. Assessing each other's work (peer assessment) gives further experience of identifying what they are learning. As the researchers point out, 'engaging in peer and self-assessment entails much more than just checking for errors or weaknesses. It involves making explicit what is normally implicit, thus increasing students' involvement in their own learning' (p. 66).

But how these processes are conceived and carried out, is the critical factor, as research carried out by Tunstall and Gipps (1996) has shown. These researchers made a distinction not only between descriptive and judgemental feedback from teachers to children but between different kinds of descriptive feedback. On the one hand, types of feedback that they classified as either specifying attainment or specifying improvement were what they called 'mastery orientated': the children's work was evaluated against the specific predetermined criteria, owned by the teacher. On the other hand, the researchers also identified more constructive feedback ('constructing achievement' and 'constructing the way forward') that included discussion with the child and a shared approach to the development of the children's learning: 'This type of feedback provided children with strategies that they could adopt to develop their own work and encouraged children to assess their own work'. Here, the criteria were developed more collaboratively. The process was described by the researchers as learning-oriented, rather than performance or mastery orientated 'in that it includes many of the strategies described in constructivist approaches to learning, as well as self-regulating strategies'. This is an important distinction that shifts the focus from what otherwise can result in simply telling children, ever more precisely and prescriptively, what to do and how to do it.

Situated learning – assessment *as* participation

When seen in this constructive way – as a shared practice – self-assessment is consistent with the participative view of learning I have been discussing in earlier chapters. It embraces exploratory talk rather than running the risks of the superficiality and circularity I described above. This approach to self-assessment takes us back to the practices of enquiry that generate knowledge and that constitute learning for those who participate in them (see Chapter 7). It may help children to gain a greater insight into the principles of the modes of enquiry and educated discourses they are engaging in. By learning to engage with the internal criteria of a disciplined mode of thought or enquiry, they are raising their meta-cognitive awareness of what counts and what doesn't within the community of those who practise it. In helping them to learn how to learn in this way, it also gives them the means to learn more independently – to become self-regulating learners. Again, when learning is seen not as a 'purely interpersonal phenom-enon' (see Chapter 5) or the 'acquisition' of new knowledge or skill (offered, delivered or transmitted by others); when it is not presented as the achievement of pre-set goals or the fulfilment of *given* 'success criteria', but is viewed instead as participation in practices, then the potential for this kind of self-monitored learning can be seen more clearly. When learning is understood as engagement in the forms of reasoning that are implicit in, for example, scientific activity or artistic endeavour; when the children's activity is seen as legitimate peripheral participation as newcomers, alongside others, in these, and other cultural practices, this joint activity can be understood as providing the grounding for children to undertake these activities themselves. They have got started in these activities and they are finding out how things are done, alongside mature practitioners. They can begin to work out for themselves and with their peers how to take their activities and their learning in fruitful new directions.

From this perspective 'assessment for learning' must be embedded in activities and discourses; children must fully engage with what counts as valid in different practices, including different modes of enquiry within the 'teaching' curriculum. I would suggest that what is involved here is more than merely providing the child with examples or models, or providing clear feed-back. Again, children must *see themselves* as participants in 'communities of practice' with their more experienced teachers; their learning is a matter of collaborative activity – of getting things done with their teachers. To do justice to the theories of learning that Black and his colleagues invoke (Black et al. 2003 p. 78); to ensure that assessment for learning does not 'just add on a few techniques here and there', as they warn against (p. 79); to ensure that teachers do not merely follow the letter of AfL strategies, but engage in the spirit of them (Alexander 2010; Wyse and Torrance 2009); to ensure that AfL organises 'the whole teaching and learning venture around learning' (Black et al. 2003 p. 79), then AfL arguably must be seen as part of the broader contexts of learning – in other words as integral to participation in social and cultural practices. It is these practices and the multifarious forms of interaction, feed-back and meaning making that constitute them, which should be recognised as the contexts for the practices of 'assessment for learning'.

In this way, assessment can be seen as integral to learning in a much deeper sense: the relationship between the two implies teachers' full engagement with children as active meaning makers (see Chapter 1). In shifting the focus from teaching to learning, the argument leads back to the important contribution of Mercer, Alexander, Wells and others in emphasising the role of dialogue in learning (see Chapter 5) – and hence in assessment – in making explicit the principles underlying what is being learned (see Chapter 7). It endorses the centrality of participation and the sustained discourse between children and their teachers – of the kinds discussed in earlier chapters – with the intention of providing contexts where children can take the next steps in their own learning. It also points to the role of interaction between children themselves and the importance of children's voices.

To recap and summarise, as 'situated cognition', learning is seen as the process of children collaboratively *building* their understandings of the criteria for what counts with the participants in the particular community of practice, rather than *acquiring* them. Seeing learning from this perspective should help to deepen interpretations of the suggestion made by Black and his co-researchers (Black et al. 2003 p. 41) that children can contribute to the *development* of criteria. Not only are they building understandings of the criteria but they are also, as I have suggested in earlier chapters, contributing to *building those criteria* – they are contributing to the communal practices (Cobb and Bowers 1999). Again, this needs to be carefully construed to avoid the distortions of the performative, mastery orientation. It is now common in some primary classrooms, for example, to ask children to 'set their own success criteria'. I have explained above the difficulties in relation to assessing themselves against given criteria. From the performative, mastery perspective, to ask children to set their own objectives or goals may be to invite them, first, merely to set random criteria or criteria that they do not understand. Even though they may have a superficial knowledge of what the criteria should be – the children may have encountered some criteria through the teacher either sharing the objectives of a lesson, or (another practice that has become quite common) specifying exactly what they are looking for – they may make very different sense of them than their teacher had intended. Second, it may encourage the children to set criteria that they have already mastered. As the explanation above suggests, 'setting their own success criteria' will not necessarily extend children's learning in the anticipated way, at least in the context of performative, linear approaches to teaching and learning.

As participants in *shared activity*, on the other hand, children's contribution can be taken more seriously, and as a contribution to the creative transformation of practice. For instance, their own analysis of a range of stories, including their own, can lead to the construction of some ideas about what makes a good plot, from their point of view. Their own ideas will of course be informed by the stories of experienced story writers that they are reading, and their conversations with their teachers, but the children will bring something of their own to how the criteria are constructed. So, rather than seeing the analysis of plot in stories or the ability to construct plot in their own stories as the development or application of skill, informed by the acquisition of understanding of predetermined criteria, learning is engagement in the practices of plot construction along with other, more-established members of the community of story writers.

Challenging the performative, linear model

I would suggest that the term 'success criteria', itself, points in the linear, performative direction. It suggests the achievement – or mastery or acquisition – of a given end point; learning is a successful performance, rather than participation in the process of constructing knowledge. The term suggests that the end point is the starting point – and endorses the objectives-driven approach to teaching and assessment. It starts with the goal and the criteria for its successful achievement. The alternative is to begin by becoming aware of the child's actions as a learner and scaffolding these through engaging children in the available and valued activities and discourses, always being mindful of the openness of the outcome and its negotiated quality (guided participation – see Chapters 3 and 7).

What I am suggesting here is that the 'objectified discourse' of assessment for learning is replaced by the discourse of 'learning-as-participation' (Sfard 2009). The different kinds of feedback identified by Tunstall and Gipps (1996), that I referred to above, provide an example of the contrast between these two discourses. Although the Assessment for Learning project brought teachers to think differently about their teaching, it nevertheless seems to have remained embedded in a goal-orientated approach. The AfL researchers saw positive changes in teachers' thinking: the teachers involved in the project did come to see their teaching as 'a series of learning goals rather than a series of activities [tasks] to be completed' (Black et al. 2003 p. 91). This is a step away from curriculum coverage. Nevertheless, it retains the metaphors of mastery. There may be questions, therefore, to ask about how far it actually challenges the existing, narrowly defined, *performance*-orientated practice. The AfL conception of the curriculum as a set of goals seems to conflict with its own aims of allowing the children to take control of their learning – at least, if this is to be realised in its fullest sense.

This tension emerged in the AfL project in the perceptions of secondary teachers in different subject areas: it was apparent to those involved in the research that teachers of arts subjects, for instance, found the assessment for learning strategies less challenging to their existing practices than teachers of science or maths. This was attributed in part to the more open-ended nature of the tasks: in arts subjects outcomes are not predetermined in the same way as they might appear to be in the sciences; learning in these areas already involves participation in the process of making qualitative judgements: 'part of the nature of the subject is to assess quality and learn how to apply those judgements to one's own work. Much of the role of the teacher is to apprentice students into this process' (Black et al. 2003 p. 71). The project encouraged teachers of all areas of learning, including those subjects that were apparently more 'closed', to set open-ended tasks and to adopt forms of questioning that encouraged children to learn how to learn – tasks that helped them to understand, in mathematics, for example, how strategies could be applied in different contexts and to everyday problems. This inevitably led back to the issue that, in mathematics, 'an understanding of the criteria of quality is harder to achieve and may require an iteration in discussion between examples and the abstract criteria which they exemplify' (ibid.). I would argue that this again points to the need for children and their teachers to see themselves as joint participants in communities of practice in everyday contexts where mathematics can be applied, as well as in the discrete context of the form of enquiry itself. When seen as situated in this way, activities and purposes are not solely determined by the goals set by the teacher – rather, intentions and values of both parties emerge through participation in negotiated, purposeful activities, in jointly getting things done and solving problems. This can hold true for mathematics and for science, (as Bruner suggested), as much as for the arts (see Chapter 7).

This alternative view might also help to resolve the debate as to whether children's learning should take place in the context of 'authentic tasks,' where children are pursuing their own ideas and intentions. It was noted by Black and his colleagues (ibid.), for instance, that there was discussion amongst teachers, in relation to art, around whether the child making something of value to themselves might take precedence over the basic learning of skills. If it did, the child's own activity and quest for meaning in the context of their everyday lived experience would be setting the direction of the learning, with the teacher acting as guide, introducing skills and ways of understanding as and when they would be of use to the child. If the debate is resolved in terms of the child's active meaning making in the context of social practices, then this, once more, has implications for a shift in orientation, away from a view of teaching and assessing within a narrowly conceived 'teaching curriculum', understood as the achievement of pre-determined goals or objectives, towards a view of learning-as-participation – in the context of this particular example, in the social practice of making art.

An interpretive model

Steven Rowland (1984; 1987) presented a clear articulation of an alternative to the linear approach to teaching and learning some time ago, which he referred to as an 'interpretive' model. I am introducing it here as it helps to clarify the implications for assessment of a shift in focus towards learning-as-participation. Rowland would not have known, when he was writing, that the culture of teacher-directed transmission would continue to prevail and that objectives-driven teaching would become so accepted in the primary classroom as to virtually eradicate other forms of practice. His description of it still resonates today and depicts the kind of practices that the AfL initiatives are addressing now, more than twenty years on:

> It is the teacher who is really active, keeping control of the children's behaviour and the substance of their learning. All the instruction and stimulus is defined by the teacher in the language of the teacher. It is the teacher's knowledge and skill which the child attempts to copy, and success is measured in terms of the match between the two.
>
> (1987 p. 129)

By contrast, at the heart of his interpretive approach 'lies the idea of the interaction between teachers and learners as essentially an attempt by each party to interpret the expressions of the other' (p. 131).

His description of his encounter with 10-year-old Dean, who was inventing a way of classifying caterpillars, illustrates how the child, in grappling with the problem of how to record the features of his collection of these creatures brought him to a much deeper understanding of taxonomy than he could have achieved as a result of Rowland's direct instruction – and, in the process, sharpened Rowland's own understanding of taxonomy. Dean rejected or modified Rowland's interventions: 'There is little doubt that had Dean uncritically followed my original suggestion of tabulating his invented names for the caterpillars against my selection of attributes, he would never have confronted problems of classification and taxonomy in such depth' (p. 125). But Rowland was not advocating an approach that relied only on exploratory activity, with the adult standing back. He fully acknowledged the social nature of learning and the important part he played in the child's emerging understanding. When Dean himself had a need for instruction, then Rowland could act as what he described as a 'reflective agent' in the child's learning.

On Rowland's interpretive model,

> the initial stimulus for activity may come from the child or from the teacher. In either case, it is vital that it is the child's interpretation of that stimulus which motivates the activity. Only then can the child's control be assured. She is not trying to guess what's in the teacher's mind in responding to the teacher's resources, but formulates her own ideas. Once the activity is underway, the teacher's role is then to act as

a reflective agent, aiming to help the child identify concerns and needs, and also to provide positive yet critical feedback to the student. The child, in turn, critically responds to the teacher's contributions. Neither is 'right' or 'wrong'.

(p. 131)

Formative assessment is central to learning and teaching as Rowland conceived it, as the teacher's 'deliberate interventions' into the learning are based on the teacher's interpretations of the child's existing conceptions and knowledge. (p. 122). Assessment is the starting point for the teacher's interventions in a much more responsive way than the planned interventions of objectives-driven teaching. Where the teacher is 'planning to objectives', her focus for base-line assessment is determined by her teaching programme. By contrast, on Rowland's interpretive model, the planning is more open-ended and may well find its origins in the authentic concerns of the child and their own purposeful activities and self-initiated problem solving.

Participatory assessment

Such an approach may leave a teacher who is used to planning and assessing to objectives with a sense of insecurity. How can she know what to assess and how to assess it, if the child is in control of their learning? I have seen student teachers face this contradiction, particularly in the Foundation Stage. They have seen a dilemma in, on the one hand, wanting to allow the children to pursue child-initiated activities, as the Foundation Stage curriculum encourages, and, on the other, assuming that the only way to achieve a secure assessment of progress is to teach to objectives, as learning seems to be more readily and definitively assessable that way. To deviate from the adult-led, objectives-driven approach does indeed require of the teacher wide-ranging understanding of modes of enquiry and familiarity with educational discourses that, in the previous chapter, I suggested is necessary for teachers. Earlier in this chapter, I discussed the need for the teacher to know what learning opportunities were available in the activities they might plan to meet specific learning objectives. From this different perspective, the teacher needs not only to be able to analyse her own planned tasks – she needs to be able to analyse the child's own activities (whichever direction they go in), to understand what learning opportunities they might be providing and to be able to assess the nature of the learning that might *actually* be going on. This is a complex process: it demands of the teacher not only wide-ranging knowledge and understanding of the modes of enquiry that might be considered important for children to learn and of their under-pinning principles but also the need to be perceptive and analytical and to be able to draw on this wide 'repertoire' (Alexander 2010) of knowledge to identify the learning going on.

Much more is involved, however, in making these judgements if teachers are to move beyond the idea that assessment is simply about looking for evidence that children are 'acquiring' such knowledge. There is a great deal that adults take for granted about what is 'common knowledge' that must be looked at critically and analysed in relation to the child's own actions and thinking. To return to Rowland's example, what might have seemed eccentric about Dean's classification of his caterpillars may only be so because, as adults, his teachers 'have never enquired into the internal logic of the problem with which Dean was concerned' (Rowland 1987 p. 126). More specifically, I would suggest, they might not be inclined to enquire into how Dean, in particular, was trying to address this problem. If they did, then they would avoid referring to children's 'misconceptions'. Rather than judging children's conceptions unfavourably, as deficient in comparison with the 'correct' conception, they would engage more closely with children's specific activities and with their reasoning and meaning making.

Clearly, from the perspective of learning-as-participation the teacher must have a breadth of awareness of context and what that means for learning that goes well beyond the narrow attentiveness to the evidence of cognitive development in 'performance' that is matched to 'objective'.

As Cobb and Bowers (1999) point out, from the situated learning perspective, diversity in children's reasoning is related to the ways in which they participate in communal activity; that reasoning is not 'solely an internal mental phenomenon' but an act of participating in communal practices – and its diversity reflects the 'qualitatively distinct ways in which individual students participate in particular practices'. This, again, highlights the need for teachers to be acutely aware of the situation as a whole and of the impact this can have on how assessments are made. It was clear in the 'giving change' example above that how the task was framed as a practice affected the children's performance. From the learning-as-participation viewpoint, and to follow Cobb and Bowers' analysis, assessment in that situation and reflection on how to improve it would not be based exclusively on the children's responses, or only on the teaching strategy, but on how to ensure, as these researchers put it, 'that all students are "in the game"'. What this entails is to 'attempt to adjust the classroom participation structure, classroom discourse, and instructional activities on the basis of ongoing observations of individual students' activity' (p. 10).

From this viewpoint, assessment for learning is more about the judgements that the teacher makes about the situation in its entirety, than it is about an individual child's performance. Assessment is integrally related to how children participate in particular activities. Interpretation of the evidence is seen as inextricably bound up with the way those interpretations are constructed within specific social situations. Thus teachers do not only need a repertoire of knowledge, but a range of strategies in making assessments that is rather different to what might traditionally be expected. It is crucial for them to consider both what to interpret, and how. They need to be good observers: they need to be alert to what children are *doing* and how they are going about it; they need to watch carefully how children are using the cultural tools and resources at their disposal to represent their thinking, to carry out practical tasks and to solve problems; they need to be able to listen closely to what children are saying and to pay attention to the marks they make and the artefacts they construct. They need to consider the nature of the feedback they give and its contribution to the learning situation; how it draws children inside the culturally valued practices through which knowledge is constructed. They need to be able to interact with children in much more collaborative ways than when they are simply 'measuring' children's level of performance. Whatever evidence is directly presented by the child needs to be seen much more broadly than in terms of the outcomes resulting from particular teaching input. It is worth noting again that it is instructive for teachers in primary schools to look to the changing practices in the Foundation Stage in this regard. They can learn from the new focus on observation of children, of the shift to include more child-initiated activities and for constructive interventions, based on teachers' own participation in and observations of the learning going on.

In the context of a view of learning as active meaning making and learning-as-participation, these assessment practices are *embedded* in the processes of interpretation. It is not possible to neutrally observe what children are doing. 'Seeing' what children are doing entails interpreting. Teachers need to become aware that they themselves are bringing their own conceptions to the situation and that this influences what they see. Their 'prejudices' cannot be 'put to one side': they are a part of who they are – part of their identities, which are shaped through their own participation in social practices, including those of the classroom. This presents layers of complexity for the teacher's assessment of children's understanding and knowledge in the classroom: their assessments are always 'provisional and context-related' (Filer 1997 p. 97).

Concluding reflections

Arguably, children's learning and their lives are impeded by the performance-driven culture because it prioritises a very narrow view of assessment. Within a different classroom culture, where assessment is integral to learning-as-participation and where it is seen as the construction of criteria for knowledge building, classroom life and learning might indeed flourish. Assessment can contribute to all participants' awareness of what goes on in school so that it can be improved to ensure that school activities are not centred on schooling but around education.

Such changes on a local level within the classroom require a re-conceptualisation of learning and, as Rowland suggested, of teaching itself – as 'a task of active observation and interpretation, rather than one of performing and instilling' (Rowland 1987 p. 121). Black and his team (et al. 2003 p. 123) have argued, however, that the challenge to change the culture of teaching is dependent on changes in national policy. While teachers may recognise that the obsession with performance is misguided and the goal of objectivity is unattainable, this needs also to be acknowledged by policy makers. Wyse and Torrance (2009 p. 217) note the recent signs

> that the 'standards' agenda is becoming exhausted and that top-down control has run its course. Test results have plateaued since 2000 . . . and across the public services any benefits which centrally imposed targets may have produced are perceived as diminishing rapidly.

The reinstatement of trust in teachers that has been withheld in the culture of performativity (Elliott 2001) is part of the Coalition government rhetoric, at least – 'responsibility for improvement rests with schools' (DfE 2010a p. 22) – but to pave the way for real change at classroom level the hold of targets and testing needs to be released. Whether this will materialise is, currently, uncertain. While the stated intention is to 'end current centralised target setting' (p.10), at the same time it is asserted that 'Government should certainly put in place the structures and processes which will challenge and support schools to improve' (p.22).

Wyse and Torrance (2009) point out that 'professionals may be at least as informed and effective as governments in taking decisions about curriculum and assessment'. I have been developing the argument that, at the level of the classroom, there is scope for teachers themselves to re-conceptualise and reconstruct their practices. If teachers adopt a different vision of learning, as participatory and collaborative, this not only changes the way they might implement formative assessment; it could again also help to shift power relations within the classroom, as from this perspective, these assessment practices imply – to use Gipps' (2002 p. 78) distinction – 'power with' rather than 'power over' the child. Again, when the individual is seen as part of a community and it is acknowledged that outcomes will be shaped by all participants in the specific social practices of school life, children can be seen as more equal partners with adults.

Issues for teachers

- To what extent do the difficulties and issues around objectives-led assessment discussed in this chapter resonate with your own experience?
- How does the dominant goal-orientated culture shape your own formative assessment practices or your implementation of Assessment for Learning strategies?
- From the socio-cultural perspective of learning-as-participation, what might you do to develop your awareness of children's activities and their specific contexts, in order to assess their learning?
- How might this inform your planning and teaching?
- How do you see children's contribution to assessment? How does this change when seen from the learning-as-participation perspective?
- What practical steps could you take to embed assessment in collaborative activities in your classroom?

9　End piece

There is no shortage of new initiatives in the world of education. These are often sold to teachers in classrooms in the way that any other goods are marketed – through a catchphrase or acronym. Whether it is 'excellence and enjoyment'; 'creative curriculum'; 'thinking skills'; ELG (Early Learning Goals); AfL (Assessment for Learning) or APP (Assessing Pupil Performance), teachers must stay up to date with new language and new products. The problem is that teachers can end up with a shopping bag of discrete items all of which must find their place in the classroom somehow, with the danger that the whole collection can become an untidy heap with too little time and space available to teachers to organise it into some sort of coherent offering. I have attempted in this book to provide a framework to support teachers in facing this challenge.

I have tried to show that these initiatives are being interpreted within a context that is largely dominated by performance. The practices and values of policy makers, who have embraced an intensely competitive market-driven system over the last 20 years, are shaping teachers' actions in the classroom. In this regard, teachers are less powerful players in the educational community. I have also tried to show, however, that their approaches enact long-standing beliefs about teaching and learning that constitute a culture of schooling that stretches back much further. Teachers have been complicit participants in those practices for perhaps as long as the idea of schools and teaching has existed. As members of the community of teaching practitioners, teachers today (and I include myself in this) help to construct and re-construct those practices in these habitual ways.

But teachers can help to build a new community of practice – one that might be referred to as the 'reflective community'. Sources and resources for teacher learning are not only to be found in this particular social context of 'the school' and its dominant partners such as policymakers. Teachers might also belong to and identify with a wider community – of educators. Moreover, developing one's practice is not just a matter of articulating and understanding principles in the practices that are prescribed. Unless practitioners engage with the principles that they themselves routinely enact in their classroom teaching, and challenge them, they may yet interpret any new initiatives from their established perspective. As Stenhouse argued (1975 p. 39), the improvement of professional practice comes about as a result of 'systematic study of one's own teaching' in the contexts in which it takes place. There is good reason for teachers to seize the initiative to improve their own practice in these uncertain times by examining and changing their practice.

The wider educational community includes parents and other educators. The professional reflective community, in which teachers can collaboratively participate and learn, includes researchers and theorists who are collectively building a different understanding of learning – which may already be implicit in the practices of other educators. On this understanding, as I have tried to show, learning is not so much a matter of the consequences that result for the individual from an interpersonal pedagogical relationship that prioritises cognitive processes. It is participation in the social practices of the cultures that constitute life as it is lived. This has implications for both children and adults. It means that children learn how to 'be' as well as to 'do' in the worlds in which they find themselves – teachers have the power to shape how children see themselves as both a person and a learner through contexts which they have the power to create and through the kinds of classroom activities that children participate in. A teacher who enacts the more established, transmissional understanding of learning may, by default, provide narrow activities that are limited by a focus on mastery and may discourage divergence, on the part of the children, from the teacher's 'schooling' agenda. By contrast, the alternative view of learning acknowledges that the child exercises agency in constructing meanings and coming to know, and this is situated in collaborative activities with their teachers where the adults can provide the necessary cultural tools to support that. First, it entails a more active, or 'participative', participation than is afforded in the established classroom culture – given that, as I have shown, children are participating in whatever social situation they find themselves in, even those where they have no obvious active role. A teacher who enacts these principles understands the value of collaborative activity that is wide open to the collective resources of the culture and the interests of the cumulative meaning making of both children and teachers. Second, it is one where children are more equal partners with adults. Activities in schools are thus re-configured, I would argue, as educational practices.

The alternative view is challenging – it requires the teacher to foster the children's enquiring frame of mind and to develop the same in themselves. To know what to do next in any situation will not be a matter of following the linear template. Decisions on how to act will not be made on the basis of how best to arrive at a specific end point. Instead they will be made on the basis of a broad knowledge of the possibilities – of how to construct and make possible as yet unpredicted purposes and how to use the range of cultural tools and resources in realising them. Decisions about what to do as a teacher – how to interact; how to construct the curriculum; and how to assess learning – will be made in the context of a classroom and school community where adults and children participate in different ways, but in a climate of equal respect for their contributions. All, however, will be engaged in the activities because they have meaning and purpose in their lives, as people, whether children or educators.

I am reminded of a sequence from a video (Kolbe 1985) which for many years I have shared with pre-service teachers. It shows two children using drawing to construct a narrative. They have drawn a complex construction of builders' scaffolding, tunnels and ladders. In one corner there is an enormous monster. There are several tiny figures climbing around the structure. The teacher, looking at their drawing, invites the children to share their story with her. One of them tells how some of the figures are going to escape past the monster and explains how one man has become trapped and has been reduced to a skeleton. The child points to another of the figures who is escaping: 'He's trying to find a rope to go up there.' The teacher asks: 'How is he going to get out of there in the end? Do you know?' The child replies: 'I don't know. I haven't made up the story yet.' Here is a teacher who understands that she does not determine all the answers. She is attentive to the children's ideas and open to their own resolution of the plot. The sequence is an example of meaning making in progress in the here and now and also a powerful representation of how children – in the company of their teachers, amongst others – make up their story of what they learn and who they are.

References

Alexander, R. (1992) *Policy and Practice in Primary Education*. London and New York: Routledge.

Alexander, R (2004) 'Still no pedagogy? Principle, pragmatism and compliance in primary education' *Cambridge Journal of Education* 34(1).

Alexander, R. (2008) *Towards Dialogic Teaching: Re-thinking classroom talk*, 4th edn. York: Dialogos.

Alexander, R. (ed.) (2010) *Children, their World, their Education: Final Report and Recommendations of the Cambridge Primary Review*. London and New York: Routledge.

Alexander, R., Rose, J., and Woodhead, C. (1992) *Curriculum Organisation and Classroom Practice in Primary Schools*. London: DES.

Auld, R., (1976) *William Tyndale Junior and Infants Schools Public Inquiry*. London: ILEA.

Bakhtin, M. M. (1981) *The Dialogic Imagination: Four essays by M. M. Bakhtin*. Austin: University of Texas.

Bakhtin, M. M. (1986) *Speech Genres and Other Late Essays*. Austin: University of Texas Press.

Ball, S. (1994) *Education Reform: A critical and post-structuralist approach*. Buckingham: Open University Press.

Ball, S. (2001) 'Performativities and fabrications in the education economy: Towards the performative society' in Gleeson, D. and Husbands, C. (eds) *The Performing School: Managing, Teaching and Learning in a Performance Culture*. London and New York: Routledge Falmer.

Ball, S. (2004) 'Education Reform as Social Barberism: economism and the end of authenticity' *Scottish Educational Review*, 37(1).

Barnes, D. (1976) *From Communication to Curriculum*. Harmondsworth, UK; Ringwood, Australia: Penguin Books Ltd.

Barnes, D. (1992) *From Communication to Curriculum*, 2nd edn. Portsmouth, NH: Boynton/Cook- Heinemann.

Barnes, D. (2008) 'Exploratory Talk for Learning' in Mercer, N. and Hodgkinson S. (eds) *Exploring Talk in School*. London: Sage.

Barnes, D. and Todd, F. (1977) *Communication and learning in Small Groups*. London: Routledge and Kegan Paul.

Barnes, D. and Todd, F. (1995) *Communication and Learning Re-visited*. Portsmouth, NH: Heinemann.

Barton, D. and Hamilton, M. (1998) *Local Literacies: Reading and writing in one community*. London and New York: Routledge.

Bastiani, J. (1987) (ed.) *Parents and Teachers 1: Perspectives on Home-School Relations*. Windsor: NFER- Nelson.

Berger, P. and Luckman, T. (1966) *The Social Construction of Reality: A treatise on the sociology of knowledge*. New York: Random House.

Black, P., Harrison C., Lee, C., Marshall, B., Wiliam, D. (2003) *Assessment for Learning: Putting it into Practice*. Maidenhead: Open University Press.

Black, P., Harrison, C., Lee, C., Marshall, B. and Wiliam, D. (2004) 'Working Inside the Black Box: Assessment for Learning in the Classroom' *Phi Delta Kappan*, 86(1), pp. 9–21.

Black, P. and Wiliam, D. (1998a) *Inside the Black Box: Raising Standards Through Classroom Assessment*. School of Education: Kings College.

Black, P. and Wiliam, D. (1998b) 'Assessment and Classroom Learning' *Assessment in Education*, 5(1).

Blenkin, G. M. and Kelly, A.V. (1981) *The Primary Curriculum*. London: Harper and Row.

Bloom, B. S. (ed.) (1956) *Taxonomy of Educational Objectives 1: Cognitive Domain*. London: Longmans.

Board of Education (1931) *Report of the Consultative Committee on the Primary School* (The Hadow Report). London: HMSO.

Bottery, M. and Wright, N. (2000) *Teachers and the State*. London: Routledge.

Boyle, B. and Bragg, J. (2006). 'A curriculum without foundation' *British Educational Research Journal*, 32(4).

Brehony, K. J. (2005) 'Primary Schooling Under New Labour: the irresolvable contradiction of excellence and enjoyment' *Oxford Review of Education*, 31(1).

Brookes, M. (2009) 'Irresponsible to end the humiliation of SATs?' *Times Educational Supplement*, 1st May 2009.

Brown, A. and Palinscar, A. S. (1989) 'Guided co-operative learning and individual knowledge acquisition' in L. Resnick, (ed.) Knowing, Learning and Instruction. Hillsdale NJ: Erlbaum.

Brown, G. and Wragg, E. C. (1993) *Questioning*. London: Routledge.

Bruner, J. S. (1977) *The Process of Education*. Cambridge Mass.; London: Harvard University Press.

Bruner, J. S. (1986) *Actual Minds: Possible Worlds*. Cambridge Mass; London: Harvard Press.

Bruner, J. S. (1996) *The Culture of Education*. Cambridge Mass; London: Harvard Press.

Burke, P. J. and Hermerschmidt M. (2005) 'Deconstructing Academic Practices Through Self Reflexive Pedagogies' in Street, B. (ed.) *Literacies Across Educational Contexts: Mediating Learning and Teaching*. Philadelphia: Caslon.

Byron, T. (2009) *We see children as pestilent. Guardian* 17.3.09.

Central Advisory Council for Education (1967) *Children and their Primary Schools* (The Plowden Report). London: HMSO.

Cobb, P. and Bowers, J. (1999) 'Cognitive and situated learning: Perspectives in theory and practice' *Educational Researcher*, 28(2).

Cole, M. and Griffin, P. (1983) 'A socio-historical approach to re-mediation' *Quarterly Newsletter of the Laboratory of Comparative Human Cognition*, 5(4), 69–74.

Cox, C. B. and Dyson, A. (eds) (1969) *Fight for Education*. London: Critical Quarterly Society.

Cox, S. (1998a) 'Oral History – Primary Children and Older People Working Together' *Education 3–13*, March.

Cox, S. (1998b) 'The Primary Curriculum – The State of the Art' *Forum*, June.

Cox, S (2005) 'Intention and Meaning in Young Children's Drawing' *International Journal of Art and Design Education*, 24(2).

Cox, S., Currie, D., Frederick, K., Jarvis, D., Lawes, S., Millner, E., Nudd, K., Robinson-Pant, A., Stubbs, I., Taylor, T. and White, D. (2006) *Children Decide: Power; Participation and Purpose in the Primary Classroom*. CfBT/School of Education and Lifelong Learning University of East Anglia Research report, available from Libby.Allen@uea.ac.uk.

Cox, S. and Robinson-Pant, A; with Elliott B., Jarvis, D., Lawes, S., Millner, E. and Taylor, T. (2003) *Empowering Children through Visual Communication*. CfBT/ University of East Anglia, www.cfbt.com/research/projects/emp_vis_com.html.

Cox, S. and Robinson-Pant, A. (2005a) 'Communicative Practices and Participation in Schools Councils in Primary Schools in the United Kingdom' in Street, B. (ed.) *Literacies Across Educational Contexts: Mediating Learning and Teaching*. Philadelphia: Caslon.

Cox, S. and Robinson-Pant, A. (2005b) 'Challenging Perceptions of School Councils in the Primary School' *Education 3–13*, 33(2).

Cox, S. and Robinson-Pant, A. (2006) 'Enhancing participation in Primary School and Class Councils through Visual Communication' *Cambridge Journal of Education*, 36(4).

Cox, S. and Robinson-Pant, A. (2008) 'Power, participation and decision making in the primary classroom: children as action researchers' *Educational Action Research – an international journal*, 16(4).

Cox, S. and Robinson-Pant, A. (2010) 'Children as Researchers – a question of risk?' in Cox S., Dyer, C., Robinson Pant, A. and Schweisfurth, M. (eds) *Children as Decision Makers in Education*. London: Continuum.

Cox S., Dyer, C., Robinson-Pant, A. and Schweisfurth, M. (eds) (2010) *Children as Decision Makers in Education*. London: Continuum.

Daniels, H. (2007) 'Pedagogy' in Daniels, H., Cole, M. and Wertsch, J. *The Cambridge Companion to Vygotsky*. Cambridge: Cambridge University Press.

Daniels, H., Lauder, H., and Porter, J. (eds) (2009) *Educational Theories, Cultures and Learning: A critical perspective*. Abingdon; New York: Routledge.

Daugherty, R., Black, P., Ecclestone, K., James, M. and Newton, P. (2008) 'Alternative Perspectives on learning outcomes: challenges for assessment' *Curriculum Journal*, 19(4), pp. 243–54.

DCSF (2003) *Excellence and enjoyment: A strategy for Primary Schools*. London: DCSF.

DCSF (2007a) *Letters and Sounds: Principles and practice of high quality phonics*. London: DCSF.

DCSF (2007b) *The Children's Plan: Building brighter futures*. London: DCSF.

DCSF (2008) *Statutory Framework for the Early Years Foundation Stage: Setting the Standards for Learning, Development and Care for children from birth to five*. London: DCSF.

DCSF (2009a) *Independent Review of the Primary Curriculum: Final Report* Nottingham: DCSF Publications (Rose Review).

DCSF (2009b) www.dcsf.gov.uk/everychildmatters/earlyyears/surestart/whatsure-startdoes/(Accessed 24/08/10).

Dearden, R. F.(1967) 'Instruction and Learning by Discovery' in Peters, R.S. (ed.) *The Concept of Education*. London: Routledge and Kegan Hall.

Dearden, R. F. (1968) *The Philosophy of Primary Education*. London: Routledge and Kegan Paul.

Dearden, R. F. (1976) *Problems in Primary Education*. London: Routledge and Kegan Paul.

Dearing, R. (1993) *The National Curriculum and its Assessment: final report*. London: SCAA.

Dent, M. and Whitehead, S. (2002) *Managing Professional Identities: Knowledge; performativity and the 'new' professional*. London: Routledge.

Denvir, H. and Askew, M. (2001) 'Pupils' participation in the classroom examined in relation to interactive whole class teaching', in Rowland, T. (ed.) *Proceedings of the British Society for Research into Learning Mathematics*, 21(1) March 2001.

DES (1978) *Primary Education in England: a survey by HM Inspectors of Schools*. London: HMSO.

Dewey (1916) *Democracy and Education*. Toronto: Collier-Macmillan Canada, Ltd.

Dewey (1938) *Experience and Education*. New York: Collier Macmillan.

DfE (2010a) *The Importance of Teaching: Schools white paper* DFE: www.education.gov.uk/b0068570/the-importance-of-teaching/(Accessed 11.03.11).

DfE (2010b) *Key Stage 2 Testing and Accountability Review – Call for Evidence* www.education.gov.uk/consultations/index.cfm?action=consultationDetails&consultationId=1739&external=no&menu=1 (Accessed 3/12/10)

DfE (2010c) *Free Schools* www.education.gov.uk/schools/leadership/typesofschools/freeschools (Accessed 22.11.10).

DfEE (1998) *The National Literacy Strategy: framework for teaching*. London: DfEE.

DfEE (1999a) *The National Curriculum: handbook for primary teachers in England*. London: DfEE/QCA.

DfEE (1999b) *The National Numeracy Strategy: framework for teaching mathematics from Reception to Year 6*. London: DfEE.

DfES (2004) *Every Child Matters: Change for children*. Nottingham: DfES.

DfES (2007) *Every Parent Matters* (White Paper). London: DfES.

Dickens, C. (1969) *Hard Times*. Harmondsworth: Penguin.

Donaldson, M. (1978) *Children's Minds*. London: Fontana Press.

Drummond, M. J. (2003) *Assessing Children's Learning*. London: David Fulton.

Earl, L., Watson, N., Levin, B., Leithwood, K., Fullan, M. and Torrance, N. (2003) *Final Report of the External Evaluation of England's National Literacy and Numeracy Strategies*. London DFES; Toronto: Ontario Inst. for Studies in Education.

Eberbach, C.E. and Crowely, K. (2009). 'From Everyday to Scientific Observation: How Children Learn to Observe the Biologist's World' *Review of Educational Research*, 79(1).

Edwards, A. (2009) 'Becoming a Teacher' in Daniels, H., Lauder, H., and Porter, J. (eds) *Educational Theories, Cultures and Learning: A critical perspective*. Abingdon; New York: Routledge.

Eisner, E. (1969) 'Instructional and Expressive Educational Objectives: their formulation and use in the curriculum' in Popham, W., Eisner E., Sullivan H. and Tyler, L. *Instructional Objectives*. American Educational Research Association Monograph Series in Curriculum Evaluation. No. 3. Chicago: Rand McNally.

Eisner, E. (1985) *The Art of Educational Evaluation*. London: The Falmer Press.

Elliott, J. (2001) 'Characteristics of performative cultures: their central paradoxes and limitations as resources for educational reform' in Gleeson, D. and Husbands, C. (eds) *The Performing School: Managing, Teaching and Learning in a Performance Culture*. London and New York: Routledge Falmer.

Fielding, M. (2001a) 'Beyond the Rhetoric of Student Voice: new departures or constraints in the transformation of 21st century schooling?' *Forum* 43(2).

Fielding, M. (2001b) 'Students as Radical Agents of Change' *Journal of Educational Change*, 2(3).

Fielding, M. (2004) 'Transformative Approaches to Student Voice: Theoretical Underpinnings, Recalcitrant Realities' *British Educational Research Journal*, 30(2).

Fielding, M. (2009) 'Interrogating student voice: pre-occupations, purposes and possibilities' in Daniels, H., Lauder, H. and Porter, J. (eds), *Educational Theories, Cultures and Learning: A Critical Perspective*. London, Routledge.

Fielding, M. and Rudduck, J. (2006) 'Student voice and the perils of popularity' *Educational Review*, 58(2).

Filer, A (1997) 'Assessment and the Function of Children's Language in Their News Session' in Pollard, A., Thiessen, D. and Filer, A. (eds) *Children and Their Primary Schools*. London and Washington DC: Falmer Press.

Freire, P. (1972) *Pedagogy of the Oppressed*. Harmondsworth: Penguin.

Gallimore, R. and Tharp R. (1990) 'Teaching mind in society: teaching, schooling, and literate discourse' in Moll, L. (ed.) *Vygotsky and Education*. Cambridge: Cambridge University Press.

Galton, M. (2007) *Learning and Teaching in the Primary Classroom*. Los Angeles; London: Sage Publications.

Galton, M., Simon, B., and Croll, P. (1980) *Inside the Primary Classroom*. London: Routledge and Kegan Paul.

Galton, M., Hargreaves, L., Comber, C., Wall, D., with Pell, A. (1999) *Inside the Primary Classroom: 20 years on*. London and New York: Routledge.

Gipps, C. (2002) 'Sociocultural Perspectives on Assessment' in Wells, G. and Claxton, G. (eds) *Learning for Life in the 21st Century*. Oxford: Blackwell.

Gleeson, D. and Husbands, C. (2001) (eds) *The Performing School: Managing, Teaching and Learning in a Performance Culture*. London and New York: Routledge Falmer.

Goodman, N. (1976) *Languages of Art*, 2nd edn. Indianapolis: Hackett.

Goodman, N. (1978) *Ways of World Making*. Hassocks, Sussex: Harvester Press.

Hall, K., Collins, J., Benjamin, S., Nind, M. and Sheehy, K. (2004) 'Saturated models of pupildom: Assessment and inclusion/exclusion' *British Educational Research Journal*, 30(6).

Hamlyn, D. W. (1978) *Experience and the Growth of Understanding*. London; Boston; Henley: Routledge and Kegan Paul.

Hargreaves, D. (2006) *A New Shape for Schooling?* London: Specialist Schools and Academies Trust.

Hargreaves, L., Moyles, J., Merry, R., Patterson, F., Pell, A. and Esarte-Sarries, V. (2003) 'How do primary teachers define and implement interactive teaching in the national literacy strategy in England?' *Research Papers in Education*, 18(3), pp. 217–36.

Herne, S. (2000) 'Breadth and Balance? The Impact of the National Literacy and Numeracy Strategies on Art in The Primary School' *International Journal of Art and Design Education*, 19(2).

Hipkins, R., Reid, A., Bull, A. (2010) 'Some reflections on the philosophical and pedagogical challenge of transforming education' *The Curriculum Journal*, 21(1).

Hirst, P. H. (1973) 'Liberal Education and the Nature of Knowledge' in Peters, R.S. (ed.) *The Philosophy of Education*. Oxford: Oxford University Press.

Hirst, P. H. (1993) 'Education, Knowledge and Practices' in Barrow, R. and White, P. (eds) *Beyond Liberal Education: Essays in Honour of Paul H. Hirst*. London: Routledge and Kegan Paul.

Holma, K. (2009) 'The Strict Analysis and the Open Discussion' *Journal of Philosophy of Education*, 43(3).

Houssart, J. (1999) 'History and Numeracy', Keynote address to Northamptonshire Humanities Conference, July 1999.

Howe, C. and Mercer, N (2007) *The Primary Review – Research Survey 2/1b: Children's Social Development, Peer Interaction and Classroom Learning*. Cambridge: University of Cambridge Faculty of Education.

Hughes, M., Andrews, J., Feiler, A., Greenhough, P., Johnson, D., McNess, E., Osborn, M., Pollard, A., Salway, L., Scanlan, M., Stinchcombe, V., Winter, J. and Wan Ching Yee (2005) *Contexts, communities, networks: Mobilising learners' resources and relationships in different domains*. ESRC Teaching and Learning Research Programme (TLRP) Thematic Seminar Series: Seminar One, 15–16 February 2005, Glasgow Caledonian University 'Exchanging Knowledge Between Home and School to Enhance Children's Learning'. www.leeds.ac.uk/educol/documents/151720.doc (Accessed 27.2.11).

Hughes, M. and Greenhough, P. (2006) 'Boxes, bags and videotape: enhancing home–school communication through knowledge exchange activities' *Educational Review*, 58(4), pp. 471–487.

Illich, I. (1971) *Deschooling Society*. New York: Harper and Row.

Independent, The (2010) *Ministers under pressure to scrap Sats* www.independent. co.uk/news/education/education-news/ministers-under-pressure-to-scrap-sats–2042009.html (Accessed 18.08.10).

Kellogg, R. (1969) *Analysing Children's Art*. Palo Alto: National Press Books.

Kern, L. and Clemens, N. H. (2007) 'Antecedent strategies to promote appropriate classroom behaviour' *Psychology in the Schools*, 44(1).

Kolbe, U. (1985) Video: *The Image Makers*. Sydney: Institute of Early Childhood Studies: Sydney College of Advanced Education.

Kress, G. (1997) *Before Writing – Re-thinking the paths to literacy*. London: New York Routledge.

Kuhn, T. S. (1996) *The Structure of Scientific Revolutions*, 3rd edn. Chicago: University of Chicago Press.

Lave, J. and Wenger, E. (1991) *Situated Learning: Legitimate Peripheral Participation*. Cambridge: Cambridge University Press.

Lawton, D. (1994) *The Tory Mind on Education 1979–1994*. London: Washington DC: The Falmer Press.

Marley, D. (2010) 'SATs "breach pupils' human rights"' *The Times Educational Supplement*, 9th April 2010.

Matthews, J. (1999) *The Art of Childhood and Adolescence: The Construction of Meaning*. London and Philadelphia: Falmer Press.

Matthews, J. (2003) *Drawing and Painting: Children and Visual Representation*. London: Paul Chapman.

Matusov, E. and Hayes, R. (2002) 'Building a Community of Educators versus Effecting Conceptual Change in Individual Students: Multicultural Education for Pre-Service Teachers' in Wells, G. and Claxton, G. (eds) *Learning for Life in the 21st Century*. Oxford: Blackwell.

Maybin, J. (2006) *Children's Voices: Talk, knowledge and identity*. Basingstoke: Palgrave Macmillan.

Mercer, N. (1995) *The Guided Construction of Knowledge: Talk amongst teachers and learners*. Clevedon; Philadelphia; Adelaide: Multilingual Matters.

Mercer, N. (2000) *Words and Minds: How We Use Language to Think Together*. London: Routledge.

Mercer, N. (2002) 'Developing Dialogues' in Wells, G. and Claxton, G. (eds) *Learning for Life in the 21st Century*. Oxford: Blackwell.

Mercer, N. and Littleton, K. (2007) *Dialogue and the Development of Children's Thinking: A socio-cultural approach*. Abingdon: Routledge.

Mercer, N. and Dawes, L. (2008) 'The Value of Exploratory Talk' in Mercer, N. and Hodgkinson, S. (eds) *Exploring Talk in School*. London: Sage.

Mercer, N. and Hodgkinson, S. (eds) (2008) *Exploring Talk in School*. London: Sage.

Moll, L. (1990) (ed.) *Vygotsky and Education: Instructional implications and applications of socio-historical psychology*. Cambridge: Cambridge University Press.

Moll, L. and Greenberg, J. (1990) 'Creating zones of possibilities: Combining social contexts for instruction' in Moll, L. (1990) (ed.) *Vygotsky and Education: Instructional implications and applications of socio-historical psychology*. Cambridge: Cambridge University Press.

Mortimore, P., Sammonds, P., Stoll, L., Lewis, D. and Ecob, R. (1988) *School Matters*. Wells: Open Books.

National Advisory Committee on Creative and Cultural Education (1999) *All Our Futures: Creativity, Culture and Education: Report to the Secretary of State for Education and Employment; the Secretary of State for Culture, Media and Sport*. NACCCE.

Neill, A. S. (1962) *Summerhill: A radical approach to education*. London: Victor Gollancz.

Nudd, K. (2006) ' "Sharing Decisions." Project report' in Cox, S; Currie, D; Frederick, K.; Jarvis, D.; Lawes, S.; Millner, E.; Nudd, K.; Robinson-Pant, A.; Stubbs, I.; Taylor, T.; White, D. (2006) *Children Decide: Power; Participation and Purpose in the Primary Classroom*. CfBT/School of Education and Lifelong Learning University of East Anglia Research report available from Libby.Allen@uea.ac.uk.

Nystrand, M., Gamoran, A., Kachur, R., Prendergast, C. et al. (1997) *Opening Dialogue*. New York: Teachers College Press.

Ofsted (2002a) *The National Literacy Strategy: The First Four Years, 1998–2002*. London: Office for Standards in Education.

Ofsted (2002b) *The National Numeracy Strategy: The First Three Years, 1999–2002*. London: Office for Standards in Education.

Ofsted (2009) *Annual Report 2008/9* http://www.ofsted.gov.uk/Ofsted-home/Annual-Report–2008–09/Main-summary (Accessed 19/9/10).

Onthespot(2010)www.guardian.co.uk/education/2010/apr/27/primary-education-cambridge-review (Accessed 10/6/10).

Peters, R. S. (1958) *The Concept of Motivation*. London: Routledge & Kegan Paul; New York: Humanities Press.

Peters, R. S. (1966) *Ethics and Education*. London: George Allen and Unwin Ltd.

Peters, R. S. (1969) *Perspectives on Plowden*. London: Routledge and Kegan Paul.

Peters, R. S. (ed.) (1973) *The Philosophy of Education*. Oxford: Oxford University Press.

Pollard. A. with Filer, A. (1996) *The Social World of Children's Learning: Case Studies of Pupils from Four to Seven*. London: Continuum.

Pollard, A. (2001) 'Towards a New Perspective on Children's Learning?' in Richards, C. (ed.) *Changing English Primary Education*. Stoke on Trent: Trentham Books.

Postman, N. and Weingarter, C. (1969) *Teaching as a Subversive Activity*. New York: Dell Publishing Co. Ltd.

Pring, R. (1976) *Knowledge and Schooling*. London: Open Books Publishing Ltd.

Reay, D. and Wiliam, D. (1999) ' "I'll be a nothing": Structure, agency and the construction of identity through assessment' *British Educational Research Journal*, 25(3).

Reimer, E. (1971) *School is Dead. An essay on alternatives in education*. Harmondsworth: Penguin.

Resnick, I. B. (1999) 'Making America smarter' *Education Week Century Series*, 18(40), 38–40.

Richards, C. (1999) *Primary Education – At a Hinge of History?* London: Falmer Press.

Rogoff, B. (1990) *Apprenticeship in Thinking: cognitive development in social context*. Oxford: Oxford University Press.

Rogoff, B. (1994) 'Developing Understanding of the Idea of Communities of Learners' *Mind, Culture and Activity*, 1(4), pp. 209–29.

Rousseau, J. J. (1762) *Émile, or On Education*, trans. Allan Bloom (1979). New York: Basic Books.

Rowland, S. (1984) *The Enquiring Classroom: An Introduction to Children's Learning*. London and New York: The Falmer Press.

Rowland, S. (1987) 'Child in Control: Towards an Interpretive Model of Teaching and Learning' in Pollard, A. (ed.) *Children and Their Primary Schools*. London; New York and Philadelphia: The Falmer Press.

Rudduck, J. and Flutter, J. (2000) 'Pupil Participation and Pupil Perspective: "carving a new order of experience"' *Cambridge Journal of Education*, 30(1).

Rudduck, J. (2003) *Pupil voice and citizenship education – article for the QCA Citizenship and PSHE Team, March*. Cambridge: University of Cambridge.

Sanders, D., White, G., Burge, B., Sharp, C., Eames, A., McEune, R. and Grayson, H. (2005) *A Study of the Transition from the Foundation Stage to Key Stage 1* (DfES Research Report SSU/2005/FR/013). London: DfES.

Schon, D. (1983) *The reflective practitioner: How professionals think in action*. New York: Basic Books.

Schools Council (1972) *With Objectives in Mind: Guide to Science 5–13*. London: Macdonald Educational for the Schools Council.

Sfard, A. (2009) 'Metaphors in Education' in Daniels, H., Lauder, H., and Porter, J. (eds) *Educational Theories, Cultures and Learning: A critical perspective*. Abingdon; New York: Routledge.

Shepherd, J. and Williams, R. (2010) *Primary heads scupper league tables with out-of-date Sats tests* www.guardian.co.uk/education/2010/may/10/sats-boycott-by-headteachers (Accessed 18.8.10).

Shulman, L. (1987) 'Knowledge and Teaching: foundations of the new reform' *Harvard Educational Review*, 57(1).

Simon, B. (1983) 'Why no Pedagogy in England?' in Simon, B. and Taylor, W. (eds) *Education in the Eighties: The central issues*. London: Batsford.

Siraj-Blatchford, I., Sylva, K., Muttock, S., Gilden, R. and Bell, D. (2002) *Researching Effective Pedagogy in the Early Years (REPEY)*. London: DfES

Skinner, B. F. (1938) *The Behaviour of Organisms*. New York: Appleton-Century-Crofts.

Smith, F., Hardman, F., Wall, K. and Mroz, M. (2004) 'Interactive whole class teaching in the National Literacy and Numeracy Strategies' *British Educational Research Journal*, 30(3).

Stenhouse, L. (1975) *An Introduction to Curriculum Research and Development.* London: Heinemann Educational Books Ltd.

Stetsenko, A. (1995) 'The Psychological function of Children's Drawing: a Vygotskyan Perspective' in Lange-Kuttner, C. and Thomas, G. V. (eds) *Drawing and Looking.* New York: Harvester Wheatsheaf.

Street, B. (ed.) (1993) *Cross-cultural Approaches to Literacy.* Cambridge: Cambridge University Press

Sylva, K., Melhuish, E., Sammons, P., Siraj-Blatchford, I. and Taggart, B. (2008) *The Effective Provision of Pre-School Education [EPPE] Project Final Report. A Longitudinal Study Funded by the DfES 1997–2004.* London: DFES.

Taylor, T. (2006) 'Exploring Power Sharing in the Classroom' in Cox, S; Currie, D; Frederick, K.; Jarvis, D.; Lawes, S.; Millner, E.; Nudd, K.; Robinson-Pant, A.; Stubbs, I.; Taylor, T.; White, D. *Children Decide: Power; Participation and Purpose in the Primary Classroom.* CfBT/School of Education and Lifelong Learning University of East Anglia Research report available from Libby.Allen@uea.ac.uk.

TDA (2007) *Professional Standards for Teachers: Why sit still in your career?* London: Training and Development Agency.

Tizard, B. and Hughes, M. (1984) *Young Children Learning.* Cambridge, Mass: Harvard University Press.

Tizard, B. and Hughes, M. (1987) 'The Intellectual Search of Young Children' in Pollard, A. (ed.) *Children and their Primary School: A new perspective.* Lewes; Philadelphia: The Falmer Press.

Torrance, H. (2002) *Can Testing Really Raise Educational Standards?* Inaugural professorial lecture: University of Sussex.

Troman, G., Jeffrey, B. and Raggl, A. (2007) 'Creativity and performativity policies in primary school cultures' *Journal of Education Policy,* 22(5).

Tunstall, P. and Gipps, C. (1996) 'Teacher feedback to young children in formative assessment: A typology' *British Educational Research Journal,* 22(4), pp. 389–404.

Tyler, R. W. (1949) *Basic Principles of Curriculum and Instruction.* Chicago: University of Chicago Press.

United Nations (1989) Convention on the Rights of the Child Geneva: UN General Assembly Resolution 44/25. http://www2.ohchr.org/english/law/pdf/crc.pdf (Accessed 22/11/10).

Vincent, C. (1996) *Parents and Teachers: Power and Participation.* London; Washington DC: Falmer Press.

Vygotsky, L. S. (1978) *Mind in Society.* Cambridge Mass; London: Harvard Press.

Vygotsky, L. S. (1987) 'Thinking and Speech' in Rieber, R. and Carlton, A. (eds) *L.S. Vygotsky: Collected Works (vol. 1).* New York: Plenum.

Webb, R. and Vuillamy, G. (2006) *Coming Full Circle? The Impact of New Labour's Education Policies on Primary School Teachers' Work.* London: Association of Teachers and Lecturers (ATL).

Wegerif, R. and Scrimshaw, P. (1997) *Computers and Talk in the Primary Classroom.* Clevedon; Bristol, PA; Toronto; Artaman: Multilingual Matters Ltd.

Wells, G. (1986) *The Meaning Makers: Children Learning Language and Using Language to Learn.* Portsmouth NH: Heinemann.

Wells, G. (1999) *Dialogic Enquiry: Toward a Socio-cultural Practice and Theory of Education.* Cambridge: Cambridge University Press.

Wells, G. (2004) 'DISCUSSION: Narrating and Theorizing Activity in Educational Settings' *Mind, Culture, and Activity,* 11(1).

Wells., G. (2009) *The meaning makers: Learning to talk and talking to learn.* Bristol: Multilingual Matters.

Wells, G. and Chang-Wells, G. L. (1992) *Constructing Knowledge Together.* Portsmouth NH: Heinemann.

Wells, G. and Claxton, G. (2002) (eds) *Learning for Life in the 21st Century.* Oxford: Blackwell.

Wells, G. and Arauz, R. M. (2006) 'Dialogue in the Classroom' *Journal of the Learning Sciences,* 15(3).

Wells, G. and Ball, T. (2008) 'Exploratory Talk and Dialogic Inquiry' in Mercer, N. and Hodgkinson S. (eds) *Exploring Talk in School.* Los Angeles; London; New Delhi; Singapore; Washington DC: Sage.

Wenger, E. (1998) *Communities of Practice: Learning, Meaning, and Identity.* Cambridge: Cambridge University Press.

Wertsch, J. (1991) *Voices of the Mind: A socio-cultural approach to mediated action.* Hemel Hempstead: Harvester Wheatsheaf.

White, D. (2006) ' "Time for a cat stamp" Project Report' in Cox, S., Currie, D., Frederick, K., Jarvis, D., Lawes, S., Millner, E., Nudd, K., Robinson-Pant, A., Stubbs, I., Taylor, T. and White, D. *Children Decide: Power, Participation and Purpose in the Primary Classroom.* CfBT/School of Education and Lifelong Learning, University of East Anglia Research report available from Libby. Allen@uea.ac.uk.

White, J. (1990) *Education and the Good Life; Beyond the National Curriculum.* London: Kogan Page.

White, J. (1982) *The Aims of Education Restated.* London: Routledge & Kegan Paul.

White, J (2005) 'Reassessing 1960s philosophy of the curriculum' *London Review of Education,* 3(2).

White, J. (2007) *What schools are for and why,* Philosophy of Education Society of Great Britain IMPACT Paper No 14.

White, P. (1996) 'Civic Virtues and Public Schooling: educating citizens for a democratic society' in the Advances in Contemporary Educational Thought Series, New York and London: Teachers College Press.

Whitty, G. (2002) *Making Sense of Educational Policy.* London: Sage.

Whitty, G. and Wisby, E. (2007) *Real Decision Making? School Councils in Action.* Research Report DCSF: RR001, London: Institute of Education University of London.

Wilson, P. S. (1971) *Interest and Discipline in Education.* London: Routledge and Kegan Paul.

Wittgenstein, L. (1953) *Philosophical Investigations*, trans. G. E. M. Anscombe. Oxford: Basil Blackwell.

Wood, D. (1986) 'Aspects of Teaching and Learning' in Richards, M. and Light, P. (eds) *Children of Social Worlds*. Cambridge: Polity Press.

Wood, D. (1998) *How Children Think and Learn*, 2nd edn. Oxford: Blackwell.

Wood, D. (1991) 'Aspects of Teaching and Learning' in Light, P., Sheldon, S., Woodhead, M. (eds) *Learning to Think*. London and New York: Routledge, in association with The Open University.

Wood, D., Bruner, J. S. and Ross, G. (1976) 'The Role of Tutoring in Problem Solving' *Journal of Child Psychology and Psychiatry*, 17(2), pp. 89–100.

Wyse, D. (2001) 'Felt tip pens and school councils: children's participation rights in four English schools' *Children and Society*, 15(4), pp. 209–218.

Wyse, D. and Torrance, H. (2009) 'The development and consequences of national curriculum assessment for primary education in England' *Educational Research*, 51(2).

Young, M. (1971) (ed.) *Knowledge and Control: New directions for the sociology of education*. London: Collier Macmillan.

Index